F

A FIRESIDE BOOK

Published by Simon & Schuster

New York   London   Toronto   Sydney   Tokyo   Singapore

Dance
of
the
Selves

LORETTA FERRIER, Ph.D.
with MONICA DRUCTOR BRIESE

FIRESIDE
Simon & Schuster Building
Rockefeller Center
1230 Avenue of the Americas
New York, New York, 10020

FIRESIDE and colophon are registered trademarks
of Simon & Schuster Inc.

Designed by The Black Angus Design Group
Manufactured in the United States of America

10 9 8 7 6 5 4 3 2 1

Library of Congress Cataloging-in-Publication Data

Ferrier, Loretta.
    Dance of the selves / Loretta Ferrier with Monica Dructor Briese.
        p.   cm.
    "A Fireside book."
    Includes bibliographical references (p.   ).
    1. Success—Psychological aspects.   2. Intuition (Psychology)   3. Reasoning
(Psychology)   4. Femininity (Psychology)   5. Masculinity (Psychology)   I.
Briese, Monica Dructor.   II. Title.
BF637.S8F428 1992
158—dc20   91-33636

ISBN: 0-671-72839-3   CIP

In loving memory of my parents,
Robert and Virginia Ferrier

Acknowledgments

While the presentations in this book are uniquely mine, I have been strongly influenced by the great teachers in my life, the hundreds of classes I have taken, and the thousands of books that I have read.

I thank Charles Fillmore and Unity, for teaching me how to be fully human and live with God. Here I learned to transcend my personal issues and to not let circumstances spoil my bliss with God.

Shirley Gehrke Luthman in Sausalito, California, enhanced my knowledge of the masculine/feminine process. She has been one of the top innovators in this field for a long time and has written several very fine books. One of my favorites is *Collections*. You can receive information on her books by writing to Mehetabel & Co., P.O. Box 2611, Sausalito, California 94965.

Shakti Gawain and I have been exposed to many of the same teachings. Therefore, some of the concepts in Shakti's book and in mine will have a similar ring, although we treat the theory very differently. I highly recommend *Living in the Light* as a fabulous addition to your understanding. Shakti, thank you for being such a light in the world.

Thank you to the men I have co-led workshops with: Don Hanson, Mark Sato, Larry Jenson, and Tim Heath. You have positively influenced my personal development and my work. You will see yourselves and your influence on the pages of this book. There is nothing like an exceptional man and to me you are all exceptional.

A special thank you to Martin Cohen, who invited me to use his work when I met him in Sedona. It added greatly to my insights.

You can reach Martin Cohen by writing to 420 Lexington Avenue, Suite 620, New York, New York 10170.

My heart is full of loving thanks to all of my dear friends who believed in me and encouraged me in every possible way. A special note of love to Mya Lit, Jon and Patricia Diegel, Eric Lehrman, Bunky Bowman, Alex Handy, Diane Clair, Melba Beals, Vonnie Brenno, Theresa and Peter Mahoney, Jeannie Hooper, Ann Watts, Myra Anderson, Ann Riggs, Barry Mann, Jonathan Hirshfeld, Russel Frischella, Barbara Bissell Howell, Ann Louise Gittleman, and John Desgrey, without whom I wouldn't be alive today. Thank you for your extraordinary gift of love and friendship during my tragedies. Great gratitude to Ann Brawley and Jane Bower, who were the catalyst for my beginning to teach again and enjoy life.

Thank you, Howard Franklin, for encouraging me to develop my mind all those years ago, and for never failing to be there for me when I really needed you. You are family to me and occupy a special place in my heart.

My love and gratitude to Laura Huxley, who touched my heart from the day I met her. She is an extraordinary woman who has been unbelievably generous to me and continues to inspire me.

David Lee has been there for me in a way that no one else ever has. David, you have given me sound business advice and encouraged me until writing has become my passion. I cherish your friendship and your support. You and my dear friend Sindja Ming pored over and edited this manuscript so many times that you know the material almost as well as I do. Thank you, Sindja, for your great heart.

Most of all my gratitude and appreciation go to three very special women. These women helped me to keep on keeping on. The first of these is Monica Briese, who wrote this book with me. Monica did not realize when we began that she would literally have to become an intern in order to write the book. We have worked side by side and developed a terrific friendship and partnership. Good for us for surviving all the pitfalls of writing with hearts full of love.

Next is my agent, Regula Noetzli, who is a magnificent woman. She has from the beginning taken me under her wing, read and made invaluable suggestions, with much kindness and encouragement. Regula, you are a true miracle worker and tops in my book.

Last but not least is Barbara Gess, our editor at Simon & Schuster, who went way beyond the call of duty. Barbara, thank you for taking such a personal interest in this book and for being such an inspiration. You helped us to reach beyond our limits and make this a wonderful experience. You helped us to refine this book until it became something that we are proud of.

I cannot end without thanking all of my students and clients throughout the world who have taught me so much. As you grew and learned, you challenged me to go deeper into my understanding of my own work. We have had a wonderful journey together.

God bless you one and all. I love you.

Thank you, Heavenly Father, Mother, God for your many blessings.

Contents

Introduction

For a long time we have worked and lived according to an accepted formula for success and happiness. We were brought up believing that if we put our nose to the grindstone and worked hard, all our dreams would come true. But that formula for creating success and happiness has been unbalanced for many generations because it forgot to include a very necessary aspect of our inner strength—our intuitive/creative self. It is our intuitive self that gives us those golden moments of utter wisdom. It helps us to solve our problems and steer our lives. We have forsaken this part of ourselves in order to fit into the status quo of business and success, but that is changing. John Naisbitt and Patricia Aburdene write in their book, *Megatrends 2000*, that intuition will be the catalyst for self-determination and individual initiative in the nineties. They state:

> The new golden era where humankind earns its daily bread through the creativity of the individual instead of as a beast of burden already exists in the developed world, which is now entering the global economic boom of the 1990's. In a high-wage information economy, people are paid for what is unique to them—their intelligence and creativity, not their collective brawn.

Naisbitt and Aburdene use the word creativity whereas I say "intuition." When they mention intelligence it corresponds with my "logic."

We're discovering that it takes more than intelligence and elbow grease to succeed. In order to survive in today's world we will have to shift from the dictates of previously imposed guidelines to a more precise guidance that will have to come from within. Our intuitive nature *is* that internal guidance. We will have to balance old-fashioned logic and reliability with a more sensitive/intuitive nature. Successful people in today's world utilize their intuition as well as their logic. This is often an automatic skill, but if it doesn't feel automatic to you, you can learn to enhance your intuition and reasoning abilities so that they work in what I call "The Dance of the Selves." Your intuition and logic will learn to work with one another so gracefully that their continual movement will feel like an exhilarating dance inside of you. This book will show you how to develop both your intuition and your logic, and to teach them to dance together.

I have been teaching the use of intuition and its integration into life in a practical, grounded way for the past twelve years. During that time I have repeatedly had students ask me when I was going to write down my theory so they could share their new information with friends and associates. In the past I always said, "I am too busy teaching." Many years and many thousands of students later, I realize that it's now time to make this information more available; not just to my students, but to people all over the world.

That's because your inner dance is the foundation for all of your ideas and actions concerning success, relationships, and life. It is the basis for your creativity and passion. Through the internal dance you will be able to know exactly what actions to take, when to take them, and how to successfully complete your projects with more excitement and enthusiasm than you have ever had. If you can embrace your internal masculine and feminine fully, you will unleash your inner passion and your life will never be the same. The dance of your intuition and logic will become so refined that you will experience what I call the "Inner Marriage." When you have achieved the inner marriage, you will experience complete balance and harmony in all aspects of your life.

It is often hard to create this balance on your own. Very few people have achieved this, so we have few role models and teachers. I was raised in an unusual family, and had no concept of balance or integration in my early life. My mother was an incredibly gifted spiritual teacher and healer, but was so raw and sensitive that she became an alcoholic and drug addict. I was highly creative and impulsive, and wanted to be an actress and a writer. My impetuosity created all kinds of problems and unhappiness for me, and I didn't have the vaguest idea of what might be causing the suffering in my life. Fortunately, I had settled down a great deal before I entered my doctoral program.

As I worked on my doctoral dissertation I became more fully aware of the power of the feminine/intuitive force. It was then that I began to look at the relationship between my own internal masculine and feminine. I discovered a dysfunctional marriage within me, and immediately began the process I share with you here. After further research and much reading, I began to focus on the relationship between intuition and logic in creating success and happiness. It was at that time that I began referring to these aspects of ourselves as our "internal duo" (our internal masculine and feminine). Over the years, I developed a process for enhancing both these aspects and the relationship between them.

When I began this book I had no idea how little of the practical aspects of feminine/masculine integration had ever been put into words. Writing it has been a tremendous challenge for me. It has forced me to clearly express what I have known on an intuitive level for a long time. This book has been immensely valuable in my own personal process, and has helped me become more succinct in my teaching. My own healing journey, as well as that of many others, is described in this book for you. Every exercise I give you is one that I have found valuable both for myself and for others.

I know that every one of you wants to actualize your potential and have your dreams come to fruition. I know that you have something to contribute both personally and professionally. There aren't any shortcuts to developing the kind of inner strength that you will need to express these gifts. What I am talking about here is a way of life that is well worth the time and effort to pursue. Determine now that you will be patient, and will not become discouraged in learning these new methods, but will instead become totally involved in the ever-unfolding process of developing your natural ability to learn, grow, and develop.

Loretta Ferrier, Ph.D.

Dance
of
the
Selves

ONE

The Foundation for Lasting Change

The mechanistic world view cannot make us healthy, because it misses the point of who we are: conscious beings passing through an evolutionary process, creative and fluctuating in nature, and able to transcend to new levels anytime we fall into entropy—never victims of our past, but instead, capable of being in the past, present and future all at once, in charge of our own destiny. If we continue to focus on the objects in our lives as "truth" (events, labels, other people, problems, and mind-sets we adhere to are all examples of this), we miss the point entirely.

—Jacquelyn Small
Transformers: The Therapists of the Future

What if I were to tell you that two very unique powers exist inside you? They are very much like two individuals, and They have a relationship just like any two people in the external world. What are these two powers? They are your intuitive/creative self and your cognitive/logical self. The relationship between these two aspects within you is the foundation for the way you live your life. If these two powers work synergistically you'll move through your life with great ease and satisfaction.

Unfortunately, most people don't naturally experience a synergy between their intuition and logic. Instead they usually experience an internal war. The result is always a lack in some aspect of their life, whether it be money, self-worth, or love. If you're one of these people you can become an inner "matchmaker" for your internal selves, and can help Them to work together. Their relationship is

the essence of your personality and is the foundation for real transformation.

Many years ago, when I first began my studies in counseling, I
discovered an interesting phenomenon in the majority of my clients.
They could intellectually grasp the changes they needed to make,
and could even successfully develop new behaviors. Yet, in the face
of a familiar and painful situation, such as interacting with their
family, my clients would invariably revert to their old patterned
reactions. How often I heard them lament, "Oh no, not again! I
thought I had outgrown this response." This was true even for clients
who had been in traditional therapy for a long time, or had been
devoted to their self-growth for many years.

Despite all their personal processing, far too many still suffered
from the very same problems they had been trying to transcend.
Attempting to change even a simple habit, such as dropping a figure
of speech like "you know" from our sentences or stopping ourselves
from picking at our fingernails, can require real work. Changing
these habits is usually quite slow. Worst of all, the change may
only be temporary. How then can we ever hope to change something
as complex and deeply entrenched as a psycho-spiritual problem,
such as a deep-seated fear of intimacy, a debilitating feeling of
worthlessness, or a distrust of our intuition or good common sense?
I began an earnest search to answer the key question, How do we
truly transform ourselves, thus creating permanent change?

As time passed I became more and more convinced that authentic and permanent personal growth involves much more than
being able to cognitively approach our particular problems and
addictions. It requires more than knowing what specific thought
forms and patterns create pain or joy for us. Many therapeutic
approaches seem to be cognitive in nature. The client explores
typical behavioral and thought forms, and searches for the reasons
behind them by digging through the past. The knowledge that your
father was an alcoholic or that your mother abused you as a child
doesn't automatically free you from the impact of the experience.
Awareness of your background and patterns is merely the first step
in the journey of release.

Other therapeutic approaches deal with the emotional debris
created by our life experiences and focus on emotional release by
encouraging crying, screaming, pounding pillows, and so on. These

activities emancipate blocked energy associated with certain traumatic situations, but permanent change requires that we go beyond
the first step of release. Once the emotional outburst is over we
may feel better, yet we are still faced with "something else" that
actually holds the key to transformation.

The twelve-step programs instituted by many addiction recovery
groups address change by connecting to a power greater than ourselves. This can be very effective work for many who suffer from
dysfunctional behavior. The basis of these programs is that we are
helpless and that only God (our higher self, etc.) can allow us to
transcend our emotional problems and dysfunctional behaviors.
However, I do not believe that a client who has undergone the
initial stages of recovery is then helpless. Far from it. While leaving
the initial process of change to a higher power is important, it is
simply not enough. If you are currently involved in a twelve-step
program, I am not denying its value to you, nor suggesting that
you should quit. Use the program to stabilize yourself and your life,
and begin the initial stages of change. Then, when you are ready
to claim your personal power, this book will help you understand
how to live beyond the recovery phase. At that time you will fully
experience your life and will manifest all of its potential.

Your personal power comes from the full development of the
two aspects I mentioned earlier: your intuitive/creative self and your
cognitive/logical self. I call these aspects your internal feminine
and your internal masculine. The theory of what I call the internal
masculine and feminine is becoming important in the highly com-
petitive twentieth century business world. It is no longer an esoteric
topic that remains in the domain of the New Age. For instance,
Roy Rowan is a business journalist who has traveled all over the
world writing for magazines such as *Life, Time,* and *Fortune.* Mr.
Rowan addresses the qualities that I call the masculine and feminine
in his book *The Intuitive Manager,* and refers to these same aspects
as "the mover" and "the motivator." He states that over the years
America's top business people have told him that they perceived
the balance of intuition and logic to be critical for business success.
Let me give you an example of an intuitive manager.

Bill owns a large, successful company on the East Coast. His
salesman, Ron, is constantly amazed by Bill's ability to sense good
business deals. Bill calls Ron three or four times a month and says,

"You had better check in with So-and-So's company. Something is happening there." If Ron asks him if he knows something in particular, Bill will always respond, "No, it's just a hunch." Every time Ron checks out Bill's hunch he discovers that the company he contacts is thinking about or has just moved in a new direction, and has problems for which Bill's company offers a perfect solution. Ron says of Bill, "The man is uncanny. Sometimes when I call the particular company, they will ask, 'What made you call? We only just discussed this issue.' I just answer 'We just had a hunch.' "

Dr. Nathaniel Branden, founder of the Biocentric Institute, has a sign in his office that reads: SEE WHAT YOU SEE, KNOW WHAT YOU KNOW AND BE WILLING TO ACT ON IT. That is a very clear statement about the integration of the internal masculine and feminine: seeing is the job of the masculine; knowing is the job of the feminine. Integrating both processes and acting on them is the mark of an individual who is truly living life in a productive, happy way.

Dr. Branden is a great proponent of knowing our internal truth and acting on it. He believes that we have the capacity within us "to be the teachers and custodians of our growth" and so do I. When we follow our internal truth, we experience what Branden calls self-esteem, and what I call integration. Your internal feminine is the teacher and your internal masculine is the custodian.

The theory of our inner masculine and feminine is deeply rooted in many oriental and Western psychological theories. According to Jung, we are born with two very important archetypes in our subconscious, our anima and animus. The anima embodies qualities such as receptivity and intuitiveness. The animus embodies such qualities as logic and aggressiveness. According to Jungian psychology, each of us displays not only behavior that is typical to our sex—i.e., women as nurturing, men as assertive—but we also display behavior that is typical of the opposite sex. (Remember that this behavior is defined by societal norms.) A woman has her "animus," and a man has his "anima." Jung postulated that in order to maintain mental and emotional health, we must balance our external self with our internal counterbalance.

I base my work on the premise that both men and women have an internal masculine and feminine, two polar forces inside us that embody creative, intuitive energy as well as logic and form. These

FEMENINE

aspects are two separate, living archetypes within us. They are very much like people we know. Each internal being has His/Her own unique personality, style, set of needs, and approach to viewing reality.

The internal feminine is creative energy, the source of our intuition, and our connection with God. She is the principle of expansion; She embraces all viewpoints and wants to include all things. In Her perfect form She is absolute knowing. Through Her guidance we receive direction for our life. She corresponds to Rowan's motivator. She is lost without our internal masculine, who takes action. The feminine must rely on His focused awareness to fulfill Her dreams. Without Him, She cannot manifest Her vision. Because of this, She must listen to His perceptions, taking into consideration what He can and can't do. She functions at Her highest level when She gives clear, concise visions and does not go beyond His ability to manifest.

Our internal masculine builds structure within us, which then reflects in the structure of our outer world. He narrows and defines. He corresponds to Rowan's mover. Our internal masculine is focused and therefore exclusive. He is the principle of contraction. When They are working together, He brings the feminine's visions to fruition through logic and order. He manifests physical reality, but functions at His highest level when He is *following* Her vision rather than trying to lead Her. He has no vision without Her. She keeps Him motivated and in motion. He follows Her blueprint to create form and physical reality.

For most people, the dynamic between the internal masculine and feminine is at its uncooperative worst. At best, They barely know one another. It is the war between our masculine and feminine that leads to imbalance in our lives and produces inharmonious relationships, poverty, and a loss of excitement about living. I believe that until we have fully integrated the internal masculine and feminine in ourselves, we will lead lives full of suffering, effort, and struggle.

By developing Their relationship to the point where They literally fall in love, we can have unlimited possibility for change. As Their relationship changes, our personal dynamic and our lives change for the better. When your intuition functions well, you are

inspired, creative, and strongly guided by hunches. When your logic
functions well, you know exactly how to organize your life and what
steps to take to fulfill your vision. Your masculine and feminine
will continue to evolve for the rest of your life. Perhaps you can
see why helping people develop a passionate love affair between
these two functions is of the utmost concern in my life and work.

I use the word *passionate* deliberately. Passion speaks of fervor,
ardor, intense emotion, and compelling action. I feel that passion
in life is an essential component in a well-integrated individual.
When we create that passion between our masculine and feminine,
we then experience fully dynamic and joyful lives that radiate from
our newfound mastery.

Before They can operate with passion together, our internal
masculine and feminine must learn to function at Their uniquely
individual best, and must simultaneously learn to live in harmony
together. Because I see Their interaction as movement, I refer to
Their dynamic as a dance and refer to the marriage of our feminine
and masculine as "The Dance of the Selves." Imagine your intuition
and logic as two dance partners trying to move together, arms
around each other. They must learn the finer nuances of communication and cooperation so they will move in the same direction
at the same time. When it is done right, the dance of self is the
most beautiful thing in the world to experience. Your life will reflect
your inner dance very poetically. If your masculine and feminine
don't master Their movements together, Their actions will become
clumsy instead of being graceful. If They attempt to function sep-
arately, with Her going in one direction and Him in another, you
will find yourself feeling separated, indecisive, and unable to take
action. If they become too disjointed, the dance may actually stop.

There is a difference, though, with the dance of the selves. It
is not the masculine who leads but the feminine. I will explain this
further. For now, remember that as the giver of guidance, your
feminine establishes the direction you are to go in. I want to clarify
that I am not talking about external men and women. I am not
saying that men should follow women or that women should wait
for men to do things for them, or that one sex is better than the
other. I am talking about the two functions that we all have inside
us. The process of integrating these two aspects is exactly the same

for men and women, although individual journeys will vary considerably. If you don't believe that the process could possibly be the same for both men and women, then I would suggest to you that your response comes from stereotypical patterns between your internal masculine and feminine. The same would be true if you responded negatively to the notion of Him following Her. If you become entrenched in your position about the sexes, you will be missing the point and will not be able to use this rapid and effective form of personal integration.

Masculine and *feminine* are terms for separate qualities within us that are equal. One is not better than the other. Either can be strong or debilitating in its own right. We use many terms other than masculine and feminine to describe this dichotomy of abilities; animus/anima, yang/yin, cognitive/intuitive, focused awareness/diffuse awareness, contraction/expansion, etc. Today we often refer to these characteristics as left brain or right brain.

The fact is that our internal masculine and feminine don't necessarily reflect the traits we usually associate with maleness and femaleness. For instance, most of us associate aggressiveness and power with masculinity, and receptivity and softness with femininity. In my theory, we reown the true power of the internal masculine and feminine.

For now, let's simply say that the power of our internal feminine is the movement and motivation in our lives. She is not necessarily soft in Her power. She can be ruthless, for She is the spirit of evolution and carries no emotional bonds in Her desire for change. She has kept mankind alive for thousands of years. She can also be impatient and impractical.

His power leads to manifestation in our lives. This power can be tough, but can also be extremely caring and nurturing. When unleashed into His true power, our masculine brings the element of compassion to our lives as He effortlessly creates according to Her vision.

At this point, I am generalizing Their individual dynamics for the sake of simplicity. However, our internal masculine and feminine have many forms in which They initially emerge, depending on our personal experiences and our archetypal structure. I will discuss this in greater detail, later.

Living Life Energetically

If you can begin to see painful situations and problems as opportunities to build His structure to match Her intuitive guidance, you can release old emotional patterns that no longer work for you. In this way you use the events in your life as feedback. You will begin to see repeated patterns as an indication of old, limiting structures within you. Then, each time you come up against another similar circumstance, you will have the opportunity to release the old pattern rather than continue its cycle. Your release of old structures allows the new structure to emerge far less painfully. Rather than working to make the limitation go away, you will be allowing a new structure that will literally push out the old one. You will become free of a past pattern and open to amazing new possibilities. Many of the exercises in this book will enable you to begin this process.

To start, learn to live life energetically. I don't mean that you must become more exuberant or physically active. I am talking about following the messages of your internal feminine by becoming aware of the energy shifts in and around you. Those feelings of deadness or repulsion you have at times and the attraction and aliveness that you have at other times are the kind of energy shifts I'm talking about. The more open we become to reading our body's energetic response to our environment, the more likely we are to experience vitality and energy rather than apathy and tiredness.

She "speaks" in vibrations or energy patterns that you experience as sensations in your body or as sounds or images. She will guide you by charging you with energy when She says yes to some action, or by a feeling of open tingling in your heart area or your gut. You are probably used to calling these "hunches" or a "gut feeling." When she says no, She will guide you by pinching your gut or giving you a heavy heart, a drop in your energy level, or a feeling of deadness. For a few of you, She may guide you with images or even sounds.

As you read this book you will learn to read and follow the signals He and She are giving you through your body. The body is a perfect feedback mechanism for Their state in any given moment. For instance, when He can't follow Her energy toward action at any moment, then He will speak to you as a pain in the back, the stress of tightness across the shoulders, or a stiff neck. You may feel angry, or apathetic, or simply burnt out. In other words, there is too much to do and He has reached the limit of His tolerance to deal with things. Through these kinds of signals you will learn to follow your intuition more successfully and to know whether or not your masculine can bring your feminine's vision to reality. Almost everyone can eventually learn to feel energetic shifts in themselves and in a group.

If we are doing what we think we should do rather than what our feminine directs us to do, then we create deadness in our lives. Being fully alive requires being in the here and now, waiting for guidance in each moment, and being willing to act on that guidance. Being in the moment means taking our cues from Her, from the world of the nebulous. Our masculine, with His world of structure and form, is often very unnerved by this. He is more comfortable when things are static, stable, and linear. It is only when He is operating in His full-powered state that He is ready, willing, and able to follow Her "juice." This means that He is willing to let go of stability and the forms to which He has become attached. The more your masculine backs up your feminine's guidance through action, the more alive and vital you become. Although life lived this way is much more exciting and rewarding, most people settle for deadness rather than aliveness. The familiar, even though dead, feels safer and easier. But once you learn to live life energetically you will be unwilling to sacrifice your aliveness for anyone or anything. You will refuse to live with that dreadful feeling of deadness and disinterest.

Inner Matchmaking

As in any relationship, your relationship with your internal masculine and feminine must begin with an introduction. They will, of course, have to get to know each other, develop a friendship, and have a courtship. This exciting courtship inside yourself will increase trust and confidence between your logical and intuitive selves. They will first learn to dance harmoniously together, and then Their passion will be released. If He and She already know each other, and have unfortunately built up a history of ignoring or even disliking each other, a reconciliation process much like marriage counseling will be necessary.

As you do this, you will develop the ability to be an educated observer of your internal dynamic. You will become your own marriage counselor. Observation without judgment is a crucial step in building toward Their passionate dance. Your job, if you are going to have more than surface change, is to become a conscious observer of the limited patterns to which you cling.

Give up the notion that you are going to change things by thinking about them. All the thinking in the world never really changed anything. You are not going to try to be different. The first step is to accept yourself now, exactly as you are. Seeing yourself as imperfect is a judgment and judgments always cut you off from Her. (Judgments usually come from a limited internal masculine.) Judgments create even more effort and struggle than you already have.

Rather than viewing change as loss and trauma, you will learn to view change as merely an ebb and flow of experience. Once you start operating from a more secure foundation, you won't feel as much fear and pain, even though your life will constantly move and change. Whether life brings you roses or lemons, you can simply observe where you are and notice what is emerging without getting emotionally bogged down in your situation.

Feeling truly alive is the greatest gift we can have. Imagine the thrill of feeling excited when you get up each morning, actually anticipating the adventures of the day ahead. As a result of working with the internal duo, I have seen major changes in my own life and the lives of my clients, both on a professional and personal level. Here's an example:

When Henry first came to me, he had been operating in a safe and secure world for most of his life. His life had security, but he wasn't happy or excited, nor was he filled with self-determination. Each time Henry ventured in a new direction he felt as if he was suffocating from fear. Even the smallest of decisions filled him with terror. His masculine was somewhat stodgy and lived according to the expectations of Henry's family. This was a family of great wealth (for six generations). His feminine was being crushed by tradition.

She wanted to cast off in new directions. Each time Henry tried to follow his feminine the terror would rise.

We had to build Henry's masculine so that He would more willingly follow the feminine. I encouraged Henry to take small risks, like going to new restaurants and talking to strangers on impulse. Henry's internal feminine began to take him in all kinds of new directions. These things were nothing major but life was a great deal more exciting than it had ever been.

His internal masculine was able to step forward and actually begin the new direction. Henry became more adventurous and the fear began to dissipate. He developed confidence and courage. Henry made a major shift through living life energetically, and by accelerating through old patterns of behavior that kept him bound to deadness. Through working with his internal masculine/feminine archetypes, he rapidly pushed the judgmental, narrow-minded patterns of his family from his cells. As his cellular memory shifted, Henry built his physical reality around his new inner vision.

The marriage of Henry's internal masculine and feminine was just the beginning of his powerful journey in transcendence. While She and He grew in mutual love, trust, and support, Henry engaged in a dynamic, new way of living. He then experienced the freedom of following his inner vision in the moment. He threw away the family road maps to life that had guided him since childhood.

A year after he came to me, Henry, with the feminine's guidance and the wholehearted approval of the masculine, sold his business and his house, bought a vintage three-masted schooner, and toured the world. He had definitely learned to feel safe and happy in the midst of constant movement. Without his former security, which was actually based on limitation, he felt much safer because change no longer frightened him.

The exercises in this book take you through the same kinds of processes Henry experienced. You can do them at home, either by yourself or with a partner. As you learn to live your life energetically, you may find in the process that you will let go of many people and things that were previously very important to you. You will find that new opportunities and new people come into your life. You will develop new interests and may even fulfill some dreams that you gave up long ago. Healing the relationship between your archetypal internal feminine and masculine and bringing them to a state of perfect union is the foundation for living life fully. The goal of this work is to create a passionate inner marriage that will result in the integration of your brain-body and spirit. You will then experience a beautiful Dance of Self. Before we do that, let me show you how the feminine and masculine originally developed.

TWO

Once upon a Metaphor: Your Inner Fairy Tale

. . . where men are men and women are women . . .
—John Wayne

*C*inderella was rescued from misery and abuse by Prince Charming. Snow White was kissed back to life by still another Prince Charming. Little Jack, who climbed the bean stalk, rescued his mother from the grips of poverty through his courage, cunning, and perseverance. What do these fantasy characters have to do with us in real life?

A lot!

Even though the stories in which these characters star are mainly sources of amusement and entertainment, the characters in our fairy tales and myths provide a wealth of imagery that mirrors the belief system of any particular age. We have set up a legacy of legends, myths, and stories and have created goddesses and gods, all depicting the various aspects of our views on femininity and masculinity. Gods have been both male and female; frightening, benign, jealous, all loving, and lusty. Until recently, our heroes have been fearless, incredibly intelligent, and able to solve any problem. Our heroines have been beautiful, very patient, understanding, supportive, and have often needed to be rescued.

You have inherited these fairy tales, whether you believe in them or not. No matter how liberated you think you are, this inheritance may be your bane as you struggle to maintain your sense of self. Even as we verbally embrace equality in intelligence, physical prowess, and independence in both men and women, we often secretly long to be like the wondrous characters we find in fairy tales, living out these fables in our own lives. Despite their own strength, many women still unconsciously search for a Prince Charming to rescue them. Sensitive men who have more interest in literature than fixing cars often chastise themselves for not fulfilling the quintessential hero image. Our inability to fit the image of our inner fairy tale or to find the perfect fairy tale relationship brings us much grief and pain.

New Understanding/Same Behavior

The experience of manhood versus womanhood has never been universally consistent. We have struggled with our concept of maleness and femaleness through the ages, never coming to a resolve. Multitudes of cultures have dealt with maleness and femaleness in many different ways, and it is obvious that many of our concepts are arbitrary and changing. Humankind has experienced cycles in which we have swung from devaluing either masculinity or femininity to exalting and glorifying those same traits.

In the aftermath of the seventies' feminist movement we have tried to intellectually embrace a different understanding of what it means to be human. More of us talk in terms of our having both masculine and feminine qualities and we have relaxed our strict rules about acceptable behavior for both sexes. However, not much has really changed in our basic nature or in the kind of people to whom we are attracted. Women still have pretty much the same complaints and problems. Men do too. While the old role models are dissolving, there is still great confusion about what it means to be a man or woman.

In 1973, Jerome Kagan from Harvard did a study in which six-year-old children were shown pictures of animals and asked to identify the animal's tendencies "toward or away from" aggression, according to sex. The children were asked to classify male and female behavior in terms of their parents and then themselves. Results from the study showed that the children had definite stereotyped attitudes. The children described themselves in the same terms that they described their parents. They believed that "a tiger is a masculine animal and that a rabbit is feminine."

You may think attitudes have changed since then. However, in random samplings of my own, I still find children respond in very much the same way as in Kagan's study. Our intellect may tell us that equality reigns, but our children don't seem to be getting the message. Nor are we getting the message as adults.

Women who have strong business skills or who are highly athletic still run the risk of being categorized as unfeminine. Men who have developed their more sensitive side are now accused of being wimps and not masculine enough. A recent article in a women's magazine showed that women still don't want men to cry. People who consider themselves to be enlightened human beings tell me that no matter how much they feel they've evolved, they still find themselves operating blindly from their stereotyped patterning. Even today, if I ask a room full of people, "What is masculine or what is feminine?" I repeatedly hear fairly consistent descriptions.

MASCULINE	FEMININE
Strong	Weak
Aggressive	Passive
Logical	Intuitive
Unemotional	Emotional
Organized	Disorganized
Hard	Soft

It is obvious that the various feminist movements over the years haven't changed our deeper levels of consciousness.

The Development of Our Internal Masculine/Feminine

If we were merely linear beings born to fulfill a one-dimensional destiny based upon our being male or female, life might be simpler. We could then fulfill the fantasy expressed by John Wayne of an era "where men are men and women are women." This is obviously not the case. For generations we have absorbed this one-dimensional message. Where did that come from?

There are several theories as to what happened to us as we developed psycho-spiritually. One is that we started out as whole beings and then became divided and incomplete at some point in our development. *The Encyclopedia of Religion* states that many stories from the world's religious texts describe the original human as being androgynous, and then later separating into the two sexes, male and female. You can find these accounts of androgynous human beings in Native American stories, in Eastern Indian philosophy, and in folktales from Africa and the Pacific Islands. Other examples are tales of the Australian Aborgines, ancient texts from Mesopotamia, and even the account of Adam and Eve in the Bible.

I see the story of Adam and Eve as an allegory of the time when we were whole. Part of their original wholeness included what I call the integration of our internal masculine and feminine. Remember that our internal feminine correlates to that part of ourself that is diffuse and intuitive, whereas our internal masculine correlates to the focused, logical part. I hypothesize that there was originally a wholeness in each of them, and because of this, they lived in perfect harmony together. The eating of the apple symbolizes their becoming polarized and incomplete. Adam became one half of the polarized experience and Eve the other. When this happened, Adam and Eve lost their full connection with God, who is the quintessence of integration, and thus were cast out of the Garden of Paradise. Being incomplete, Adam and Eve began to seek their wholeness outside themselves. Eve started to rely upon Adam for those qualities She lost and vice versa. They were, of course, doomed to failure.

It is possible that as we evolved physically and mentally, from that moment in time, our internal masculine/feminine also evolved. Bronowski, in his book, *The Ascent of Man*, suggests that the forerunners of man began to be nimble with their hands in making tools and clever with their brains in planning them. With the invention of the tool came the creative urge that separated humans from the lower animal kingdom. Bronowski correlates the drive that led man to make tools with the drive to create a community. As we became hunters instead of gatherers, the nomadic way of life evolved and the necessity for community emerged out of that.

Community survival required communication and social inter-action. Culture, as we know it, began to develop 50,000 to 100,000 years ago. Cultural evolution soon became as important as biological evolution. At some point the male as hunter began to dominate and became the protector. The more clever and skilled a man was in creating tools, the more mates he could attract. Conversely, woman's primary role became mother and home keeper in support of her hunting mate. Her producer-of-life role placed her back at camp, vulnerable and needing protection. The word *vulnerable* is defined as "open to damage" and that is how women began to be perceived. Men became the planners and the powerful.

The emergence of role differences created "good matches" along with its converse, "bad matches"; thus we began to view others as desirable men and women verus undesirable men and women. With this division of expectations for the sexes we became more polarized in our thinking and abilities. We started on a long journey of rules and expectations.

As community consciousness became more and more important to human development, the roles of the sexes were further differ-entiated in order to maintain peace and order. Our culture dictated how we should act as male or female. Depending on our gender, we were molded to display either aggressiveness or passivity, emo-tionality or lack of emotion, logic or intuition—but not both. In order to achieve social acceptance, we felt compelled to disown that part of us that did not fit in with our society's definition of proper behavior, thus denying one half of ourselves. We repressed any thoughts or abilities that contradicted the ones we were sup-posed to display, and developed stories or fairy tales to transmit our society's role beliefs to the new generations. The repeated trans-mission of these concepts from one generation to the next developed into what Carl Jung referred to as genetically inherited archetypes.

Jung discussed humankind's thoughts and behaviors in terms of archetypal images, which are genetically encoded and transmitted from one generation to the next. Thus we are born with an image of what reality is and how we are to function in it. Some of those images are: good/evil, God/Satan, and mother/father. To Jung, archetypes are essential building blocks, and form the basis of in-stinctive thoughts and behaviors common to all mankind. He re-ferred to archetypes as: "Pieces of life itself—images that are

integrally connected to the individual by the bridge of the emotions." Therefore these archetypes compose the psyche of men and
women, coloring our very thoughts and reactions. In creating this
paradigm, Jung went beyond the contemporary theory of environmental influence—that we are what we've learned in this life—
and added that we are also what we've mentally/emotionally inherited.

Cellular Transformation

My exploration of our internal masculine and feminine integration
led me to realize the full impact of Jung's theory that we genetically
inherit archetypal information. If we transfer genetically stored
mental/emotional concepts such as archetypes, then surely we also
store our own mental-emotional patterns. I began to realize that
the reason we couldn't transform patterns and emotional reactions,
even after years of therapy, was because those emotional patterns
are actually a part of our bodies. They are in each and every cell,
and won't change just because we want them to. In other words,
our emotional experiences are actually imbedded in information
that is stored in our cells. This stored information then becomes a
program that is the basis of our reactions and dysfunctional patterns.

I call these stored patterns and thought forms "cellular" or
"internal" structure. Cellular structures or patterns are the very
source of repetitive behavior, and result in preset ideas and even
religious dogma. These are the thought patterns that keep us going
in circles. They generate a set of limiting expectations and unconscious behaviors that become our reality and keep us from realizing
our full potential. When we attempt to change our psycho-spiritual
awareness without pushing the old and limiting structure from our
cells, the change is never complete. Thus we continue to repeat
past problems and to act out in the old ways.

This is not really a revolutionary concept. Since 1930 there
have been many others who have explored this idea. Only now is
scientific research being done that will help us to understand the
process of transformation. Let me give you a few examples of how
this work has been demonstrated over the years.

Wilhelm Reich, a student of Freud, was close to the concept

of cellular memory in the early thirties when he introduced a new concept that he called "body armoring." Armoring develops when we continually store emotional energy in patterns in our muscles. These patterns literally become a part of us, and they develop into muscular armoring in an attempt to protect us. That is what happens when we develop certain body postures, habits, etc. Reich believed that unless the armoring in our muscles was released we would not really benefit from psychoanalysis, because the basic blocks would remain. If we free the body from its armoring we activate our body's natural ability to heal itself.

This was a profound realization at the time, but now we know that releasing the muscular armoring alone will not bring about the depth of change that we might desire. That change must occur within all of our body's cells, not just particular parts of our body. While it is true that as armoring dissolves it has a freeing impact on the cells, it is only part of the solution. We must allow our consciousness to accept the fact that all our cells have intelligence and can change.

Our cellular intelligence is turning out to be far more important than we ever dreamed. Marilyn Ferguson, in her book *Pragmagic*, talks about the work of neurologist Israel Rosenfeld. Rosenfeld does not agree with the commonly accepted notion that the brain is a computer that stores information. He instead agrees with Nobel Prize–recipient Gerald Edelman's theory, which defines memory as being comprised of a variety of "maps" and that the very first map forms in the embryo. These maps might be seen as a gathering of like information. The maps "speak" to one another, and in the process form categories. In the Edelman model, cells develop and relate to one another dynamically, establishing "neuronal groups." These neuronal groups alter with history and with changing context. Edelman claims that these individual groups would "be an unreliable storage unit" if they operated alone. However, in concert, the groups can create categories of information. By matching and overlapping categories, they can place a new stimulus into an appropriate context. In other words, the "memory is assembled" and changed as we continually amass new information and experiences.

Drs. Stein and Belluzzi, who are studying addiction, from the University of California at Irvine, are finding interesting results that might support my theories. While exploring what they call the "mindedness" of isolated brain cells, Stein and Belluzzi have discovered that a single brain cell can be trained in a laboratory setting, in much the same way as a rat can. A rat rapidly learns to push a button that will result in a reward of food. Similarly, the research of Stein and Belluzzi has proven that a brain cell can learn that it will receive dopamine or cocaine each time it registers an electrical discharge. As the brain cell becomes addicted, it will deliberately increase its electrical discharges in order to get more of the drug. Stein states, "If what we found is valid, then nerve cells are capable of goal-directed behavior. It's a wild idea, but that's what our results are telling us." This may explain why it is difficult to overcome addiction and to make lasting change in our personalities. We might need to address the addiction found in individual cells.

If we store the memories of our life experiences in our cells, and if our cells indeed collectively react to external stimuli in a particular learned pattern, then we had better start looking at behavioral changes on a cellular level. It stands to reason that we must physically extricate ourselves from our limiting patterns in order to experience true change. To do this, we must release our cellular memories so we can make room for more healthy, positive responses.

In my view, *true change occurs only through cellular transformation, in conjunction with an intelligent restructuring of our belief systems.* Unless we work with cellular transformation, we are just exchanging one limiting pattern for another. For example, if you continually end up with the same kind of man or woman in your relationships, it may not be simply wrong choices on your part. It may be that your choices are more a reflection of a cellular pattern that is within you.

I began to research the possibility that the real value of integrating our internal masculine and feminine has to do with building new patterns in our cellular memory. Your internal masculine and feminine are initially part of your inherited archetypal imagery. They then change over time, based on the way you live your life. Memories stored in your body's cells have affected the ability of your internal masculine and feminine to function in their full power.

Since our masculine and feminine are genetically inherited, no matter how sincerely we try to change ourselves we will usually fall back into former modes of thought and behavior. They are part of our inner fairy tale, which gnaws at us as we try to maintain our theories on being the "new woman" or "new man." For example, your intuitive nature may be asleep, just like Snow White, who was kissed back to life, or it may be like Cinderella, who was abused and needed to be rescued by the prince. Your masculine, being cognition and logic, may operate according to His belief that the feminine power, like the Sirens or Medusa, will destroy you if you venture too near.

As your internal masculine and feminine change, which They will when you work with Them, you will be releasing stored information that is no longer useful, creating new memory patterns that will lead to cellular transformation. Your inner fairy tale will dissolve and you will create a new reality for yourself, one without the shackles of fear.

← vibration

THREE

The Internal War

He is playing masculine. She is playing feminine.
He is playing masculine because she is playing feminine.
She is playing feminine because he is playing masculine . . .

—Roszak and Roszak

Theodore and Betty Roszak begin the poetic introduction to their book *Masculine/Feminine: Readings in Sexual Mythology and the Liberation of Women*, with these lines. The poem continues to describe the intricate web of action and reaction that we weave in our relationships. This web, based on our inner fairy tale, grows increasingly oppressive as we build a history of interactions with our romantic partners, who reflect qualities that we've had to deny within ourselves:

He desires her for her femininity which is his
femininity, but which he can never lay claim to. She
admires him for his masculinity which is her
masculinity, but which she can never lay claim to.
Since he may only love his own femininity in her, he
envies her her femininity. Since she may only love her
own masculinity in him, she envies him his
masculinity. The envy poisons their love . . .

The Roszaks eloquently describe a dynamic fairly common to relationships between men and women. For the past thirty years, through the human potential and freedom movements, we have attempted to transform this dynamic. As a result, we see small changes creeping into the mass consciousness. Just as our ancient myths reflected older dynamics, our modern stories clearly reflect our new dynamics.

For instance, there is a new focus in the way television and movie roles depict men and women. The heroines of today's movies are much more spunky, feisty, intelligent, capable, and human than the heroines of yesteryear. Take a comparative look at the characters portrayed by Mary Tyler Moore in *The Dick Van Dyke Show* versus her own television series many years later, *The Mary Tyler Moore Show*. In *The Dick Van Dyke Show*, Ms. Moore played the worried housewife; in her own show, the harried businesswoman. Compare the character portrayed by Donna Reed in her show years ago with that of Roseanne Barr. Did we ever hear Donna's character raise her voice to her husband? Donna never struggled to balance her needs with her family's, nor did we see her work outside of the home. Ms. Reed and her television contemporaries were far different from Roseanne Barr's television character or the female characters on other current television programs.

The roles men portray now are not always strong, wise, and all-powerful heroes. They are shown as bumblers as often as they are competent, they are sometimes rescued by women, and they are even portrayed as being successful in the role of homemaker. For example, the movie *Three Men and A Baby* is the story of three bachelors who are all successful businessmen. They suddenly wind up with a small baby at their doorstep and, through the trials and tribulations of balancing their professional lives with the needs of the baby, they become adept at caring for her.

The external stereotypes in our movies and television shows are changing because our internal dyamic is changing. In the introduction to his book, *SHE!*, Robert Johnson states that myths ". . . are the product of the collective imagination and reflect the experience of an entire age and culture. Myths seem to develop gradually as certain motifs emerge. They are then elaborated upon, as people tell and retell certain stories that catch and hold their interest. Thus themes that are accurate and universal are kept alive." These themes are much more than the description of external relationships; they describe our internal dynamic as well.

Our fairy tales have been rewriting themselves over the past twenty years and new myths are forming in order to accommodate these changes. However, regardless of the changes we are now experiencing, the shadows from the original dynamic, as expressed in the Roszak poem, are still entrenched in us. Many of us live as if a full-scale war is still raging within us. We are like the old Japanese soldier who was found hidden in the jungles of a remote island, years after World War II had ended, acting as if the war was still going on.

The shadows of those old myths we still experience are merely fragments of old patterns remaining in us. They point out where we, as individuals, have stopped in our human development. We can use those internal myths and fairy tales to start us on our personal archaeological dig where we can uncover the things that we need to change inside in order to change our external reality.

The Swinging Pendulum

Our internal masculine/feminine have developed as humankind has progressed throughout historical time; but Their individual development within each of us has not necessarily progressed at the same rate of speed. Our feminine might be very wise and knowing, while the masculine is very young and impetuous, or just the reverse: She might be frivolous, while He is wise. One may be old, the other younger. One may be patient and the other outraged, etc. They are exactly like real people, and They tend to have certain body stances and patterned facial responses.

I will talk about this dynamic in much more detail later, but for now, realize that the constant shifts in the growth of our internal feminine and masculine and our attitudes with respect to that growth are reflected in our external attitudes and behavior. (Remember that the external is a reflection of the internal.) At different times in our history we have collectively tended to be more dominated by one or the other of the internal duo. In one era we have honored Him—distrusting both the intuitive world and those who possess heightened intuitive natures. In another era we have distrusted the logical manifester's world and those who live comfortably there. Like a clock's pendulum trying to establish equilibrium, we have swung back and forth, from one extreme to the other, trying to create a balance. As a result, we've created cycles of misogyny (the hatred of women) or misandry (the hatred of men) as we project our fears of the masculine and feminine principles onto our external reality. In either case, both sexes now struggle with internal misogyny and misandry by suppressing either our intuitive or our logical sides.

Why does the pendulum continue to swing back and forth? Because most people are not spiritually and psychologically developed enough to listen simultaneously to the "voices" of their internal masculine and feminine. Generally, we tend to predominantly listen to one and fear or distrust the other.

We've seen a very big swing of the pendulum in the last three decades. We have shifted from denying our feelings and our intuitive side to the opposite—ridiculing logic, power, and material success—then back to admiring logic, power, and success. With the rise of the technological age, men and women have progressively learned to deny their own internal feedback and sensitivity and have also accepted that denial as normal. That led to rejection of the feminine principle and the rigid establishment of the masculine principle. In the sixties, we reacted to this rigidity established by the masculine principle and started to reject His domain, swinging back to the feminine principle. As growing numbers of people dismissed the masculine principle, we embraced the opposite extreme of perception. Anyone who wanted money was a "capitalist pig."

During the eighties, we entered the era of Yuppies, where achievement and financial success were once again admired. Interestingly enough, the New Age movement also grew in the eighties, capturing the attention of many. Information about alternative methods of psychology, spirituality, and health began to make its way into popular magazines and other media. However, there was a growing skepticism about the New Age. There were too many ungrounded people in the New Age movement who were trying to "manifest" their rent through meditation rather than rolling up their sleeves and working. With the simultaneous rise of Yuppies and New Agers, I saw our masculines and feminines trying to achieve Their full potential at the same time, but not necessarily doing it together, as a couple. The nineties, more than at any other time in history, are more about balancing these two aspects of ourselves.

The Roots of Our Misogyny

Let's look in depth at the various shifts in our internal growth so that we may go on to balancing ourselves. We have inherited very conflicting messages about the feminine/intuitive principle. On one hand, intuition is recognized as a strong power; but that power has no definition and is not obviously controlled. Such ominous power would have to be feared, denied, and contained. Some early religions believed that women had the power to turn men into animals. The witch hunts of Europe and early America, however reactionary they were, are an example of the extremes to which our fears and denials can drive us.

On the other hand, the feminine/intuitive principle involved receptivity. Receptivity translates to vulnerability and therefore we have often avoided it. We assigned receptivity and vulnerability to the domain of women. The domain of women has often been depicted as overly emotional, uncontrolled, and therefore, neither as functional nor as desirable as the domain of men.

In Retrospect

In the original order of things women or motherhood were associated with the earth, and men or fatherhood with the heavens. The power of the heavens (i.e., the penetrating sun, the forceful wind, etc.) were identified with the masculine principle. The masculine principle became more important in our values, with the receptive earth taking a back seat. Humans equate the earth with females because of their receptivity and their ability to bring forth life. When humans began working with agriculture and controlling the productive faculties of the earth, this was extended to the attitude and treatment of women. Susan Griffin writes of this in her brilliant work *Woman and Nature*:

> And it is decided that the angels live above the moon and aid God in the movement of celestial spheres. "The good angels," it is said, "hold cheap all the knowledge of material and temporal matters which inflates the demon with pride." And the demon

resides in the earth, it is decided, in Hell, under our feet. It is observed that women are closer to the earth.

Major religious texts and dogma display distaste and fear of women. Many of the earliest religions believed that women led to man's downfall. The great Buddhist teacher Chogyam Trungpa writes in *Maitreya* about one of the Buddhist sects that also believes that women led to man's downfall and to the downfall of Buddhism itself:

> . . . Buddha was compelled to ordain his female cousin. Because women were accepted by the Order, the reign of the Buddhist teachings was supposedly shortened by five hundred years. Also, a woman's body is considered the unfortunate result of bad karma.

Even though a number of modern religions and cultures verbally affirm the power and divinity of the feminine principle, their practices seem to denigrate women. There are several Native American tribes, for example, that are matriarchal in their structure. However, their custom dictates that women not look a man in the face, especially when she is serving him meals. The women are also expected to wait until after the men are completely satisfied and finished with dinner before they are allowed to eat. They are excluded from tribal activities while they are menstruating and are considered dirty at that time. So they are not actually held as equal and honored. Many of these same customs have been held by Western and Eastern societies over many centuries.

An interesting aspect of this is that some of these practices actually originated out of respect for women or the feminine principle. Through the ages, however, as we further divorced ourselves from our original state of wholeness, we perverted these practices because of our own renouncement of our internal feminine. For instance, there is the Hassidic rule of imposing the separation of men and women during their worship and the practice of keeping the teachings from women.

I spoke about this with Rabbi David Zellor, formerly of the Institute of Transpersonal Psychology in Menlo Park, California. He said that many people think that women were initially separated

from men because they were considered to be lower in status. Rabbi
Zellor stated that, on the contrary, this practice originated from
the belief that women were in touch with the spiritual teachings
naturally and didn't need as much instruction as men. He com-
mented: "As the soul takes its traditional form there are two basic
forms that it comes into—one being male and one being female.
As an allegory you have a population of people fifty percent of
which suffer from an acute and terminal disease called 'masculinity.'
Originally masculinity was a disease which separated one from the
Divine. . . . The treatment of that disease is a strict regime of
intensive hours of meditation and Torah. Manifestation of the
Divine—of the Word—helps a man to realign. Females did not
suffer from this disease."

Rabbi Zellor went on to say that at one time the Jewish people
believed that this disease (masculinity) was not communicable to
any woman. I feel this "disease" is a dysfunctional masculine archetype that is transmitted at birth through the genetic encoding I
mentioned earlier and it *is* transmitted to women.

Misandry

Don't feel confused if this is the first time you've heard the term
misandry. You won't find it in the dictionary. In fact Dane Rudhyar,
celebrated philosopher/writer, created the word for me while I was
working on my doctoral dissertation. I was doing a study on successful female entrepreneurs. In the course of that research, I also
looked at less successful businesswomen. I found a phenomenon for
which there was no word. It was the fear and/or hatred of men, or
more accurately, the fear of the masculine principle.

Misandry is real, whether we choose to recognize it or not, and
has come about in a more complex manner than misogyny. Male
images have been traditionally depicted as heroes, as bigger than
life. "He" was the savior, the wise one, the all-powerful, all-know-
ing one. When real men turned out to be less than those images,
women secretly despised them. It was a jarring discovery to realize
that our vocabulary includes a word to denote the hatred for women
but there is no correlating word describing the hatred for men.
What does this show about the hidden thought processes in our

society—that hatred for men, i.e., the masculine principle, is of no consequence? It is as if we have had no clue that the masculine principle in us could possibly be as feared and hated as readily as our feminine principle. As we lost faith in them, our onetime heroes rattled around in rusting armor, trying to figure out how to be strong and how to attain the hero image they were supposed to already possess.

I began to understand why, until recent times, most women had such a difficult time being successful. We cannot develop that which we reject through fear or hatred. Since many women were filled with unacknowledged misandry, they were unable to tap into their own masculine force with love and respect. This being the case, there was no way He could make their business lives more satisfying.

Misandry arose as a backlash after centuries of misogyny and cellular memories of rape, beating, forced marriage, slavery, etc. While the masculine superstructure promised to love, protect, and cherish the family, it was also actively suppressing women. This superstructure justified its actions as keeping the home fronts safe, making life easier, or earning money. As both men and women denied the reflection of their own feminine, the masculine superstructure became trapped by the lowest level of expression—survival—and lost sight of the consequences that unbalanced change and growth had for the earth and its people. We didn't know how to achieve health, wealth, and happiness in a productive, compassionate way.

A low, seething rage against men and the masculine principle began to build in women and in the more sensitive men. We turned against Him and His world of form, logic, and order. Eventually we became disdainful of those who were successful in this domain. We grew to distrust anyone or anything that represented success in the material world or any of the other so-called masculine qualities. If we have fear and disregard for any part of the physical world, we carry our own form of internal misandry.

It was the latest women's movements that stirred misandry into its extreme. In the first movement in the early 1800s, women first grumbled about their treatment by men. One such early feminist, Sarah Grimké, said, "All I ask of our brethren is that they will take their feet from off our neck."

By the second women's movement in the late seventies, the grumbling had turned into blatant, vocal rage and hatred. Women by the thousands turned against the masculine superstructure. To the radical feminist, the primary enemy was "man." Societies such as the Society for Cutting Up Men (SCUM) arose. It has been the strongest misandry movement humankind has seen. Women like this were pretty difficult for all of us to deal with. Their anger toward men was so forceful that all they presented was rage. They wished that men, like a dying fossil, would become extinct, viewed only in zoos as rare specimens or stuffed and found in museums.

In the seventies, women sought to equalize their lives by experiencing their more aggressive, masculine force, though they might not define it as such. In order to do this, they turned on men. The result was the emergence of the repressed power of their feminine, fully enraged and dressed in war regalia. June Singer refers to this particular archetype as the "Artemis-Amazon" and says that the emergence of the Artemis-Amazon signaled a major cultural transition. It was critical for women to separate from men and learn to productively use all of their capacities. Singer says: "Had the Amazon type never broken the stereotype of 'femininity,' the independent woman of self-esteem would never have found the courage to make her voice heard."

The last women's movement was an important awakening. We had denied our true nature, with both its beauty and strength, for too long. For the first time, women in large numbers began to explore becoming truly responsible members of society and expressing themselves fully. However, many went too far to the opposite extreme, and began to embody the very attributes they could not tolerate in men. They dressed like "the enemy" and often acted like men, adopting the toughest, most uncaring characteristics.

While women were moving into their power, men were challenged to change as well. Men, too, had their Artemis-Amazon archetype. It was the long-haired, hippie radical. These men turned against everything our society held dear. They were against fighting for our country, eating meat, following Western religion, and earning a good living. They didn't drink but they used mind-expanding drugs. They didn't look like the men we were used to seeing and they didn't act like them.

The Amazon archetype caused more of us to become painfully

aware of our lack of soul. It was then that parts of society shifted to the other extreme, downgrading success, family concerns, and organization. The sexually liberated view became popular and many of us began endlessly examining our emotions in order to transcend the pain of old standards and expectations.

New role models of sensitivity and ability for both men and women emerged and traditional role models were publicly degraded. Men were challenged to show the depth of their feelings, nurture their children, participate in housekeeping, and still be a professional success. Women were challenged to make a living outside the home, and became embarrassed to say they were "merely" housewives.

As a result of the feminine rejection of the masculine principle, both men and women regarded the masculine principle as evil and overbearing. His energy had dominated the world for centuries, its rampaging ego attempting complete control and creating destruction in its wake. As a result, we became suspicious of anything resembling the masculine. We hated men and we hated masculine structure. Men too began to despise even the more positive aspects of who they naturally were. For instance, several years ago, a marvelous thirty-four-year-old man came to see me at the recommendation of a professional friend. He was sweet, soft spoken, spiritually devoted, and a loving, gentle father. He was in the process of a divorce in which he felt very much at the mercy of his attorney and the legal process. He refused to stand up for his rights to the point where he wasn't confronting his attorney for some very important mistakes that would cost him a lot of money as well as custody of his child. This young man felt he had no power over the situation.

You might guess that his internal masculine was weak but that was not the case. Both his masculine and feminine were strong and capable. However, the internal feminine did not like the internal masculine. Although the masculine loved the feminine and pursued only Her, She had no use for Him, especially during conflict. As a result, the masculine would disappear in the face of conflict, leaving the feminine to handle it.

I pointed out to the young man the importance of accepting the warrior in us and that it was imperative that his internal masculine come forward to match the abilities of his feminine. My

client told me that he was afraid of that part of himself, because
he knew it had such great brute force and he didn't want his ego
to take over his life. He was fourteen when the feminist movement
was in full swing and felt his feminist mother was far too aggressive
at that time. He had interpreted her aggressiveness as masculine
and vowed at an early age that he would never be like her.

When I pointed out to him that it may not have been the
masculine in his mother that was harsh but her internal feminine,
he was shocked. I reminded him that the feminine can be even
more harsh than the masculine when She is in control. Intuitively,
I saw his mother as a woman with a weak, hiding masculine, and
an outraged feminine. Since the age of fourteen, when he made
that vow not to be like his mother, my client had worked diligently
on his feminine side but had never healed the part of him that was
like his mother, so he avoided any behavior that closely resembled
her. In trying to avoid what he saw in his mother, this young man
was actually developing the very same internal structure she had.

Although all the changes in our gender roles were very important steps in our psycho-spiritual genesis, it's not news that the
women's movement has missed the boat, as do most movements.
Although the feminist movement definitely opened our eyes to the
separate prisons that men and women were living in, it didn't
produce any real answers. The self-exploration it encouraged only
further intensified each sex's underlying fears and confusion.

We didn't make the transition too easily, experiencing great
confusion about what was expected of us as men and women. The
changes necessary to break from the stereotyped roles were formi-
dable to accomplish, so we became dismal failures at simply being
human. Women tried to develop their masculine, assertive side,
but they were dealing with the same stereotypical patterns they saw
outside of them. Men were their role models. As a result, women
tried to emulate men and were not a pretty sight. They intellectually
embraced equality but didn't know how to live it.

Suddenly women had to take care of their professional careers
and the home front, as well as find time to be glamorous for their
men. Most of their spouses were unwilling to help with the housework, and they began resenting men even more. As a result of too
many pressures in wearing too many hats, the "Superwoman Syn-
drome" developed. Many women separated even further from men,

and denied their basic desire for a loving relationship in order to survive.

Right now we are in another evolutionary shift. Men have been trying to develop their feminine aspect, having only us as their role models. Because of this, many have become too soft and too emotional. They are where women were thirty years ago, and again it is not a pretty sight. More and more women come to me complaining that men are too feminine. As a result, we are seeing a backswing to the ultra-macho warrior in our movies through characters portrayed by Arnold Schwarzenegger, Sylvester Stallone, and kung fu movie star, Steven Seagal.

To Shift Our Reality

We have been looking outside ourselves and accusing the opposite sex of being impossible. We began to believe that it was men and the patriarchal structure or women and the matriarchal structure that we had to conquer. We even turned away from God as "He" had been distorted by the masculine superstructure in the building of churches and organized religions. Each sex tried to change, and as it did we said, "No, that wasn't what I wanted; that doesn't make me happy either." We were blind to the truth that our external world is a mirror of our internal dynamic. The external war has always merely reflected the tragedy of our deep, internal war.

The imbalance is inside us and that is where the correction has to be made. The only thing that will heal these problems is creating a new context within which we can view life. Individual emancipation ultimately comes only when we cease casting the problems of our inner masculine and feminine (our wholeness) out there upon other members of our society.

It is sometimes hard to accept that separation is inside us rather than out there. In order to heal ourselves, we must first transcend any of our inbred views of the masculine and feminine principles. Those views create the norms by which we attempt to live. That's why the Roszaks' poem at the beginning of this chapter is so powerful. It blatantly points out to us the ridiculous norms by which we have tried to live. These norms prevent us from actualizing our divine internal masculine/feminine.

There are now fewer and fewer guidelines for behavior, with the continual shifting of roles and attitudes, so our natural integrity has to arise from within. Natural integrity, however, is not possible without awareness of our internal guiding pulse. The internal feminine is that guiding pulse and She acts as our barometer of truth. She leads us forward to live beyond the confines of the moment. With Her guidance we can transform our habitual way of responding.

Let me give you my favorite analogy of how your feminine and masculine should work together. Think of a wagon wheel for a moment: the axle of the wheel appears motionless, while the outer rim appears to move faster and faster as its speed increases. The axle, which centers and holds the entire wheel, is also the power that allows the wheel to turn effectively. As we move progressively toward the wheel's outer edge, movement appears to increase, even though the entire wheel is making the same number of rotations.

You can liken your life to that of a wheel. If you learn to live in the center of the wheel where the inner masculine and feminine have their eternal relationship, you will be operating from the center of your existence, holding all that is in your life in total harmony with ease. The further away you get from the center of the wheel (or your inner relationship), the more movement you will have to make to achieve the same amount of success and progress. If you get caught living your life on the outer rim of the wheel you will find yourself expanding more and more energy in an attempt to operate further and further away from your essential nature.

Most of us have lived our lives on the outer rim, running frantically to keep up with the pace we've set for ourselves. Exhausted, we can no longer hold on. If you are one of those people, I am inviting you to return to the axle, to that place that fully empowers you to live your life without effort or struggle.

Natural Integrity Requires Forgiveness

Before you can establish a relationship between your internal masculine and feminine, it is important to heighten your receptivity by preparing your mind and heart. The journey of true integration begins with learning to forgive ourselves and others. This is because we are either weakened or strengthend by our thoughts. Judgment, guilt, blame, and resentment block our ability to listen to our feminine. Thought patterns, even if unconscious, are stored in our cells and unless we release them, we will endlessly repeat the cycles they produce.

If you think that you have no anger or blame toward others or yourself, please look again very carefully. Denial is a powerful force. It is easy to fool yourself, especially if you have done a magnificent job of repressing anger for years. I suggest that if you are not clearing your pain and anger on a regular basis, you will find that it has once again built up. Until we are enlightened, it is doubtful that we have cleared our emotional hooks. It may be that you have done a great deal of psycho-spiritual work on yourself and the following exercise may be too elementary for you. If you've really searched for hidden anger and truly find none, then you are very fortunate and very rare. If this is the case, please continue past the Releasing Anger and Resentment exercise.

Kinesthetic Muscle Testing

There is a rather simple way to test yourself for anger and weakening thoughts. It's called Kinesthetic Muscle Testing. The muscle test checks your body's reaction to people, things, or thoughts. Your body can actually tell you who and what is good for you and what is harmful to you. It can tell you if it wants to do something or doesn't want to do something. It will tell you which thoughts weaken or strengthen you. For instance, anger, held in any form, will weaken you. Your body will literally become physically debilitated, and that will reflect in the muscle testing. There are two ways to test yourself; one you can do alone, the other requires another person.

TESTING WITH A PARTNER
1. Stand facing your partner. It is best if you are a little to the side of one another so that you aren't completely face to face. Look straight ahead and don't make eye contact with your friend.
2. Hold your left arm straight out to the side, at about shoulder level. Have your friend put her left hand on your right

shoulder and her right hand just above the wrist of your extended arm.

3. Have your friend lightly push down on your wrist while you resist her effort to push your arm down to your side. Have her tell you to "resist" just before she pushes down. The point is not to trick you but to give you fair warning so that you are not caught unaware. Your partner should be pushing down just enough so that you are required to exert a little effort to keep your arm up. This has nothing to do with brute strength. Don't make this a contest of wills.

Once you have gone through this initial test you will understand what I mean. In a moment you are going to have your friend lead you through a list of people who have played important roles in your life: your family, employers, lovers, friends, etc. Do this one person at a time. Your friend tells you, "Think of your mother; resist." Then she will press lightly but firmly down on your extended arm.

Notice each time what happens. Was it easy for you to keep your arm up? Were you helpless against your friend's push on your arm, so that your arm weakened or even collapsed against the side of your body? If your arm weakened, thinking of that person is weakening to you and you may have unresolved feelings about him or her. In this case, even if you think you have done a great deal of work on your relationship with that person, then doing the anger letter I discuss below would be beneficial. Repeat the test with the rest of your list. Your common sense will tell you which of these people you need to forgive and which of them generate guilt in you, pointing out the need for self-forgiveness.

TESTING ALONE

You can do this same type of test on yourself using the fingers of one hand to pry apart the fingers of your other hand. If your fingers open easily, it is a sign of weakness. If they resist opening, it is a sign of strength. Here is how you do it:

1. Place the tips of the thumb and first finger of one hand together so that they form a circle. You will have something that looks like the A-OK signal. Make sure that the back of your hand is down and your palm is up.

2. Now place the thumb and forefinger of the opposite hand

together as if pinching something together. You will use
these fingers like levers to attempt to pry open the circle
of the thumb and forefinger of the opposite hand.

3. Slip these fingers inside the circle you've created with
the first hand. Now make a statement and push the two
"lever" fingers apart. Resist with your circle fingers just
as you resisted with your arm when someone else was
testing you.

The same principle applies with this exercise. If you are thinking
a thought that weakens you, it will be easier to pry your circle
fingers apart than if you are thinking a thought that strengthens
you. Test yourself initially so you will know how you register weak
and strong. Ask your muscles, "Show me strong," and then ask,
"Show me weak." If that doesn't work, think of your favorite thing
to do and test yourself. Then think of something awful, like getting
fired or having a terrible argument. The more you do this exercise,
the more you'll learn to read your muscular reactions to situations.
When you are first learning to follow the feminine, you can also
use this as a reality test. For instance, you can say, "I'm going to
buy a new car." Test. Then, "I'm not going to buy a new car."
Test.

Establishing Forgiveness

Now you are ready to deal with forgiveness. Most of us have experienced a number of incidents that have left us feeling betrayed,
abused, or unloved. The most common reaction when we experience abuse or betrayal is to become angry at the person, the situation, or even at God. If we don't release that anger, we repress
it, burying it in our cells where it turns into self-negation or depression. Over time that unresolved anger builds up, blocking our ability
to experience the full range of our emotions. We cannot simply
block out so-called negative feelings without also blocking out positive feelings. Block out anger and you also block your ability to
experience love. One of the ways to liberate yourself from this
deadness is through the act of forgiving those whom you perceive
have harmed you.

You, in turn, might have someone who is angry or disappointed
with you. Your denial that your actions may have been harmful to
yourself and to another can lead to guilt and self-abuse. Again
forgiveness is the first step in moving toward healing. For most
people, forgiving others is actually easier than self-forgiveness. We
are often our most severe critic.

Once you have really examined your mind and heart, you may
find that while you do not have any anger, you still have a "charge"
when you think of a particular person, and that you would like to
be free of even that small response. If so, you may want to simplify
the exercise. Shift it from anger to merely expressing any thoughts
you still have about that person and about your behavior with that
person.

FORGIVENESS

Follow these instructions exactly. Do not attempt to compress
all three days into one. If you do, you will not have the full
impact of the exercise. It would be like taking three days' worth
of medication in one day. Emotional release and detoxification
are like physical detoxification. It takes time to let go of the
toxins that are stored in your body's cells whether those toxins
are chemical or emotional.

Don't let time lapse between day two and day three. Many
people want to delay going on with the last step, forgiveness.
I have been told by clients that they found they weren't willing
to forgive someone and let go of that person's influence. Delay
will only generate disruption in your life. Before you begin the
exercise, please make sure that you have paper and pen or
pencil, and find a time to be quiet and alone on each of the
three days. On the third day you will want to plan a burning
ceremony. Decide before you begin where you will want to do
that and how you will burn your paper. If you are going out
into nature, be sure to take a pan to burn paper in or make a
small fire in an authorized area. At home, many people use
their fireplace. PROCEED UNTIL YOU FINISH.

Day One
Determine the person with whom you are the angriest.

Write a letter to that person and say every mean thing you
ever wanted to say. Don't pull any punches. Don't hold back—
be as freely angry as you can.

Hide the letter so your subconscious mind knows that some-one would have to really search to find this letter.

Day Two
Take the letter out. Cross out words and make them worse. Write more if you need to but keep intensifying the anger and the pain. Now hide the letter once more.

Day Three
Go to the place where you plan to have your burning ceremony. Make sure that it is safe and quiet. Make something beautiful, almost like a prayer alter. Use music that always moves you and allows you to open your heart. Take the letter out again, this time with the pure intention of forgiving.

Take a few deep breaths and get into as relaxed a state as possible. If you pray or meditate, do that now and get as calm and centered as you can. TAKE YOUR TIME because your internal state is the key to the success of this exercise.

1. When you are quiet and open, ask nature, your higher self, the universe, or God to release you from your anger and pain and to release these heavy feelings from your brain-body and heart.
2. Now begin to reread the letter. Each time you feel the anger and resentment coming back again, turn it over to a Higher Power.
3. Continue doing this until you have finished reading the letter. Make sure that you stay in contact with a Higher Power as you tear the letter up and burn it. As the smoke rises say out loud, "I know that these negative feelings are now being transmitted to the light."
4. When the smoke stops and the paper is thoroughly burned, close your eyes and do the following visualiza-tion: Imagine that a beautiful white cloth is placed under the ashes. See yourself tying it into a knot. Now imagine that a beautiful white bird flies down from the left, scoops up the bundle, and flies off to the right. As the bird disappears just say, "I now let go and let God" or "I now let go and am free from these feelings."

5. Slowly become aware of your surroundings. Open your
    eyes and take the real ashes and either flush them down
    the toilet or bury them in the ground.

If you finish the exercises and find that you are still really angry
with the person to whom you have been writing, you may have
to repeat the exercise. Wait at least three days before doing so.
Most often someone else will come to mind. Again, please allow
three days to one week before proceeding on. You need this
time for integration.

Forgiveness is extremely important in rectifying your internal war. Sometimes you have to forgive yourself, sometimes the
opposite sex, sometimes your friends and/or family. The stored
anger and resentment may be from many areas of your life. It
can also be passed down through your family. Releasing anger
and resentment can create the atmosphere of love and openness
that you will need to work toward peace with your internal
masculine and feminine. If you are consumed by anger and
resentment, it is difficult to find peaceful resolutions for your
own internal war. I'm not suggesting that a simple exercise will
remove all of your anger and resentment, but it is a beginning.
Remember that forgiveness must often be done in layers. Just
when you think you've forgotten and forgiven, another layer of
anger or resentment bubbles up. Check yourself often for these
feelings and do the releasing exercise whenever you need to.

Forgive all that is outside you and all that is inside you, and
you will not only quell the internal war, you will also develop
compassion for yourself and others. You don't have to live with
the emotional bondage that limits your life.

FOUR

Following the Bread Crumbs

Much suffering comes into the life of one who tries to be anywhere but here in the present moment—right nows are all you have.

—Sujata, *Beginning To See*

We don't often receive guidance like Moses did or the other figures from our spiritual literature who spoke to God. Rarely does a booming voice give us messages; nor do we receive stones emblazoned with rules to guide us. No bolt of lightning is likely to come down out of the sky to get our attention. Most people expect their inner guidance in the form of a voice or an unmistakable sign from the heavens. We don't usually hear voices, but we can receive more subtle messages about how to direct our lives in a very practical and dependable way by working with our internal feminine and masculine.

We receive guidance through energy shifts in our bodies. If you become aware of subtle shifts in your body, you will become sensitive to the messages from Her and Him that will guide you in all aspects of your life. I like working with the allegory of Him and Her because I find it a very workable method that leads to increased awareness and stability.

I also like the metaphor of an internal masculine and feminine because it allows you to honor your particular version of God, the universe, or your higher self. In other words, Catholics, Hindus, Jews, Buddhists, even atheists and agnostics can find this process useful. Regardless of your spiritual beliefs, you can train your body to be a finely tuned reading instrument that will serve you well in each moment. When you develop the ability to respond immediately to these shifts, you can be fully adept at analyzing and acting upon each new situation you encounter. Just like the samurai warriors you see in the movies, you can exist in a state of constant preparedness for mastering all obstacles. In fact, many of the martial arts trainings, some of which I share with you in this book, work on integrating the feminine with the masculine.

Our goal is to follow our feminine and to use our masculine to bring Her guidance into physical reality. Following your feminine means acting when you feel open and energized and not acting when you feel closed down or in pain. Your body will feel energized when She is saying yes, and suddenly drained of energy when She is saying no. One of the primary places for reading Her is the area that encompasses the solar plexus. You may have a tight, pinched feeling in your stomach. You may feel a heaviness on your upper chest or around your sternum.

Following Her means that you commit yourself to acting only when the juice is there, or when your solar plexus feels open and relaxed while your back feels comfortable. We often get tight, pinched feelings in our stomach or our back and are used to ignoring these feelings. I have learned to pay attention to those feelings. There have been many times I received a message from my feminine to stop what I was doing. I could tell by a tight feeling in my stomach. If I didn't stop immediately, I then experienced a loss of energy. So, now, when the juice isn't there, I don't act. I do nothing until I feel the juice moving again.

Aside from learning to follow Her direction, you need to take in His feedback and to back off from Her impulses if He can't back Her up. For purposes of the metaphor, when your masculine is having trouble backing something up, He will often let you know by a tightness or pain in your back, neck, and shoulders. In this case, you simply ask Her to slow down. When He can easily fulfill Her visions, you will find that your neck and back feel quite comfortable.

It will become progressively easier to read the signals your body gives you as you begin to pay attention to Their messages. If you don't initially pay attention to those messages they will grow stronger and stronger. Let me give you an example of paying attention to the energy.

A few years ago I met in private session with some people from South Carolina. They called a couple of weeks later and wanted me to fly there and work with their friends. It was the middle of the summer, and I knew it would be hot and sticky there. I went anyway, trusting the spark of energy I felt in my gut. The people were charming, and rarely have I enjoyed any journey more. I made several good friends there who have added delightful new dimensions to my life. That trip also led to work in several other cities. My trust in both my masculine and my feminine really paid off. You want to have a strong intuitive; but you also want to keep Her in perfect balance with a strong masculine.

Following Her changes in direction is very hard for most of us because we feel our decisions are commitments that are cast in stone. When you think your decisions are permanent, you automatically stop following your inner voice. She often asks you to move in new and unfamiliar directions, doing things that make no sense to His logic. He often gets stuck in a particular mode of operation because he has previously been able to manifest something using that mode. Unfortunately, by the time He is certain of something and has manifested it to His satisfaction, She may have already moved on to another vision.

Let's say that She wants to build a store and the masculine builds a store that becomes very successful. The masculine then becomes enamored with His ability to manifest and builds a chain of stores across the country without consulting Her about it. He then goes on to build shopping centers. She, on the other hand, wanted to build only two more stores, one in Florida and another in Hawaii. He quit listening to Her. In other words, the logical self got carried away and stopped paying attention to intuition. If He continues in His same direction rather than following Her, the result will almost always be some kind of complication in that person's life or a feeling of quiet despair and emptiness.

Once you begin to listen to your feminine's signals, you must learn to temper the masculine's left-brain drive to adhere to far-reaching plans, no matter what. You want to use His valuable ability without letting it dominate you. His job is to make plans but his weakness is to stick to them stubbornly. Sometimes, your feminine wants you to move in a certain direction but only for a period of time. She is using the new direction to dislodge you from your rigid patterns. Once you are more flexible, She is able to guide you in a way that might have been too frightening at first or something for which you were not yet prepared. Never assume that where you are headed is where you will wind up.

It will be very important for you to learn to follow Her moment-by-moment instructions. You may find this difficult in the beginning, so you might make a lot of plans that you will have to cancel. For instance, you may go out for dinner with friends you usually like being with. You'll get there and you'll feel as dead as last year's Christmas tree and you'll wonder what you're doing there. If you are really following Her, then you will tell your friends that you love them, but it won't work for you to get together with them that night. You'll often find that the others feel the same lack of juice to be there but didn't have the courage to speak up. Eventually, you will be able to read Her signals far enough into the future that you won't have to change many plans.

The Bread Crumbs

When you live following your feminine, you get your directions in small increments, which I call "following the bread crumbs." The bread crumbs are messages that will appear to you one at a time. I always say this is because vultures will get the crumbs before you can reach them if a long trail is laid out. The vultures are an analogy of what happens when you look too far ahead of yourself for your life plan. Too many events can happen between now and the date you arbitrarily set to achieve your goals. Looking too far ahead can be confusing and can lead you away from Her unfolding guidance. You must be on the alert to pick up each message and then wait until the next one appears.

Another point to remember is that you often don't know exactly where She will take you. You may follow one small piece of guidance that changes many other parts of your life. I remember many years ago when a young woman came to me. She was recently divorced and very upset about having to return to work, afraid that her work skills were gone after years of non-employment. It was obvious from her sessions with me that Her feminine really wanted her to go back to work. My client learned to trust that message fairly rapidly and a couple of weeks later she found a good job. She was still very upset about the divorce, but was doing better. As time passed, my client began to want another relationship. After she had been working at her job for a year and a half, her boss's wife passed away quite suddenly. Their business relationship remained the same until about six months later when she and her boss began to date each other. A year later they were married. My client has a remarkably good marriage and now lives a life of luxury.

The Balance of Following the Bread Crumbs

One of the people I know who truly follows the bread crumbs is a lovely unassuming women. She was extremely successful in the business world when she had a hunch that she needed to live a quieter life. About ten years ago, she moved to the little town in which she now lives. Now she wakes up each morning and just does what she is guided to do. Her behavior is an authentic demonstration of following the feminine in the moment. When I mention her to people they say, "Well, that is fine if you are financially well off or a spiritual teacher, but how is it possible for the rest of us who have families to support and full-time jobs with bosses who tell us what to do?" It is possible, no matter what your circumstances are in life, to follow your intuitive as long as you are disciplined, practical, and willing to go through changes.

Obviously, it takes enormous courage to do this. You think that everyone is expecting you to keep your commitments or they will consider you a failure and unreliable. Commitments *are* important and people do expect you to keep them. This is especially true with business deals. But if you don't follow your gut, you will end up creating an empire that has no meaning or you will wind up always struggling. Have you ever had a sinking feeling as you got ready for a meeting or event, but went through with the original plans, only to have that meeting blow up in your face? When you get that sinking feeling, your feminine is trying to avoid a potential difficulty. You think you are being a coward or a failure if you change your plans, but sometimes retreat or no action is the strongest move.

I vividly remember one of my many work trips to Boston. I love Boston and it is always a joy to go there, so I had been looking forward to this particular trip. For several days I had been feeling unusually tired, and I wondered if She was telling me not to go. Each time I thought about how tired I was, I attributed that tiredness to my busy schedule, and so ignored it. I could barely pack my bags, and on the morning I was to leave, even dressing myself was an exhausting chore. I continued with my plans to leave, dismissing my growing weakness and developed a splitting headache. Upon stepping out of the cab at the airport, I found I was barely able to walk. I went immediately to a phone and called my friend Laurie to tell her I couldn't come. I said, "The juice is dead." She responded, "Well it's funny, people are canceling here, too." I returned home and later that day Boston had a terrible snowstorm that caused a whiteout. None of my clients would have been able to reach me. A day later, I was asked to replace a speaker, at the last minute, in Hawaii. This was one of those times when my masculine's courage to follow Her led to some lovely surprises.

When I started losing energy around going to Boston, my internal masculine at first refused to follow those signals. He didn't want to lose the money that would result from canceling the trip. He had to step out in faith when He decided to back up the message and cancel out. The ensuing Hawaii trip turned out to be more financially beneficial, but my masculine had no way of knowing that when He agreed to follow my feminine.

Let me give you a different kind of example. Monica, my coauthor, and I had a contract to get the manuscript for this book in to the publisher by a particular date. We were ahead of our schedule by several months. The feminine had Her own schedule, and trusting it, we pushed ahead. We did, however, get out of balance with the rest of our lives.

Family and business needs pulled Monica away from the book for several weeks. When Monica's other responsibilities settled down, we planned a new schedule for continuing the work on the book. The day before our new schedule was to start, northern Arizona had the most terrific snowstorm in forty-two years, which meant the nearest ski resort was loaded with fresh powder. Monica, on changing commitments -

an avid skier, had not gotten a chance to ski all winter due to all her responsibilities. Even though her feminine was screaming to get out on the mountain, Monica's masculine wanted to keep His commitment to me. Knowing how important skiing was to Monica, and sensing what her feminine wanted, I called her to tell her to go play, commitment or no commitment. She was already on her way to my home.

When she arrived, much to her surprise, I gave her a short lecture on following her inner guidance and renegotiating commitment, then sent her on her way. She told me a few days later that as a result of my giving her the freedom to follow her feminine in the new direction, she experienced a major shift in her energy. She realized that as the demands of her life had become more complex, she had begun to focus on the needs of others rather than following her internal feminine. The new energy that she was able to give to writing the book was quite apparent, so in the end we both got what we wanted and needed. It's very important for us to be dependable, but our dependability needs to be based on Her guidance rather than on our crystallized ideas.

Obviously you can't always ignore your commitments every time She wants you to, but there is often something you can do that will allow you to keep building with Her and still be responsible. As Monica (and her feminine) watched the snow fall that day before she came to work, Monica told her feminine that she knew She wanted to go skiing, but her feminine would have to wait until another time. The feminine had understood and Monica lost the charge about going skiing. She had done this so successfully that when I told her to go skiing, she actually had to debate with herself about it. One would think that Monica would have been able to jump at the chance but her masculine was still learning to follow the feminine impeccably.

Three weeks after her first ski trip, Monica once again went skiing. On the way there, Monica got feelings that maybe she shouldn't go that day after all. She wrote those feelings off as her imagination and continued on. The day was beautiful, with fresh, new snow and a crystal clear blue sky. Monica hadn't been on her skis an hour before she had a freak fall and pulled a calf muscle. For the first time in all her years of skiing, Monica had to have help getting down the mountain. With a wry smile, she told me she would be limping around the next few days as a reminder that her internal feminine doesn't always want to go skiing. It was Monica's masculine who wanted to go on with the plans even though the feminine was giving messages not to go!

The Joy of Following the Bread Crumbs

The joy of following the bread crumbs is that you will have unbelievable vitality. Problems no longer seem insurmountable and you live life as an adventure. As a result of following her internal feminine to go skiing, several personal issues with which Monica had been struggling suddenly became very clear. She experienced following the trail of bread crumbs, and found a creative way to solve her problems. Several weeks later, she jokingly told me, "I'm worried. I've been in a euphoric state for several days now and I'm beginning to get concerned. Am I becoming manic-depressive? It doesn't feel natural." We *can* have that continual state of joy and passion. It is the natural state of joy that we experience before the age of two but is now quite foreign to us.

In order to attain that state of joy and passion, you will have to drop the guidelines that you used to follow as a blueprint for your life. You'll need to develop the courage to live life in what I call the state of freefall—committing yourself to stepping out in space and expecting a path to build beneath your footstep.

There is a wonderful scene in the movie *Indiana Jones and the Last Crusade* where Indiana must cross a deep chasm with water raging far below to get to a cave in the cliff on the opposite side of the ravine. This cave holds the Holy Grail, the same Grail that mankind has coveted and sought for centuries. It is the end of an arduous journey for Mr. Jones, who has been searching for the Grail along with his father. There is no visible bridge to step onto, but Indiana was told by an oracle that by "leaping out . . . will a man prove his faith." He stands there, looking down into the deep ravine, considering the prophetic words and struggling with his faith. With one deep breath, he finally steps out into the ravine, and immediately a translucent path to the cave meets his feet.

This is the same dynamic that we are asked to demonstrate. It is very unnerving for our logical internal masculine, and therefore our body, to step out in faith. For those who need certainty and control, this can be a harrowing journey. In fact, for most people it is so frightening an experience that they won't even attempt that first step of faith. Even if we make an attempt to step out in faith, what usually happens afterwards is that our mind, full of old structure and expectations, comes back in to take control, especially if things don't turn out well. Our internal masculine fears what He perceived as Her chaos. Actually, there is always an orderly movement in Her creativity, although it is not always apparent.

Let me tell you a personal story about this. One summer my internal feminine began telling me that She wanted me to leave California, my home for over forty years. There were a number of other cities where I had friends and my work was well received; but Boston, Massachusetts, and Louisville, Kentucky, kept pulling me. Eventually I decided I would move to Boston and start a Transpersonal Institute.

The messages from my feminine grew stronger, yet my internal masculine was dragging His feet. Several months after I had first gotten messages from Her to move, I still had not even begun the process of selling my home. My mother had been living with me and had recently passed away. I was exhausted from nursing her through her transition, but the feminine was ready to move on— She wanted action now! I could feel my body resisting Her guidance. At this time, I had approximately 3,000 students and clients in California. This kept me very busy. Slowly my private practice dwindled, until one day my phone just quit ringing. I am not exaggerating; suddenly no one called for appointments. That woke me up and I got busy fast. My house sold in two months and I was then ready to move, but where?

My internal masculine was feeling very insecure, so I stayed with a friend while He built His ability to follow Her. One morning I woke up and He was ready to go. I loaded the car and began driving East. As I left California I could feel that my whole body was in motion, which meant that She was leaping and He was matching. Leap/match, Leap/match . . . moment by moment. It was so exciting to feel the motion in my cells rather than a kind of heaviness or deadness.

My internal feminine kept telling me that She wanted a Jeep. Every time I saw one on the road, I would feel Her strong surge of energy. My masculine balked at that. He kept saying, "Why would I want a Jeep in Boston or Louisville?" But She insisted, and reluctantly, while I was visiting a friend in Los Angeles, He traded in my car for a Jeep Cherokee. He grumbled for a few days but then He began to enjoy it as much as She did, although He still didn't know why one was needed.

My next stop was Sedona, Arizona, with its magnificent red rocks and hilly terrain. I had three close friends there and wanted to see them before moving so far away. I was only going to stay two days but found after those two days had passed that I couldn't seem to leave. My feminine was saying "This is home." Four days passed, and then ten days, but still I couldn't leave. Finally, I faced the fact that She really wanted to stay in Sedona. Since I knew that He had trouble backing Her up in the past, I asked my masculine if He could do it. He assured me He could. I must admit that I didn't totally trust Him, given His past performance. As a safeguard, I challenged Him. I said, "If you can really back this up, I want to find a home like the one I loved in Carmel. I want it to be reasonably priced and I want to close escrow in ten days." The third house I looked at was very much like the Carmel house, and I loved it; but I figured that I couldn't close escrow in ten days. Despite the fact that it was a seemingly impossible feat, escrow closed in ten days and two days later the movers were unloading my furniture.

My feminine had a strong vision and my masculine was in full agreement with Her. This couldn't have happened if my feminine was chaotic and impulsive, as She once was. When He follows Her fearlessly, yet tempers Her, there is absolute harmony. It is when He doesn't follow or when She is out of control that the trouble begins. Life will definitely let you know when you are off track.

OBSERVING

The following is an adaptation of a samurai training exercise. I use this process to calm the internal masculine and develop confidence and ability in following Her guidance and direction.

Go to a busy place such as a crowded downtown street, shopping center, or fair. Walk through the crowds of people, moving only as She commands. She may give you messages about going into particular stores or stopping at certain counters to look for something. Check each time to see if She wants you to continue on in the store, to buy or not buy. As soon as the juice dies at a counter or in a store, move on. Do not interact or make eye contact with anyone, unless She compels you to do so. If you do receive a strong "hit" to talk to someone, do so. This is a safe place to practice because you are not likely to run into people that you know. If She guides you to make a connection with someone and you do, you will be able to more fully understand how She is trying to teach you. Do this for at least thirty minutes. Repeat the exercise a couple of times and then increase the time to one hour.

In order to follow the bread crumbs, you will have to heighten your ability to become more sensitive to both your internal masculine and feminine. This means you will have to spend time getting acquainted with Them and understanding Their individual communication patterns. Just as in any relationship, the quality of the interactions increases with time and effort. So, if you are ready, let's meet your masculine and feminine. I will show you how to contact them. Then, afterwards, I will give you exercises for building Them to Their highest abilities.

FIVE

She: In Her Archetypal Form

> To be responsible for yourself, you must trust yourself.
> When you know your inner world as well as you know
> your face in the mirror, you will gain this trust in your
> intuitive or preconceptual self.
>
> —Jack Schwarz, *Voluntary Controls*

You have a direct connection with a universal creative source. This is your intuitive self or your internal feminine. She is the spirit of evolution, always expanding and moving toward the unknown. She is that part of you that is spontaneous and takes risks. She is the catalyst for change in your life. In Her perfect form, She is all knowing, dynamic, powerful, and exciting. Your internal feminine gives you the direction for the unfolding blueprint for your life. She is the source of your visions and dreams.

Have you ever known a visionary person? His or her visionary quality might be demonstrated as a heightened creativity, an uncanny sense of the future, or an unusual ability to pick up information without any discernable clues. Such people constantly astound us with their insight, imagination, and originality, whether it is expressed through an amazing painting, a song, a prophecy, or an invention that changes the world. How do such people get their incredible ideas? It is as if these people communicate with a world that is invisible to us. Why are they better at creating or perceiving than others?

Whether someone is an artist or a scientist, those who are creative, inventive, or intuitive are very much in touch with their internal feminine. She is diffuse awareness and embodies creativity and new ideas. Visionary types are somehow able to instinctively reach into that aspect of their being and hear or know their internal guidance.

Your intuitive aspect, whether or not you listen to it, speaks to you moment by moment. You often get whisper-soft messages, visions, or even physical sensations that are your internal feminine's attempts to guide you when you are pondering problems or considering a change. It is not unusual to think that those messages have no bearing on the situation at hand. The response of the average person is to brush Her messages aside as meaningless phenomena or to simply ignore them, judging those messages as one's imagination.

If you were to give more attention to the visions you receive and sensations you experience, opening to their energy instead of wrestling with the cognitive processes that want to shut those messages out, you would find that Her messages will grow stronger and more direct. Your visionary attributes will then become an important part of your daily life. Those cognitive processes and preconceived evaluations are your internal masculine trying to shut out your intuitive aspect. Jack Schwarz, in his book *Voluntary Controls*, states: "Preconceived evaluations blind us and limit our experiences to what we already know. If we wish to learn and grow, we need to remove all the restraints on our perceptions."

Every time you ignore Her message, you devalue and diminish Her. It actually isn't the big issues that devalue Her the most, but rather the hundreds of small ones that occur every day. She says, "Call Glenda." You say, "I'm too busy now. Maybe tomorrow." It may turn out that Glenda was the source of an important opportunity for you, but you missed hearing about it. Your feminine says, "We need to go for a walk now," and you say, "Don't be ridiculous, I'm too involved now." It might be that if you had gone for a walk, you would have found a resolution to that difficult problem you were wrestling with. All of these incidents add up and soon your feminine will become angry and/or stop giving you guidance.

It is imperative to learn to follow Her guidance in every area of your life. When I first began to follow my feminine, I would talk to Her all day long. I would start my work in the morning by asking Her, "What do you want to do first: the correspondence, work on the book, or make phone calls?" Together we would arrange my day. I no longer have conversations with Her, as Her impulses are so strong I simply follow them. There are still times when I can't follow my feminine's suggestions, but I always tell Her why it's impossible, so She knows She isn't being ignored.

Her messages will often seem like your imagination until she grows stronger in you. Practice following those vague thoughts or discomforts as often as you can. Sometimes still, even for me, the messages are almost too subtle to be recognized. Let me give you an example. My office was getting ready to send out a large mailing. The circulars were being printed on Friday. As I watched TV Thursday evening, I had the vague thought "I wonder if they used the right bulk-rate mailing stamp." The thought carried no urgency, so I forgot about it. The next morning the printer called to check something and I didn't even remember the slight message of the night before. I walked out the door to run errands and a message hit me like a bolt. "The bulk stamp isn't on the mailer." We called the printer, and he said, "No, there is no bulk stamp but we have already run the fliers." I asked him to be sure and he came back to the phone to tell me, "It seems you called just in time. We haven't run that side of the flier yet."

Your internal feminine can make the difference between your knowing what to do and trying to guess what to do, thus avoiding serious mistakes. She can, in a diffuse way, point the direction to all that you desire in your heart. You may find Her nebulous nature disconcerting at times, yet once She is developed in a healthy way She will not mislead you. How might things look different for you when you follow Her? You will become more flexible and open to the moment. You will become more adventurous and more of a risk taker. You will live a life full of excitement rather than boredom. With Her, you will never be bored. She makes things happen on all levels. Let me give you an example.

Two sisters in one of my workshops were leading lives of what could only be called quiet desperation. On the outside, Sharon and Charlotte were hard to approach. They answered any questions in short responses and didn't show any emotion or enthusiasm. They hardly spoke up during the exercise. At one point in the workshop they admitted they were very lonely and felt very bored with their lives. Things remained pretty much the same for Sharon and Charlotte during the entire workshop until the next-to-last day. I had been asking them all week to be more adventurous, to let themselves go, open up and see what happened. They couldn't imagine doing that, even though they wanted to. I encouraged both Sharon and Charlotte to dress the way their feminine would want to dress. They learned that both their feminines wanted them to dress more flamboyantly and act more outgoing.

On the last full day of the workshop Sharon and Charlotte appeared with major changes in their hairdos. They had also bought some new jewelry and were wearing their new prizes along with more dashing outfits. As they saw everyone's positive response, they became open, excited, and unbelievably playful. Instead of the meek, unresponsive persons we had seen all week, we saw smiles and outgoing natures beginning to peek through. At one point, on that last day, one of them cracked a really funny joke and the rest of the group sat stunned with surprise at the source of the joke and then roared.

The feminine is a powerful force for good on earth. She cares about animals, the forests, the water, and about starving or abused humanity. She wants to lead all of humankind toward reverence for life and toward unity. As more and more people throughout the world get in touch with the feminine there is a growing concern for our environment. She is divine wisdom when She functions in Her perfection. She literally becomes the voice of God, personalized in you. She can flawlessly direct you on your life's path. She is the key to unlocking any kind of limitation in your life. The trick is learning to follow Her and no one else.

When Mirah first came to see me her face was strained from trying to suppress her agitation. Mirah was dressed in a very subdued way. Her hair and even her eyes were dull and lifeless. Her speech lacked any animation. Gone was the beautiful sensuous woman she had once been. When I asked her how she had gotten into this state she said that her husband was very much on the spiritual path, and that he hadn't made love to her for a couple of years in order to enhance his spiritual growth. Mirah had always placed great importance on her spiritual growth, so she went along with her husband's directive on their asexual relationship thinking that his advice was good for her. But being a sexual/sensual person, Mirah began having problems with her marital chastity.

We discovered that despite Mirah's very sweet outer demeanor, her feminine was enraged because Mirah had followed the husband's wishes rather than Her desires. Mirah began to listen to Her intuitive during our sessions. She was guided to continue her spiritual journey, but in a slightly different way from her husband's. She was guided to change her diet and begin exercising again. As she did this her hair took on a healthier sheen and her eyes began to glow.

Mirah began taking an interest in the way she looked again. She finally told her husband that she couldn't live without fun in her life anymore and began going out dancing. She started wearing brighter, more attractive clothes, which not only cheered her up, but also began to draw the attention of men. Suddenly Mirah's husband decided that sex was important to him. However, in the process of his renewed sexuality, he began to have an affair. For Mirah that was the final straw. They divorced and she is now happily in love with an earthy, passionate man. Her husband is still trying to find himself.

The more intimate you are with your feminine the harder it is to follow anyone else. We spend a great deal of our time listening to others and trying to please everybody in our lives. As we develop our internal relationships, we discover how much happier we are when we are following our own inner guidance. Just as with Mirah, you might experience shifts in your relationships as you start listening to your feminine. However, in the long run, you and everyone else will be happier. Now let's meet your feminine.

Introducing . . . Her!

I always like to get in touch with the feminine first because She is often more subtle; therefore, She is often more difficult to reach, especially if your masculine is highly controlling.

As you do this exercise, let Her emerge exactly as She is rather than predetermining what She will be like. Allow yourself to be open and nonjudging about the emergence of your true feminine. Often She is not at all as you would imagine. Chances are you will be surprised by what you see. The feminine usually appears in vivid images for most people. When the form of the feminine is clear, you can talk to Her and She will usually talk back.

Find a time when you won't be interrupted. Also find a quiet place to do this process. You may find it easier to do all of the exercises with someone else so that you can take turns reading the directions of the exercise to each other. If you do this with someone else, simply decide which of you is going to meet your feminine first. Go slowly and give each other time to contact your feminine and to get to know Her. I would also suggest that you each have your own audio tape and that you record the meetings. You will find this very useful for your ongoing work.

ENCOUNTERING HER
1. Get into a comfortable position in a chair. Become aware of your breathing. Now begin to deepen your breathing, breathing slowly in and out. Notice if you are tight anywhere in your body and breath into those places, one at a time.
2. Relax your toes and your feet . . .
Relax your calves, your knees, and your thighs . . .
Relax your stomach muscles and your abdomen . . .
Let go of the muscles in your chest and your neck . . .
Let go of the muscles in your arms and your hands . . .
Relax the muscles in your back and again in your neck . . .
Relax your face muscles including your ears.
3. Now let your attention go into your heart/solar plexus area. Notice the energy you feel there or the lack of it. Is it comfortable or uncomfortable? Do you feel strong or weak?
4. Allow that feeling to grow and take you over. Allow it to form into a character called The Feminine.
5. Imagine for a moment that you are backstage in a beautiful theater. You can see the audience waiting for the opening of a play called *Life*.
6. Immerse yourself more and more in the character that has emerged and allow Her to walk on stage. Notice what She looks like and what She is wearing. Notice Her age. She may not necessarily be your chronological age.
Sometimes She appears as a symbol or a color. If this happens you will need to translate what that might mean to you. Let's say a purple triangle appears. In this case, you would ask yourself what the color purple means to you. Then ask the purple color

what it wants to tell you. You may not hear a voice, but merely get a sense of the message that comes to you. As you talk to the color or form, it may change. Keep asking the same questions of the new, emerging forms.

7.   Now talk to your feminine. You will want to have a real conversation with Her. You might begin by asking Her, "How are you?" When she responds, talk to Her just as you would talk to any person when you engage in conversation. For instance, if She says, "I am very light and playful and He's sort of boring," I might ask, "Why is that?" She might answer, "Because He never wants to have any fun. He is so serious." I would then ask, "Does He listen to you when you give Him guidance?" She might answer, "Sometimes," and so on. When She answers, be sure to respond in a way that She knows you are really listening to Her and really care about Her opinions. I might ask, "Can you tell me when He really does listen and when He doesn't?"

Below are some of the questions that you might ask Her:

- What is life like for you?
- If you could be different than you are, how would you like to be?
- What keeps you from being that way?
- Do you know what you want in the next few months?
- Do you know you have a masculine counterpart?
- Do you like Him?
- Does He follow your visions? If She says no, ask Her why not. If She doesn't know, then find out if She gives Him clear messages.
- Are you willing to give Him clear messages?
- (If She is very weak) What worries you about giving Him your visions?
- Are you willing to give Him one or two visions?
- (If She is very strong) Are you willing to slow down for Him so that He can build to match you?
- Are you willing to be His passionate lover? (If not) Are you at least willing to learn to cooperate with Him and perhaps become friends? Talk to Her about the way They were created to work together. Tell Her that She was created to have the vision and He was created to manifest that vision.

8. Before you leave Her, let Her know that you intend to work with Her and Him to build a stronger relationship between Them.

9. Prepare to return to your normal state of consciousness. Thank Her for coming and for revealing Herself to you. See Her walk offstage.

10. Now feel yourself blending together, becoming whole. Slowly come out of your wakeful, dreaming state.

11. Become aware of the seat you are sitting in.
Become aware of the floor beneath your feet.
Become aware of the sounds in the room.
Take a nice deep breath and when you are ready, open your eyes.

12. Stand up and stretch.

13. At this point, it is helpful to make some notes, or to record your thoughts on an audio tape. Make comments about the following:
   - In what form did your internal feminine emerge?
   - What kind of answers did you get to the questions you asked?
   - Did She know He existed? If so, how did She like Him?
   - Was She willing to be supportive of Him?

You want to get to know Her and to know how She operates in your world so you can truly learn to utilize Her function. If you don't see or experience your feminine, or there is no conversation between the two of you, don't give up. Eventually you will sense Her clearly, and will be able to know instinctively what She wants.

Once you have a clear sense of your feminine, you can contact Her at any time. At first, it will probably work best to find a quiet space and then contact Her like you did in the exercise above. Then you can talk to Her, get to know Her, and ask Her any questions you might have at any time. Eventually, you'll find that She is simply there, a part of you that you can easily access whenever you wish. If you lose touch with Her, briefly go back to the initial contact exercise above. Ask for Her and She'll appear, even as you go about your daily business.

After your first meeting, do no more work with Her for now. I want you to meet Him before you work any further with Her. It is important for you to have a better understanding of what They are each like, and how They are working (or not working) together in order to help Them develop individually. A little later in this book, I will give you very clear guidelines so you can do ongoing work with Them and bring Them to Their fully-realized selves.

The Archetypes You Might See

For numerous reasons, our feminines are rarely operating in Their perfection. Their abilities to accomplish Their ordained tasks of intuition and guidance are as varied as our family backgrounds. Just as we genetically inherit our eyes, hair, and nose, we also inherited a legacy of archetypal images from which our feminines emerge.

These archetypal images often create the patterns, values, and mores established in our family roots. For instance, Robert Johnson states in his three books *He, She!,* and *We,* that many of the images we hold about men and women come from medieval history. This is why fairy tales have such a strong impact on us. I certainly see these fairy tale characters as I work with my clients. The internal masculine will often be seen with a suit of armor riding a white horse, while the internal feminine, more often than not, appears with long, blond hair and a flowing dress. However, these archetypal images are merely a compilation of our internal development and our inherited imagery.

In addition to Her image being a result of our heritage and archetypal superstructure, our internal feminines are also a product of our own unique life experiences. It is through a combination of all of these factors that She can become imbalanced. She may become too weak, too strong, or a multitude of manifestations, rather than Her fully emerged form. We can even go so far as to completely disown our internal feminine just as we can with our internal masculine.

Renowned psychologist Nathaniel Branden, with whom I interned, writes about disowning parts of ourselves. He states, "Sometimes it (the disowned self) is experienced as a feeling of self-estrangement, sometimes as the feeling that one's self is only a dark question mark or a guilty secret. Many people suffer from a sense of personal unreality, that they have lost touch with themselves, that too often they do not know what they feel, that they act with numb obliviousness to that which prompts or motivates their actions."

The consequence? Your feminine is often thwarted from a passionate union with your internal masculine and from actualizing your ultimate purpose. However, just as with your internal masculine, you can work with your internal feminine in order to bring Her to perfection. You can get in touch with Her by paying close attention, both to the feedback that life gives you and to the musculoskeletal responses of your body. It is a matter of your learning how to communicate with your feminine, read Her messages, and make needed corrections.

My clients most often reveal one of the following feminines when they initially contact Her: The Child Feminine who could be a Shrinking Violet, The Brat, a Crybaby, or Miss Sugar and Spice. Other common archetypes are: The Free Spirit, The Amazon, the Seductress, the Banshee, Mrs. Nice, Miss Mousey, Her Royal Highness, The Crone, and The Wise Woman. Instead of encountering an archetype, the image of a wife or girlfriend might appear. Regardless of how She appears, we need to reassure and nourish our feminine into Her perfection and to guide Her in developing a good relationship with the masculine.

Your feminine may resemble your mother or another female in your family, or a girlfriend or a mate, past or present. When this happens She will give you a clue about why you act as you do, and why you keep attracting the same kind of people. As long as you have this internal dynamic, She will continue to pull in people who match Her. Let's discuss each of these feminine archetypes.

✱THE CHILD FEMININE This feminine often emerges in the image of a girl between the ages of two and six. Most children are fully connected to the imagination and wonder of their feminine during the first two years of their lives. After that most people lose contact with Her, to one degree or another. As people grow older in a logic-dominated society, their feminine becomes more and more diminished. The emergence of a childish feminine is an indication that the person disowned his internal feminine at an early age. The more traumatic one's childhood, the more likely a person is to disown his feminine and become frozen in a slice of time (age two, five, nine, etc.).

The child feminine (as well as the child masculine) is different from "the inner child" work that is currently getting a lot of attention. It is different primarily because the child can be either masculine or feminine with no bearing on what sex the person is. Another difference is that you can use the inner mate to help with the healing process of the child archetypes. I will discuss this in further detail in Chapter 8.

The child feminine may appear in many forms. Below are four of the most common:

✳SHRINKING VIOLET   When this powerless child appears, She is timid and frightened to one degree or another. Shrinking Violet easily dismisses her thoughts, feelings, and dreams as unimportant. She doesn't realize that not only can She have thoughts, feelings, and desires of Her own, but She is actually *supposed* to have Her dreams come true. She may know what She wants, but must be coaxed to speak up.

This feminine is most often found in individuals who have been emotionally or physically abused as children. If you were such a child, you know that you never felt safe and that all the attention of your internal duo was placed on surviving the conditions of your childhood. You were rarely able to follow your own internal guidance. This can also be true for children with overly controlling parents.

If you have this feminine, you may appear to be confused, uncertain, and not really sure of what you want. You may sometimes appear to be as shy as your Shrinking Violet feminine. At those times your eyes may look slightly frightened and you may have trouble looking other people in the eye. Your voice may be barely audible, or you may not be able to answer when asked a question. You may look a little like an unnerved Bambi.

This type of feminine is usually found in conjunction with a strong internal masculine who makes sure that She never gets a chance to express Herself. For this reason, it is not unusual for the Shrinking Violet to be in abusive relationships.

Danielle had a Shrinking Violet feminine. As a child, Danielle had been repeatedly sexually molested by her father. When Danielle first came to me she did not remember the rapes. All that we knew for sure was that she was unusually frightened about something. Her inner child appeared as a five year old. We could easily access back to the age of five, but each time we tried to go any earlier into her childhood, the feminine would become hysterical.

Danielle was fine when her masculine was in charge, but became quite a different person when Shrinking Violet emerged. At that time, Danielle would sit before me with her head bowed. She would not look at me at all as I talked to her. Her arms were crossed over her solar plexus. She was frightened of everything.

Once the child grew to trust me and to trust the inner masculine to take care of Her, then the memories of the rape surfaced. It took almost two years before Danielle developed a fully functioning adult feminine. We had to heal the shy, hurting child first. In cases of incest or rape the healing process can be rather slow.

If you have this kind of feminine, you will have to reassure Her. This frightened child will need to be loved toward wholeness. You will want to reparent Her in a positive way.

*THE BRAT   This little terror is usually about two years old. She is unreasonable, uncontrollable, and can be quite mean. It is not unusual for a happy, laughing child to initially appear; but under the laughter you will almost always find a more serious child who is either hurt, frightened, or angry. She has learned that having a tantrum might get others to do what she wants.

There are several reasons The Brat developed this way. She might have been quite spoiled, either by the inner masculine, or from her external life situation. On the other hand, Her life might have been very difficult and the only way She could survive was to become mean and have tantrums.

People with this type of feminine are often initially seen as very happy and loving. However, sooner or later their Brat feminine is bound to act up and create problems for that person. If you have this type of inner feminine, your face will often show signs of Her defiance and Her anger. She may often have her hands on Her on hips. Her chin stuck out, and her mouth pressed into a pouting, angry line.

Christina managed a women's apparel store in New York. She was well respected in her field. The initial impression she created was that of a happy, fun-loving, competent women. She could always stay well organized and effective at work, but her intimate relationships were always a mess.

Christina's father and mother had been very domineering and controlling. Her father served as a role model for her own masculine, who became equally controlling and domineering. Christina's feminine, with no safe harbor, became deeply angry and resentful. She withdrew, and simply stopped trying to speak up.

When Christina grew up, her romantic relationships were terribly difficult. Men would meet this capable, straightforward woman who had a wonderful, happy, childlike quality about her. She could maintain this image for about six months, but then The Brat would appear, having uncontrollable temper tantrums. Christina's partners would last only a short while before they would give up on her.

When I first started working with Christina, her feminine was only about two, and wavered between a happy, laughing child and a very angry one. When The Brat appeared, She was adorable and a bit sassy. Within minutes, though, She didn't want to talk to me, and She let me know She didn't like me. She told me She didn't trust anyone and hated me. I had to work with the Brat to help Her see that She had more of an emotional range than just happiness and anger. She would also have to learn to use Her anger in a more productive way. Then we had to help the feminine grow up. Once Christina had developed a strong, loving feminine and a powerful, protective masculine to care for Her, She began to experience loving relationships. Since He and She developed a passionate love affair, I have seen Christina slip back into the child only once, and that was with the death of her mother.

If you have this kind of feminine, you must always teach Her new ways of responding to the pressures of life. She will realize that She is no longer at war with the world. She will also need to learn forgiveness and how to get what She wants in a more adult, responsible way.

✳CRYBABY This feminine has spent most of Her existence grieving. She really has no hope in life and no dreams of possibilities other than what she has. She has become afraid to risk, because those risks always turn out badly. This feminine cries out for someone to care for Her time after time, no matter how old the client may be. Yet She is too frightened to trust people, and may whine a great deal. She, too, is often found with one of the tougher masculines.

If you have this type of feminine you have a deep, underlying sadness. Your life most likely has been difficult and you have become entrenched in grieving over the past.

When Cindy first came to me, she said her life was a mess. Nothing ever worked out as she had hoped and everything she did seemed to become unnecessarily complicated. Then when she tried to clear up the mess, it seemed that she always made foolish choices and was filled with grief and remorse over her decisions.

Cindy's mother had died when Cindy was twelve. Her father tried to give her and her two younger brothers a happy home life, but there really wasn't time enough for him to do that and also earn a living. The family never got over the sadness of her mother's death, and Cindy's feminine became a Crybaby.

As a result of having a Crybaby feminine, Cindy was deeply, deeply disappointed in the way her life turned out. At age thirty-six she felt that there was really no way she could have what she wanted. She wanted to feel safe inside. Cindy was a pleasant, young woman and quite attractive. She was the mother of two beautiful children and was a kind and loving parent. Despite all of this, Cindy would frequently call me and say "My little girl needs attention. She is sad and frightened."

After she started therapy, Cindy easily went through all of her grieving, and slowly began to let go of her attachment to her grief. Now when she calls me, a grown woman is talking to me. Not only is she grown, she can actually laugh at herself now, and she easily handles unhappy situations in her life.

To work with this inner feminine you have to allow yourself to feel the grieving that wells up inside you, and to finally put that grieving aside. This is much harder than you might imagine. People with this feminine have actually become attached to their sorrow.

Sometimes the anger letter, described in Chapter 3, helps a great deal because there is often anger beneath the grief. Once you have finished grieving you will want to retain your feminine to open up to Her visions.

You may rediscover some of your feminine's past visions that have been there for many, many years. Perhaps all that is needed to fulfill these visions would be extra training, or developing a new understanding. I will give you exercises to help Her develop later in this book.

✳Miss Sugar and Spice   She is such a good girl, so sweet and charming. She's very proper and cares very much about what people think of Her. She often stands properly and talks with a little-girl voice. She is always bright, chipper, and agreeable.

People with this feminine most likely grew up being taught all of the right things to say and do. In their younger years, these people excelled at being the perfect child: cute, smart, and with adorable personalities. It was as if they became a Shirley Temple clone. Their external mannerisms always reflect Miss Sugar and Spice's niceness and cuteness. They often make childish facial expressions, with many of the looks that were thought to be so cute as a child.

Unfortunately, the Shirley Temple routine will no longer work for you when you grow up. The charm of those cute behaviors is lost and your Suger and Spice feminine hasn't learned to use Her powers in a more adult fashion.

There is something incongruous about an adult with an inner Miss Sugar and Spice. People with a Sugar and Spice feminine seem too nice and too perfect. But that niceness can actually be self-destructive. It is based on insecurity and the desire for external acceptance. That can only lead to trouble. As long as someone has to be "a good little girl" for the rest of the world, she misses out on the freedom, the power, and the adventures of adulthood. She never stands up for herself and won't speak up on her own behalf, even if someone is walking all over her.

Rae was a beautiful woman in her late fifties. Her features were striking and she had a beautiful head of prematurely gray hair. She was tall and thin and held herself perfectly at all times. When Rae's Sugar and Spice feminine was in charge, her facial expressions were greatly exaggerated. She would cock her head to the side, purse her lips, and show her dimples. She was very cute. When Rae was really concentrating, she would push her lips out, frown, and lift one eyebrow. Her voice was quite childlike.

Rae learned that her cute "act" was getting her nowhere at the age of fifty. Even though she was well loved, Rae often felt taken for granted and used by her friends and coworkers. Rae's strong masculine had initially loved the feminine this way, but over time had grown weary of dealing with a child. He wanted Her to grow up and become Herself with all of Her power and vision. Rae's Miss Sugar and Spice feminine was afraid that people wouldn't like Her if She were no longer cute and perfect. Miss Sugar and Spice also didn't know how to behave any other way than as She had done for all these years.

We worked on building Rae's child feminine by first reassuring Her that She would be loved even if She became confrontive, as long as Her outspokenness was purely assertive, and not aggressive. Rae went through an assertivenes training class while we continued to work on the feminine. This gave Rae's feminine an opportunity to witness good communication role models. Rae's feminine learned to have opinions of her own rather than those given to her as a child. As a result, Rae wasn't quite so sickeningly polite anymore. She took voice lessons to deepen her voice. She learned to stop exaggerating her facial expressions, which eradicated her childlike appearance. Rae was then able to have a stronger influence with her friends and in her workplace.

If you have this type of feminine, it would be helpful to look at the rules accepted by and passed down through your family. Many of them you may not have consciously examined. Once you realize what they are, you might want to check them out. For instance, there is an old story about a woman who had been going to the same butcher for a number of years. Each time she bought a leg of lamb, she had him cut off about two inches of it. One day the butcher asked the women why two inches had to be cut off. She said, "That's the recipe that was passed down from my grandmother." He told her it didn't make much sense to him to lose all of that good meat. The woman called her grandmother to find out why two inches had to be cut off and her grandmother said, "Oh that's the only size pan I had."

This completes the discussion of the child feminines, so let's explore the other types of feminines.

*THE FREE SPIRIT   This feminine is not necessarily arrested at an extremely early age like the child feminines, but She is still quite young. She almost always appears younger than nineteen. She's an example of what Jung referred to as the "Puer Aeternis"; she wants to have fun and she wants to be free. She is often very creative and can usually be counted on to be very playful. She can also be very flighty and a big dreamer. Every new project is going to lead to fame and fortune. Simply because She says it is so, She believes it will happen.

This type of feminine may misguide you when you are trying to accomplish something other than having fun, being creative, or trying to start something new. She will think that the internal masculine is a real drag because He wants Her to pay attention to details and be disciplined. She will often change Her mind simply because She feels like rebelling against Him. She prefers to initiate things rather than carry them out. Having fun is supposed to be part of our lives, but most of us want to have some sense that we have accomplished something in this life, as well. We want to know and express our inner wisdom.

A client of mine, Marty, is a talented artist with a great flair for life. In some ways he seems larger than life with his dark good looks, his enormous size, and his boundless energy. He is prone to bouts of what I'll call overliving. When his feminine (who is about sixteen) is in charge, he goes on wild spending sprees. He drinks champagne by the case and lavishes his friends with presents. Everyone loves him. However, when his inner masculine takes over, Marty becomes despondent over the shambles in his life. Our journey with his feminine has been to make Her fully aware that each time She has a flamboyant episode Marty and the masculine will pay dearly. She basically has a good and caring heart and can't bear to see Her "men" suffer. She was very cooperative in correcting Her excessive habits, even though She still loved to move freely and dance.

If you have this type of feminine, you are probably greatly loved by others. You are joyful, playful, and fun to be around. However, it might be hard to have a relationship with you because you need to be taken care of. You may not be able to accomplish anything in this life, other than having wonderful visions and daydreams. A large percentage of the artistic community has this type of feminine.

In order to develop this particular feminine, you will need to develop a strong masculine who can contain Her. What I mean by this is that He will have to give Her strong guidelines and stick to them. Eventually, she will learn to settle down and take your life more seriously. She must grow in Her ability to be a responsible force.

*THE AMAZON This is an extremely powerful feminine. She knows exactly what She wants and has a very demanding nature. The problem is that this feminine holds the illusion that She can accomplish everything without the help of the masculine. She typically discounts the masculine's abilities because She assumes that He is weak. However, he may not be weak at all. He simply may not want to fight with Her. As a result of His backing off, She will take little heed of reality and will continue ahead with what She wants to do, against all odds.

Her guidance is powerful, yet untrustworthy, because She won't listen to any common sense. She may initially appear standing ready for battle like a warrior. Her eyes slightly narrowed and Her teeth clenched in preparation for any battles against Her position.

Those who possess this type of feminine are hard to work and live with. Although She is often highly capable, She often insists on doing things Her way and will not get along well with other highly controlling people. People with this feminine often find themselves thwarting authority and trying to defuse powerful people around them. They never really get anywhere with all their talent because their energy is spent in wrestling with power figures. People with this feminine might feel that She often races ahead while they are holding on to Her coattails. A typical manifestation of this feminine is a person who works and works, never really accomplishing what she could or receiving the acclaim she should. This is because She refuses to listen to the masculine and when She attempts to manifest Her visions without His help, She fails.

May tried to be the best wife and mother that she could be, but she was demanding and a perfectionist. May's feminine was always sure that She was right, and browbeat May's family and May's internal masculine into believing the same thing. She did the work of four people but would be quite nasty in the process of any project, letting others know how inefficient they were. Her friends and family wanted to confront her, but everyone felt it was better to keep quiet and suffer May's storms.

By the time May was forty her children had grown to dislike her and her husband was having an affair. She always clenched her teeth and her mouth was a hard, narrow line. She was always looking around the room to see if everything was in order. If it wasn't she would quickly rise and fix it.

When May met her feminine, May realized how she had spent her entire life acting like a warrior. She knew that this wasn't productive in her home life, but she didn't know how to lay down her weapons. We worked on getting The Amazon to take time to learn about the good qualities of Her masculine. May's Amazon learned that the masculine wasn't as stupid and ineffectual as She perceived Him to be. As He began to take over His rightful role, the Amazon began to calm down and May softened. Her husband, noticing the difference, began to pay more attention to her. Months later, he confessed to his affair and then broke it off. May's children renewed a more affectionate relationship with her and she noticed that her coworkers became more approachable.

This feminine must learn to be less independent, to not want to do everything by Herself. She must learn to value and appreciate the masculine. In a very real sense She must set down Her weapons, She must decrease Her speed, and learn to be His partner. If you have this type of feminine, you will find it useful to step back and take a good look at what you really want in your life. Notice if you have relationships that are satisfying and filled with mutual respect. Let go of the image of yourself as the only one who can do things well. Learn to turn things over to other people and to get out of their way so they do it in their own way. Otherwise, you are never really going to change The Amazon. She will just keep charging ahead.

❋Miss Mousey   This feminine is frightened by everything. She fears the world and She fears Her internal masculine. She is afraid to step out and take chances. She is also afraid not to take chances. She spends a lot of time changing Her mind. She usually appears as a nervous woman with Her body held very tightly as if in readiness to run at a moment's notice. Her face is drawn and She slightly resembles a mouse at times.

Al couldn't have fit this description more perfectly. You could almost see his whiskers twitching. His Miss Mousey feminine was very frightened of making the wrong decision, whatever it was. As a consequence, life for Al was pretty tough, as it was for everyone around him. He agonized over each detail of anything he did, ready to bolt at the first word of criticism. His Miss Mousey rarely had a vision. She was too busy scurrying around defensively. Al had never been married and had kept the same job for thirty-five years.

Al decided to buy a piece of property near a lake. He wanted it for his retirement, which was about ten years away. He called home to tell his mother, and she said, "That is the silliest thing I have ever heard. You may not even want to live there." Frightened, he hung up the phone. He said to himself, "What could I have been thinking of? I almost made a terrible mistake. But I sure love it here and it is just the kind of place I alway wanted to live. Oh, well." Al didn't buy the property. Two years later the land had quadrupled in value. That's when Al first came to me. He told me that he was angry for the first time in his life. However, his anger frightened him. I considered his anger a healthy step forward. We worked on Al's relationship with his mother and how Miss Mousey had developed very much as a function of their relationship.

When we first contacted Al's feminine, I asked Miss Mousey how She would like to change. As She tried to tell me, She changed Her mind three times. I sent Her home to watch several movies starring female characters, so She could get a feel for the many options of the feminine. After about three weeks she told me She wanted to be just like Auntie Mame, living exactly as She pleased. We had our work cut out for us.

Al decided not to see his mother for a couple of weeks while we worked together to free himself from their dysfunctional relationship and explore options as to what he really wanted. I guided him into making one decision each day and sticking to that decision no matter what. In no time at all, Al started to really like this process. It was about six months later that Al went back and bought the piece of land he had wanted in the first place.

If you have this kind of feminine, you will need to teach Her courage. It would be good to keep Her away from difficult people until She heals. You may also find that your masculine is too demanding and that He will have to stop terrorizing Her.

✳Mrs. Nice She is a genuinely nice person. She is steady and stable but not very creative and almost always practical. She tries a little too hard to make things easier for the masculine. She is always available and can become quite boring. Everything about Her—the way She dresses, the way She walks and sits and holds Her face—tells others that She is a really good person. She may have some frown lines from worrying about the welfare of Her family. Of course, She would never lose Her temper.

Goldie had been married for thirty-five years. She had put her husband through college, and then raised her children. Now she wanted something for herself, but she didn't even know what. She was now fifty-five and before she died she wanted to do something that would let her use all of her talents in a way that would be exciting to her. We worked with her Mrs. Nice feminine until She was willing to take a chance on adventure. The first thing She did was go away to a health spa for a week. When Goldie came back, she told me, "It was so luxurious. I have never gone off by myself nor been pampered like that."

Goldie's feminine became increasingly adventurous, becoming a cross between Mrs. Nice and a budding Free Spirit. Soon the feminine decided that it was time to go into business.

Goldie was thrilled. She had secretly dreamed of doing such a thing, but never imagined that it would come to pass. She knew a lot about children and loved them, so she decided that she would open a specialty shop for children. She bought everything that she would have loved for her own children when they were small. Goldie's store is now a raging success. The perfect balance between Mrs. Nice and The Free Spirit has served her well. Goldie is a very happy lady.

If you have this kind of feminine, She will have to be trained in having Her own vision and acting on it. Don't let your feminine lose Her niceness, but let Her know that life has to become more exciting.

✳THE BANSHEE Nothing is more brutal than this feminine. She lashes out at life, is extremely demanding, and eventually becomes very bitter. She tends to be uncaring about the effects of Her actions on the lives of others. She only wants to take on more of life and to have more and more experiences. She is furious when She is thwarted.

This feminine is most often furious with the internal masculine. He has usually become "castrated" by Her demanding anger. As a result, He either becomes inefficient in His job of manifesting, or refuses to have anything to do with Her. Because this feminine has so little use for the internal masculine, She (in men or women) may have little use for external men and may be a terror to women.

In business, anyone with this type of feminine shows up as a high achiever who is always spinning off more and more projects in a rather ruthless way. People assume, for instance, that a tough businesswoman is more in touch with her masculine, but more often than not the feminine is the source of the callous toughness. People think the same of a tough man. Again, this may not be true.

An example of someone with this kind of feminine is Patrick, a forty-five-year-old engineer. He was a man with a very nasty temper. He put people down and found most of them ineffective and useless. Although people thought he was a bully, his masculine was actually quite weak. Pat's feminine despised the masculine for She saw Him as weak. Patrick's internal masculine absolutely refused to talk to The Banshee. He didn't like Her and He was afraid of Her, just like the rest of the world.

In Pat's life this translated into a man who was driven by his feminine to achieve. But without the masculine strength and compassion, Pat was a hostile man filled with resentment. He was also a rageaholic and his coworkers lived in fear of him. He walked and sat in a cocky way to show his superiority. His face was a map of contempt and disapproval. His women friends were more than likely to be tough and hard driving as a reflection of his feminine.

This kind of feminine is completely out of control. She too must learn to value the masculine and to give Him a chance to grow strong so He can become Her equal. Otherwise, He becomes steadily weaker. The weaker He becomes the more outraged She becomes. She needs work on forgiveness, and needs to learn new ways of expressing Her anger. As the masculine becomes stronger, She can soften and let go of some of Her anger.

*THE SEDUCTRESS   This feminine knows exactly how to get her way, but not in a clean, aboveboard manner. She plays a very old game that once worked very well for both men and women. She tries to seduce Her masculine into getting what She wants. She finds that the seduction works temporarily, since He is intimately connected with Her. At some point, however, He becomes disenchanted with Her and begins to distrust Her. Rather than relying upon Her own internal masculine, The Seductress then turns to external men and women to get what She wants. She manipulates and entices. Every action, word, look, and article of clothing is consciously used to seduce. She may have bedroom eyes, and appears to have great sympathy for others.

People with this kind of feminine are actually quite vulnerable to being tricked and heartbroken, choosing romantic partners who have internal masculines that are either weak or bullying.

Rose was a beautiful woman who exuded sexuality. Rose wore tight dresses with very tight belts. She would lean into people when she talked to them and would tell them how wonderful they were. She made them feel as if they were the most important people in the world. She had a little-girl quality that was quite charming. She came across as quite loving and very lovable.

Her lovingness was quite manipulative and her Seductress feminine would manipulate both men and women. She had many men who believed that they would be her choice if she was available. These men gave her gifts and did anything to gain her attention. Each one, she said, was very special to her. In a way, they were—until they were of no further use to Her.

She made women in Her life feel that they were Her special friends and that She would do anything for them. The entire time She was seducing her "friends" to get what She wanted. Then She would cast them aside and never give them a second thought. She needed the attention and the talents of each new conquest.

Rose's masculine was just as much a victim of The Seductress as all of the others in Rose's life. Rose came to see me because her recently estranged husband and her previous husband had both told her that she was a user, and that she was like a black widow spider. They said she lured people into her web, made love to them, and then ate them.

Rose had to learn to accomplish Her visions by working with the masculine instead of seducing Him. She also needed to learn that if She didn't work with the masculine, She couldn't get others to do His work for Her. She would have to go about things the slow way instead of trying to get things She wanted by taking shortcuts at the expense of others.

If The Seductress is your feminine, you will find that She is difficult to change. It is so much easier to get what She wants by getting others to do it for Her. Because of this She has little integrity and is not particularly honest. She will always appear to be playing the field, although She is not really available to anyone. You will have to give Her guidelines for correcting Her integrity and for becoming honest. She doesn't necessarily want to be dishonest, but she just can't bear to act any other way. The Seductress is often found with an abusive inner masculine.

*The Crone   This feminine is very old and has been around a long time. She is well developed spiritually, and the masculine is generally nowhere to be seen. She feels that She carries too great a burden without His backup. She is not angry with Him, merely weary and sad at being alone.

People with this feminine have usually had very difficult lives. They are steady and willing but have lost a zest for life. There is a sense of resignation about them that comes from the absolute understanding that They must shoulder the burden alone. Such people may also be extremely intuitive. When I first met my feminine She was very old and barely able to walk. My masculine was afraid of Her because of Her extreme old age, just as society is afraid of the "old crone." He didn't want to look at Her or go near Her.

Daniel had this type of feminine. She was just as old as mine. Her shoulders were hunched and She could barely get around. Because of Her, Daniel seemed to lack any real energy. Everything was a burden to him. His face always had a worried look and he sighed a lot. Daniel's external marriage was beginning to show signs of cracking.

Daniel's masculine was a very nice guy but He was also somewhat fragile. He was quite repelled by the feminine and tried to stay out of Her way. The more He avoided Her, the older She became. When we got Them to speak with one another, Daniel's masculine discovered how really kind the feminine was. He decided He would be quite happy to help the old woman out. She asked Him to finish a large stack of correspondence for Her. As He did so, She suddenly became younger right before His eyes, which absolutely unsettled

Him. Daniel's feminine told the masculine to look in the mirror. He saw a stronger, more mature man. Daniel moved along quite rapidly and now has a passionate inner and outer marriage.

If you have this type of feminine, you need to do a great deal of work to get the masculine to share His part of the load. You may have a raging masculine who won't listen to Her, or you may simply have an ineffectual and confused masculine like Daniel's. The results are the same. She has to make all the decisions and carry the load.

✳HER ROYAL HIGHNESS   She is elegant, regal, and simply demands that the masculine follow Her wishes. It does not even dawn on Her that He might care to do otherwise. He is not usually angry with Her because She is, after all, acting like the queen She is.

People with this kind of feminine can be quite austere and unapproachable. They may hold themselves very, very upright and expect to be waited on. They may hold their chin high and literally look down on people. In work situations these people are often quite demanding and insist on perfection and on things being done their way. It simply doesn't occur to them that their behavior is out of place in today's world. They often wonder why they lack close relationships in their life. Royalty are treated with a certain distance and often don't have the love they seek.

Fred came from humble beginnings, which was always a mystery and a source of disappointment to him. He had a deep inner feeling that he had wound up in the wrong family. The people in his family were so uncouth and he was so very proper. Fred's Royal Highness feminine had told him since he was a small child that he was destined to greater things, and that he was intended to be surrounded by beauty. She told him that he was different and very, very special.

When I first approached Fred's feminine, She "deigned" to speak with me, but She let me know that it was beneath Her. She longed for a strong masculine to sit beside Her on the throne, but He was too busy worshiping Her. I had to get Fred's feminine to come down off Her throne so that She could at least stand as an equal with the masculine. Finally She came down to stand with the masculine, but She was in no way willing to see Him as equal. He was obviously Her inferior.

Shortly into our work the San Francisco earthquake occurred.

I had Fred fly there and volunteer. Her Royal Highness was furious. How could we endanger Her that way, and expect Her to work among the filth and common people? For the first two days She was impossible. Then She opened Herself up to the suffering of others and began to really love and care for them. When Fred came home Her Royal Highness was greatly changed. She had liked being with people. She had enjoyed helping them. She had discovered that She was one of them, and that it was much more fun than the solitude of royalty.

It is imperative that this feminine climb down off Her throne and walk among the people. She must learn about ordinary life and also about hard work. She needs to learn not to see Herself as special but rather to develop the strength of true humility and become more earthy. Have Her dig in the garden, do Her own housework, and work with battered women and children. Have Her volunteer to work serving food to the homeless.

✳THE WISE WOMAN Occasionally, a fully developed feminine appears who is the feminine we all seek to have. She is wise, kind, loving, compassionate, highly directed, clear about Her visions, and loves the internal masculine. She is gracious toward all of life. Her face shows genuine kindness and everything about Her body says that She is open, loving, and strong. This feminine can guide you to accomplish all of your dreams—if the masculine can equal Her in His power. Make no mistake, this feminine is very powerful and never fails to demonstrate that power.

Jeremy was a talented man with his hands and could have gone far with his talents, but things never quite came together. He had worked at a lot of odd jobs. People really admired and appreciated his work, but he would always do something to let others down. Jeremy wasn't happy about this but he gracefully accepted it.

Jeremy's feminine was fully developed. She was quite beautiful, strong, and wise. Because of his Peter Pan masculine, Jeremy had a charming personality and was very well loved by his friends and family. However, Peter Pan always managed to miss something, so that at the last minute the job Jeremy was working on wouldn't quite come off. Jeremy's Wise Woman had tried a number of times to just let the masculine flounder, but in the end She always picked up the pieces because She knew that Jeremy's life would suffer.

When I first worked with Jeremy, His Peter Pan masculine and

The Wise Woman feminine came to an immediate understanding. Everyone was willing to take the risk to change the dynamics that were wreaking havoc in Jeremy's life. Jeremy said that he would rather have his life fall apart for a while instead of living the way he had been. He wanted to settle down and build something in his life. He was between jobs right now, so it looked like a perfect time to do this. The Wise Woman determined She knew that the most loving thing She could do was to expect more of the masculine. For the next six weeks, The Wise Woman never once rescued Peter Pan. Soon He grew very tired and began to stop fluttering around so much. He and the Wise Woman kept negotiating and coming to agreements. Jeremy's Peter Pan finally began to fulfill the Wise Woman's visions and Jeremy's professional life became more productive.

If this is your feminine, you will find that She can really understand your masculine's concerns and weaknesses, almost to a fault. You will find that She will be very cooperative in being a catalyst for His growth when you ask Her. You see, in the past, She has simply accepted Him for what He is and has altered Her behavior to pick up the pieces when He is ineffective. The problem is working with the masculine who will most likely be ineffective for one reason or another. Use Her wisdom well, for She can creatively come up with new directions that will help Him quickly grow.

*Two or More Feminines   If two feminines should simultaneously reveal themselves, don't be concerned that something is wrong. There are a number of combinations you might experience if this happens to you. Sometimes people experience feminines that are drastically different in age. Another possibility is that the feminine will be different in their appearances or radically different in their personalities.

One of the therapists whom I taught to use the feminine/masculine work in his counseling found an interesting combination in himself. When we contacted his feminine, She emerged as two powerful women. One was a dark sorceress while the other was a large blonde, very loving, strong but sweet. The two had a cold acceptance of one another and weren't very interested in talking. Our job was to get Them to think about merging so that They could become one well-rounded being. You will want to merge your multiple feminines into one radiant being at some point, but we will do this only after you've met your masculine.

Guidance without Manifestation

Just because you decide to follow your feminine doesn't mean that your dreams will come to fruition. In fact, for most visionaries, the opposite is true. Visionaries are unique people, but they often share a similar problem: their internal feminine is functioning without the structure of their internal masculine.

If you just follow Her, with no regard for Him, then your visions will never stabilize or manifest. If you are in projects with others, then you need to see if they are stabilized by a good strong masculine. I remember many years ago when I was simultaneously working on several large holistic healing projects. I spent a lot of time traveling between Santa Fe, San Francisco, and several other cities. I always seemed to be finishing one meeting to fly off to another. I told friends how exciting it all was. At the same time, I was becoming more exhausted and something kept nagging at me. In the end, not one of the projects came into being. Now I realize that the projects were all overburdened with visionaries.

It is not unusual for a highly visionary person to have problems functioning well in the world of logic and manifestation. The world, which is mostly run by people who are only in touch with their internal masculine, often tends to think of the visionary quality as disorganized, incapable, penniless, and therefore, useless and worthless. We've heard terms like "absentminded professor" and are used to thinking of people who are strong visionaries as being eccentric and unpredictable. Unfortunately, this is too often true. The feminine operates in diffuse awareness and chaos. Therefore it is not surprising that highly visionary people often "have their head in the clouds," as the saying goes. Einstein was famous for doing things like absentmindedly walking away from someone who was in mid-sentence, telling him a story. This does not mean that visionaries are incapable. They just operate in a different world from manifesters.

Mrs. Einstein was told that her little boy Albert was mentally retarded and should not bother going to regular school. He didn't

show many of the capabilities childen his age usually had. Those
who live totally in their intuitive do not learn in the same way as
most other children. They access information differently. Yet
Einstein, who came up with revolutionary concepts that seriously
challenged our concepts of reality, has been considered the quintessential genius for decades.

Without the masculine to back up your feminine, you are more
than likely prone to be addicted to the adrenaline charge of new
creation and adventure. Her thrust is always toward expansion.
That is why She can run rampant without Him, operating from
the basic belief that more is better. There is never enough to satisfy
Her. In Her most extreme form She can be obsessive and compulsive.

As with any addiction, you will always be striving for excitement
and the thrill of it all. The result of this is usually a life filled with
drama and even tragedy, because you are moving too fast to accurately assess the steps necessary to accomplish your goals. Nothing
will burn a person out faster. I know from personal experience.
When I was in my early thirties, my internal masculine was continually running to keep up with the desires of my feminine. She
would show an interest in all sorts of projects and want to run off
in a myriad of directions so that She could do them all. I wanted
to follow Her in each moment. I didn't realize that in order to
really do this, He had to be Her equal. I spent a lot of time and
money on each new project with the hope that things might actually
work out with each new activity. I felt that my life was filled with
movement and change but in reality nothing really happened.

I had to work on getting my masculine as strong as my feminine
so that He could temper Her. As He began to grow strong, I learned
when He could really complete Her visions and when He couldn't.
She had to learn to slow down and wait for Him, so that manifestation, built on a firm foundation, could occur. My life became
more peaceful when They learned to work with one another.

The external manifestations of a feminine addicted to the
adrenaline rush of new creations are as varied as individual personalities. There is the person who has incredible ideas about projects that could be highly successful, but somehow never get off
the ground. Just about the time something might begin to work,
this visionary is off pursuing another dream.

One of my clients is very much like the slick traveling salesman so often seen on TV. He always has another get-rich-quick scheme. He is always sure that the next project is the "big one" that will make him rich. He exhausts endless hours and resources with schemes that have flimsy foundations. For instance, one day he approached a number of people in town with a very grand plan for "getting their work out there internationally." He claimed to know everything that needed to be done to really make them successful. He talked about a TV show and a school that he would develop around their work. When he came to me with the proposal, I challenged him. I said, "This doesn't feel solid to me." He couldn't understand why I felt that way, when he had everything in place—except the money. "And that," he told me, "isn't a problem." But of course it not only was a problem, it was *the* problem. Without the money, it was all just big dreams with no substance. A lot of people were disappointed when nothing concrete came through this man. They had gotten intuitive warnings but hadn't listened to them. I was not at all disappointed because I believed my feminine when She said no.

It wasn't until this "hotshot" young man was fired from several jobs and finally lost all his money that he was willing to look at the weakness of his internal masculine. He had to really pull back on his visions and learn to take small, practical steps in order to accomplish his goals. It was difficult for him, but he tried to begin projects on a smaller scale that could unfold later into larger ones. Unfortunately, before he could solidify this approach to accomplishing his dreams, another big scheme came along and my client moved out of state to pursue it. I occasionally hear from him, and he is still looking for the illusive "big deal."

Many of you will come up with archetypes that are not mentioned in this book. There are as many archetypes as there are people, so your feminine (as well as your masculine) may not be anything like those I have described. She may be a combination of archetypes or radically different in some way. If that is the case, then there are two things you can do that will help you understand Her. First, ask Her as many questions as you can. Be interested in really discovering who She is. Second, look at characters in books, movies, and plays who are like Her. How is She portrayed? What do you think these characters are really like? The discovery of your own unique feminine (and thus your inner guidance) will be very fulfilling for you.

By now you should have a pretty good sense of your internal feminine. Remember that Her function is guidance and vision. The ultimate goal in working with Her is to develop Her into becoming the wise, loving intuitive She is meant to be, giving your masculine fearless and strong guidance and working cooperatively with Him. Now we will explore the world of the masculine, and give you a chance to meet Him.

SIX

He: In His Archetypal Form

Every individual person may have something important
to communicate to mankind, because in that person
the Man-archetype is just as real—even though it be
hidden under a mountain of existential refuse and social
poisons—as in a poetic genius, a saint or a great scientist.
—Dane Rudhyar, *We Can Begin Again Together*

Whether you want to create a spectacular new poem, develop
a relationship, build a house, or start a new business, your success
in bringing these dreams to fruition depends upon your ability to
focus on the steps required to complete that vision. Without focus,
your dreams and visions will remain as seeds that lie fallow, never
to germinate and grow. The ability to focus and plan is a function
of your internal masculine. I often refer to Him as the manifester.
I speak of Him with the same honor and glory that I give Her. Your
internal masculine is not merely a workhorse, but is Her full and
equal partner. She is unable to function in Her full glory without
Him. Together They give you the opportunity to live heaven on
earth.

We each have a form of the manifester in us. He is the form
and structure in your life. He is orderly thought and His domain is
your body, your physical world. He is intended to act as a strong,
capable partner for your internal feminine using Her direction as
the blueprint for His structure. His purpose in your internal dynamic
is to manifest in the physical world in accordance with your inner
guidance.

As He begins to function in His perfection, He becomes the
master architect and contractor who brings your feminine's blue-

print into fruition. He knows how to translate Her vision into a workable plan and how to implement it. In other words, He learns to manifest in accordance with your higher purpose. He does this by following the direction of your internal feminine because She points the way.

I want you to understand the full impact that your internal masculine has in your life, along with the practical side of this metaphor. He is the generator of all that can be seen, felt, or touched. If you want your practical world to change, He is the key to that change. Your external relationships with men can only be as strong, well developed, and healthy as He is.

Just as with your internal feminine, you can work with your internal masculine in order to bring Him to His perfection. You can get in touch with Him by paying close attention to the musculoskeletal response of your body and by being sensitive to the feedback that life gives you. It is a matter of learning how to contact Him, read His messages, and make corrections as needed. Later in this book I will give you some exercises that you can use to develop your manifester. Now let's meet Him.

Introducing . . . Him!

As with the feminine, your internal masculine may appear as an archetypal image when you first get in touch with Him. Although He is not in His perfection at this point, most people still find it fun and exciting to experience Him. Very interesting images can come from the exercises later in this chapter. They are very real experiences, which often surprises even the most skeptical people.

As you do this next exercise, let Him emerge exactly as He is rather than predetermining what He will be like. Often He is not at all as you would imagine. Allow yourself to be childlike and open to the emergence of your true masculine. Chances are that you will be surprised by what you see. As with the feminine, do this when you are able to have quiet time.

ENCOUNTERING HIM
    1.   Get into a comfortable position in a chair. Place your hands on your lap and your feet on the floor.

2. Relax your toes and your feet . . .
   Relax your calves, your knees, and your thighs . . .
   Relax your stomach muscles and your abdomen . . .
   Let go of the muscles in your chest and your neck . . .
   Let go of the muscles in your arms and your hands . . .
   Relax the muscles in your back and again in your neck . . .
   Relax your face muscles including your ears.

3. Now let your attention go into your back. Become aware of the feeling of your bones. Do you feel strong? Weak? Are you rigid? Flexible?

4. Now that you are beginning to contact Him, let Him know that you intend to work with Him and with Her and to build a relationship between Them. This prepares Them for Their meeting.

5. Imagine for a moment that you are backstage in a beautiful theater. You can see the audience waiting for the opening of a play called *Life*.

6. You are playing the role of the masculine. You allow yourself to become more and more His character. Notice how He feels about Himself and what He is wearing. Notice how He feels about life. Notice what age He is. He may be your chronological age and He may not. Notice how He feels about your feminine.

Once you have a clear sense of Him, you will know how to work with Him. I usually begin by asking Him, "How are you?" Once He responds I talk to Him just as I would to any person whom I engage in conversation. If, for instance, He says, "I am just exhausted," I might say, "Why is that?" And He might answer, "Because I just can't keep up with Her." I could say, "Do you mean that She wants too many things at once?" "Yes," He could answer, and so on. When He answers be sure to respond in a real and sincere way. You want to really get to know Him and to know how He operates in your world. Only then will you be able to utilize His function.

Below are some of the questions that you might ask Him:

- Would you describe yourself to me?
- What is life like for you?
- If you could be different, how would you be?
- Can you manifest anything you want to?
- Are you aware that you have a feminine counterpart?
- Do you like Her?

- Are you willing to follow Her vision?
- What might happen if you followed Her?
- Do you know that spirit created you to be passionate lovers? (She was created to have the vision and He to manifest that vision.)

7. Now prepare to return to your normal state of consciousness. Thank Him for coming and for revealing Himself to you. See Him walk offstage. Imagine that you are standing on the stage. Walk offstage and right back into the seat you are now in.

8. Become aware of the sounds in the room.
   Become aware of the chair beneath you.
   Become aware of the floor beneath your feet.
   Take a nice deep beath and when you are ready open your eyes.

9. Now stand up and stretch.

10. It is helpful to make some notes or to record your thoughts on your audio tape. Make comments about the following:
    - In what form did your internal masculine emerge?
    - What kind of answers did you get to the questions you asked?
    - Did He know She existed? If so, how did He like Her?

The Archetypes You May See

Working with thousands of clients over the years, I have noticed certain common images emerging when we first delve into the internal masculine. Each individual has unique variations on these themes but the major groupings are fairly constant. I have grouped them into specific personality types of the internal masculine. Here are the common groupings that I most often encounter: The Child Masculine who usually shows up as one of four types: Fearful Freddy, the Monster, Sad Sack, and Goody Two Shoes. The other archetypes are Peter Pan, Mr. Nice Guy, His Majesty, Attila the Hun, Lover Boy, The Scoundrel, Methuselah, The Wimp, Bewildered Benny, and The Wise Man. Let's take a look at each one.

✳THE CHILD MASCULINE   These masculines are very similar to the child feminines, except that they have different names and

Their functions will affect you quite differently. Let's look at Them one by one.

✱FEARFUL FREDDY This child is frightened of everything. Usually He became terrified in childhood and never outgrew it. He can be found in anyone, and suprisingly enough is often found in the most successful people. No one really knows He is hiding in you, except your most intimate friends. He is sure to appear in their presence, and often acts very bad because He is so frightened. He is often found with The Amazon, The Seductress, The Banshee, or Her Royal Highness, but He could appear with any of the feminines. His face is often pinched and His eyes are quite wide and frightened looking, because He is always braced against the world.

When Lee came to me he said that his marriage was terrible because of his lack of fidelity. He had, in fact, had a number of failed relationships. His wife told me that Lee was often very tough and brutal, and at other times more frightened than anyone she had ever known. His wife was a very strong and fairly fearless woman. Lee's masculine was indeed Fearful Freddy, and his feminine was The Seductress.

The Seductress is fairly difficult for a child masculine to deal with. He is very unnerved by Her. I encouraged Lee to take small steps toward adventure, and to say no to Her when She was being outlandish. In his external life, Lee no longer tried to seduce others. Because of this, his relationships became much better and now he has actually gone very far with his career. If Fearful Freddy suddenly reappears, feeling He has to hide, Lee calls me immediately. Whenever Lee calls, I spend a few minutes encouraging him to take courage and stand up to either his wife or his inner feminine.

If you have this kind of masculine, you have to encourage the feminine to tone down Her desires and to refuse to give the vision unless He is willing to stand and be counted. Never give in to His fear, for it has crippled Him all of His life. Gently but firmly push Him in the direction of courage and moderation. Often something like aikido or jujitsu is helpful for this masculine.

✱THE MONSTER This is a very unnerving child. He can be impossible to deal with. He is always into something and He can be quite a bully. He lashes out at everyone and everything. He is highly destructive to people, things, and Himself. He may scowl a lot, or he may *pretend* to be nice to entice you, or the feminine.

But like the feminine Brat, He can't keep the truth hidden for long.

Skip was the youngest of five children. He was the baby of the family. By the time he was born, his parents were almost too old to have a child. His mother said that from the moment he came out of her womb he was kicking and screaming and causing trouble. He walked and talked early, and when he didn't get his way, he would break something. The whole family thought Skip's behavior was funny. So did The Monster.

As an adult, Skip soon found that other people didn't find this behavior amusing, and that no one really liked The Monster. Skip's feminine was Her Royal Highness and She certainly didn't want to have anything to do with The Monster. I knew She wouldn't even attempt to meet Him unless He calmed down. He thought She was an old windbag. I asked The Monster what He really, really wanted, and He said, "a fast car with no back seat." He said if there was a back seat, She would want to be driven and He didn't want Her to go. Her Royal Highness and The Monster had to be dealt with simultaneously. When The Monster got the love He needed He became quite delightful. When Her Royal Highness became earthier She was quite compassionate. Skip's Monster masculine turned into a very nice man and Skip's family saw significant changes in his behavior.

If you have this type of masculine, some old-fashioned discipline is in order. When He acts up, ask Her to stop giving Him visions. This masculine needs to become more sensitive to other people and to the reactions that He causes. He also needs to be loved by your feminine and you.

✳SAD SACK   This inner masculine child gave up a long time ago. From an early age He developed the idea that life was very sad and never believed that His life could be any different. Most often He is found with The Free Spirit, The Amazon, The Banshee, or Her Royal Highness. Any one of those feminines will contribute to his feelings of worthlessness. They have also, no doubt, given Him plenty of grief. They, in turn, are disgusted with Him. People with this masculine more than likely had a very difficult early life.

Angelica's masculine was Sad Sack and her feminine was The Banshee. These two played a game, each inciting the other to Their worst behavior. She was furious with Him and wanted to have some fun. But He was no fun at all. He was too busy being sad. Every time her Sad Sack masculine took an unsuccessful step to accomplish the feminine vision, The Banshee would immediately criticize Him. Then the masculine would become overwhelmed by His sadness.

First we convinced Angelica's feminine that She would never get what she wanted if She didn't ease up on the masculine. Then we began to deal with His sadness. Instead of telling Sad Sack to let it go, I pushed Him further into His deep well of grief. I told Angelica to visit her parent's grave because she had not gotten over their deaths. She cried for hours. She went to see her ex-husband and couldn't even talk because she was so sad. About a month later, the masculine said to me, "I'm sick of this. Let's get on with it." The Banshee breathed a sigh of relief. Over time, She became nicer and He became filled with a zest for living.

If you have this kind of masculine, do not try to convince Him that life is happy. He won't buy it. He already knows from personal experience that life is quite tragic. Ask Her to give Him visions that She knows He can easily fulfill and that will give Him joy. For instance, let's say She wants to go sailing. Maybe He has always longed to sail, but just knew that if He went He would drown. In setting up this day, make sure that He goes with someone who is a good sailor and you're sailing in fairly easy waters, with a life jacket.

✳GOODY TWO SHOES What a good boy He is! He always does everything just right. He knows He's adorable and acts like it. He can be very loving but is never really His own person. He only knows how to do what is expected and what He should do. That is pretty heady stuff for a child. What is cute in childhood will only add complications to adulthood. Goody Two Shoes is torn between wanting to follow His feminine's hunches and the powerful influence of external expectations.

Goody Two Shoes can be infuriating to an internal feminine as well as to external women. His attempt to please everyone will be so strong that He is unable to listen to His own feminine. Goody Two Shoes is just too good. He is always polite and generally a little too happy. He is often found with Her Royal Highness, The Wise Woman, or The Seductress.

Joe had a Seductress and a Goody Two Shoes. The Seductress felt She had to seduce to get anything she wanted. Joe told me

Goody Two Shoes was too busy being perfect to follow Her where She liked to go. He thought She was outrageous and never within the polite bounds of society. He couldn't stand it when she acted up. After all, what would *they* think. Goody Two Shoes was always trying to cover up what the feminine did. He wanted control, but a child is no match for The Seductress.

Joe had been in a relationship for about ten years. His lady friend was married to someone else and seemed to have no interest in leaving that marriage. One day, Joe's Seductress, bored with it all, met a new woman. Joe began dating her. Now he was in love with two women and had two women in love with him. Goody Two Shoes was grief stricken. He didn't want to hurt either woman nor did He want to lose one of them. He was tormented by His dilemma. When He was with the one woman, He wanted her. When He was with the other woman He wanted *her*. He simply could not make a decision. Now both women were angry with Joe.

When Joe came to me, all of our work was centered on getting The Seductress to calm down and give Him more ordinary visions. Reluctantly She cooperated. Goody Two Shoes didn't want visions that conflicted with His good-boy image. Once Goody Two Shoes became comfortable, He was ready to take small risks. The small risks led to greater risks, and soon He knew exactly what to do. Joe broke up with his old flame, dated only the new woman for a year, and then married her.

If you have this masculine, you will need to teach Him how to care less about what others think. You will want to guide Him into listening to His own internal feminine, rather than the dictates of society.

This completes the description of child masculines. Let's now examine the other archetypes that might appear.

✻PETER PAN This masculine expects to be taken care of. He does not take responsibility for being the manifester. He often just wants to have a good time and do what He wants to do, when He wants to do it. He wants Her to be both the visionary and the manifester. He is most often found with a very powerful feminine. He feels very put upon when you ask Him to perform His function, until you can convince Him that it isn't Her job to make the vision become real in the world.

No other masculine creates such rage in the internal feminine.

She has little use for this type and She will discount Him more and more. As a result He will become increasingly useless. Peter Pan will, in His enthusiasm, have a million good ideas. He will often create many opportunties in life. He will come very close to bringing something to fruition, but not quite. However, on close examination, people who have this type of manifester will see a long trail of shattered dreams. They may also discover that commitment is difficult for them and will repeatedly walk away from success and intimate relationships.

Just like His feminine counterpart, The Free Spirit, this masculine must grow up. He must become responsible. The feminine needs to demand that He pay close attention, learn to focus, and not run away.

Not long ago, Damien came to see me. He was an artist, not a very successful one, but certainly not a failure. His commissions were few and far between. He had been married twice and both of his wives had supported him. He was now living with a lovely young woman who also had to support him. She was, however, insisting that he "get his act together" or she would leave. His masculine didn't want to do any serious work. He wanted to spend hours in the hills getting inspiration. He wanted to spend the rest of His time in the studio. He didn't want the drudgery of everyday life to stifle His creativity. At first I couldn't even get His masculine to listen to me. He wanted to talk me into roaming the hills with Him. Damien's masculine didn't sober up until his girlfriend moved out of the house. When Damien's girlfriend left him the masculine finally listened. In order to help Him build structure rapidly, we got Damien a job in a warehouse where he had to account for every item that he packaged. He made a lot of mistakes but eventually got the feel of it. There came a point where his bills were paid and he could have quit the job, but he liked the feeling of stability. His art is now selling well enough and his masculine is stable enough that he is able to paint full time.

People with this type of masculine may be extremely disorganized, and they are often extremely creative, or guided, such as inventors, artists, musicians, and spiritual teachers and healers. Once this type of masculine was found most often in women. In recent years, however, I have found this masculine to be making more of an appearance in men. I believe that this is because men have opened up to their creative side and have let go of the stereotypical pattern of being the good provider. Perhaps some of them have gone too far.

You work with Peter Pan by only giving Him small projects that He can handle, and guide Him until He actually finishes each one before He starts another. Make the projects something He can do well, so He has a sense of accomplishment. Never venture out into large, untried projects. Keep things simple. Once He begins to realize that He can be successful with small things, He will become more confident. You can then gradually increase the complexity of projects, but not until He is very, very sure of Himself.

✳Lover Boy   This masculine hustles every person that He comes in contact with. He relies on His sexuality and manipulative abilities to get what He wants. He is very much like The Seductress, except that He is often more overt than She is. He doesn't know how to go for what He wants in a straightforward way. He is always attracted to someone whom He can use. He is often found with Mrs. Nice, The Crybaby, or Shrinking Violet.

Alice was very tough to be around. Her Lover Boy masculine was pushy and manipulative, always trying to get what He wanted. People would fall for it and then become angry when they discovered they had been used. When this happened the Crybaby feminine would appear.

People were startled at how hurt Alice became at their anger. It didn't make any sense to them. These two archetypes are very far apart, so of course people were confused. The guidelines we developed for Alice were quite strict. She was not allowed to "use" more than one person a week, with the understanding that this was only temporary. Ultimately she had to give up using people at all and seducing them to do her will.

Lover Boy found it extremely difficult not to seduce, and He didn't think life was any fun without it. Crybaby, however, began to find new hope. Without His constant seduction of others, She started to get happier.

If you have this type of masculine, then you either have had many lovers who were unfaithful or else you have been unfaithful. You try to get what you want through manipulation. The Lover Boy can be dangerous to fall in love with because He is always moving on to a new conquest. You must call a halt to Lover Boy's activities, always reminding Him that His internal feminine will become the perfect lover He has been seeking.

✱MR NICE GUY He does his job but is very sad and lonely because the internal feminine doesn't know He exists or cares little for Him. He understands the world of form, works hard all His life, but nothing He does seems to make any difference to Her. He is a genuinely nice guy and is almost always open to having a relationship with Her.

Most often, clients with this type of manifester have nice, safe jobs. They don't make a lot of money, but they build modest financial security. They are not risk takers and do not have a creative flare. They may often be seen as a little dull.

Betty was a successful lawyer. She was conservative in her views and her life-style. She came to me because she wanted to learn to be more playful. She was the eldest of six children, so life had always been fairly serious. When I asked her masculine if He was willing to have more fun, He thought that was very threatening. The feminine was more than ready to have fun. She tried for weeks to convince Him that He could have fun and still be serious about His profession. Finally, He decided to risk a little. Betty was going to a lawyer's conference in San Francisco. We went shopping together and let the feminine pick a party dress that was fun and exciting. Betty's masculine was unnerved by the dress, but went along with it. Once He was at the party, He was thrilled with the choice. They received a great deal of attention and even He liked that. And not only did Betty have more fun than ever, but she picked up two new clients as well. We then continued with our work to get Him to be a little more adventurous.

In order to develop this masculine into the type of power that will back up even Her most outrageous visions, He will be taught to take chances. Keep asking Him to stretch a little beyond what is comfortable. As He does, He will cease being dull.

✱THE SCOUNDREL This manipulating masculine knows that the internal feminine exists but He denigrates her. Even if She is equal to Him, He pretends that She couldn't possibly be as magnificent as He. He always knows that He is right and wants to be in total control. He will often follow Her vision to a certain point. Then, if He can't continue backing up that vision, He will find some way to blame Her. He creates conflicting messages of support for Her and at the same time manipulates Her to do it His way. This leaves Her confused. Eventually Her visions grow weaker and more nebulous. The weaker She becomes, the more intolerant He becomes. Because of this, Her guidance is haphazard at best; and life becomes a series of missed opportunities.

People with this type of manifester are always trying to get others to do the job for them. They seek the easy way out. They rarely address business or personal relationships in a straightforward way. They have a deep desire to be in control but are often covert about it. People in their life will almost always feel subtly controlled and manipulated.

Rebecca came to her first session with a great deal of confidence. She represented herself as highly successful and having difficulties only in her relationships with men. When I talked to her masculine, He tried to avoid my questions about His business affairs. He did not want to admit that there was a problem. When I asked Him about the feminine He vowed His love for Her, but I was suspicious.

Rebecca finally admitted that she hadn't really been successful in a very long time. Although people tended to like her and believe in her, she was never able to live up to the image she portrayed. She always betrayed those who trusted her, whether the relationship was personal or professional. She couldn't pay her bills, and left her last place of employment with ill feelings and some question about her honesty with money. She had an endless string of men because she always found the new ones more exciting than the one she was with.

The way to work with this archetype is to guide Him in becoming reality based, honest, and straightforward. As Rebecca's masculine became more truthful, He finally admitted to being extremely frightened. He admitted that relationships were difficult for Him. This was a step forward, because at least He was honest with His fear. However, He still wanted things to happen the easy way. He also wanted Rebecca to keep her fancy Porsche. He was unwilling to accept the actual condition of Rebecca's life, which was that she was poverty stricken. Rebecca left town seeking a short-term fix for the problem, before her masculine could learn the value of taking things step-by-step over a period of time.

✳HIS MAJESTY   He rules the kingdom with an iron hand. He knows that others are to serve Him and He expects them to do so graciously. He is very authoritarian and demanding. He stands ramrod straight, holding His chin up high. He may be a bit stiff necked. He is often found with Shrinking Violet, Miss Sugar and Spice, or Mrs. Nice.

Peter reflected His Majesty masculine in every step that he took. Peter was a tall man with regal bearing, who literally looked down on the world. He was charming, but took no nonsense from anyone. Things were to be His way, period. Peter had come from a modestly well-off family. He had been to the best schools and was expected to live up to the family name.

Peter's feminine, Miss Sugar and Spice, loved to please His Majesty. The problem was that because She was pleasing Him rather than fulfilling Her function, nothing new or exciting was happening. He was pretty well stuck with the old kingdom and way of life. Because of this Peter was not very creative in his work. He also felt out of sync with the rest of the world.

Our work together was to get His Majesty to be willing to be equal with Miss Sugar and Spice, and to get Her to grow up. In a way, it seemed a shame for Them to change, because They were so happy together just as They were. But Peter's life was not at all the way he wanted it to be. As His Majesty and Miss Sugar and Spice began to become more balanced, Peter became much more likable and felt that he really was a part of the human race. He also became extremely creative and began working in areas that he would never have gone into before.

If you have this masculine, He needs to be humanized and to get down to earth. Actually, once He lets go of His royal stance, His Majesty feels much happier and much freer. He must learn to rely on the feminine more and to be willing to share decisions and life with Her.

*Attila the Hun   This masculine is usually powerful and warlike. He doesn't care about Her messages or what She wants. He has His own ideas about how things should occur and He just wants Her to stay out of His way. My own Attila the Hun was magnificent. He sat savagely upon His black horse looking fearsome and terrible and He was one powerful warrior. He had his sword drawn at all times and would ride into battle for any cause.

Women are not even given a second thought and are never to be listened to. He is the most chauvinistic masculine. If She is unclear in Her messages to Him, He abhors Her lack of clarity and bullies Her into doing things His way. He ultimately despises Her for this. In His worst form, He becomes truly abusive to the feminine, who becomes an internal battered wife.

Rick was from Texas. He was the quintessential good old boy. He was full of self-righteousness and self-importance; it took quite a while before he realized that his life wasn't really working. Once he understood this, he began to work on himself. When we talked to Rick's feminine She was timid and very frightened of the masculine. The masculine was fully armored and ready to kill for Her, but totally unwilling to follow Her or give any value to Her. When I dared to suggest that He follow Her, He jumped up and began to storm around the room. "How dare you suggest that I should follow a mere woman." I said, "She has a great deal of wisdom." He roared back, "Not nearly as much wisdom as I have. Do you want others to think that I am weak?" I then asked Rick's masculine what use the feminine was. He said, "She is to love and cherish. She is to do nothing but let me care for Her." "Do you know She is unhappy?" I asked. He was stunned and sat down to listen.

This type of masculine always needs to be taught the value of the feminine and how to truly honor Her wisdom. He must learn to demand that the feminine fulfill Her function by giving Him clear guidelines. When the masculine receives clear guidelines, His anger will subside. If He is brutal, then He will need to be made aware of the price He pays for battering the feminine. More than likely He drives other people away from Him and loses many good opportunities.

It is often too difficult for Attila the Hun to change His ways. The force of Attila's archetypal roots were too strong and He soon reverted to His old behavior. However, there was one area of Rick's life that Attila was anxious to make a change in. Attila didn't like the fact that Rick had been divorced three times and that all of his wives found him to be an angry, abusive man. Rick finally agreed with them and realized if he was going to be with another woman, He would have to behave differently. He decided to be without a woman while he attempted to change. His self-realization was short lived. Rick is now back in Texas drinking and carousing once again, and has totally turned against his feminine.

Once Attila the Hun and The Scoundrel were found mostly in

men. Now, I find them in as many women as men. You will find these types of masculines in angry, driven people who are rarely satisfied with their lives or their relationships. These people will often feel that life has dealt them a tough time. They are often demanding and hard to get along with. They also usually hate the opposite sex and are difficult to love.

✳MethuSELAH   This masculine is usually old and worn out, because the feminine is irresponsible. She may be quite young or may be grown and filled with desire. This masculine is well developed, wise, and caring. Often, when I ask this masculine to follow Her, He states, "How can I possibly follow a little child?" He is right. He knows that They are intended to co-create but He is also wise enough to know that She is too undeveloped to be trustworthy. He would love to have a feminine who is His equal. He will say, "She is impossible. No one could do all that She wants." Unless we can move Her forward, He will remain old.

Theresa's feminine, Her Royal Highness, held the masculine in very low esteem. She felt He simply didn't do enough for Her. Her masculine, on the other hand, was worn out and old. She wanted so much from Him that He couldn't possibly live up to it all. In Theresa's life this appeared as a lot of expectations, some manifestations, and a lot of frustration and anger. Her Royal Highness was almost always upset. The masculine really tried to do all She wanted Him to do. In our work together, He had to learn to say no to Her. He also had to learn to negotiate with Her. In our conversations with Theresa's feminine, She was at first resistant and then more cooperative as She began to understand the problem. Part of the conversation went like this:

SHE: I want to learn to weave and do pottery and make jewelry and fix up the house.
HE: Well, since We have to make a living, I don't see how I can do all that. Which one would you like to do first?
SHE: The weaving, I think.
HE: Right, but now We can't afford a large loom. What would you think about a bead loom?

She loved the idea. He went out the next day and got a bead loom and the feminine was happy for quite a few weeks. With that exchange He became years younger. As the feminine begins to fulfill Her function, this masculine will always grow younger. Just like The Crone, Methuselah's secret to being more youthful lies in His partner's ability to work with Him and His willingness to do so. He must also be willing to let go and to not attempt to do it all. This means that He must refuse to act until She has given Him a clear vision. This is often difficult for Him, because He really loves Her and wants to take care of Her. For a while, He will be unwilling to let go of the larger visions, but as She becomes capable with the smaller ones, She will gain confidence and creativity and then be able to go on to the larger visions.

*THE WIMP   This masculine is poorly developed. He has a very difficult time manifesting the vision given by the internal feminine. The result is that the person's life may be full of vision and creativity, but there is no evidence of financial and worldly success. When asked to do something for Her, He says, "Oh, I couldn't do that." Most often, though, He actually fears Her. Usually He will be tied to a very strong feminine. People with this type of internal masculine will be wishy-washy when it comes to making decisions and not very adventurous.

Jason was a hard-working man. He was honest and moderately creative. He dreamed of writing a book and teaching classes, but each time he thought about it, He became painfully shy. Jason's dream would remain unfulfilled unless his masculine developed courage. I asked Jason's internal masculine to think about the movies He had seen, and what characters were strong in His view. He said Rambo was strong. He hardly dared dream of being like Rambo. We worked a little with Jason's feminine and encouraged Her to listen to the masculine. Then I took even more dramatic steps with this client. I sent him to a martial arts school (Ninjitsu). This really gave the inner masculine a feeling of power.

This masculine must build in strength. He does this by learning to match Her guidance, but to do so only when He can. He, like Peter Pan, must initially work on small projects, so He can fulfill them and experience success. This means He will have to be strong in the face of Her desire. Each time He has a small victory He will get stronger.

*BEWILDERED BENNY   This masculine is focused more on outside women than on the internal feminine. He is constantly protecting external women and taking His cues from them. He may also be basically afraid of women and spend most of his life running away from them. By focusing on external feminine energy, i.e., listening to every word or whim of external women, He leaves the internal feminine alone and unsupported. This causes tremendous internal confusion and an unbearable tension. She becomes increasingly angry and He becomes very frightened of Her.

It is hard to depend on people with a Bewildered Benny masculine because you never know where you stand with them. They will always do what they think other people want them to do. They will make one decision when they talk to one person and then make another one when they talk to someone else. They rarely know what they really feel or what will make them happy.

Andrea was always insecure about her own guidance and never knew what was right for her. She listened to her mother, her sisters, her friends, and her psychic. Each time she started a project, she eventually gave it up because others didn't approve. For this reason, many of her hopes and dreams were destroyed. By the time Andrea came to see me she didn't have the vaguest idea how to turn her life around, because she didn't even know what she wanted anymore. She was turning into a bitter young woman. Her masculine was Bewildered Benny.

The only way to heal this archetype is to get Him to focus on Her, rather than externals. This is usually a difficult journey because He doesn't know how to do anything but focus "out there." When I asked Andrea's masculine if He could do different things that the feminine wanted, He didn't know. Even getting Him to make a choice between different-colored hair ribbons was a major feat. The feminine had opinions, but Andrea's masculine was too busy listening to others. In order to teach Him to listen to the feminine, I had Them go shopping twice a week without telling anyone. They were to make a minor purchase and were not to return it under any circumstances. Andrea's masculine had to complete only unimportant small tasks at first so that He didn't become frightened. As He did this He became a little braver. As He began to trust the feminine more, He became more certain.

It is imperative for this masculine to listen to His own feminine, make a decision, and then complete it according to Her directions. In this way He will become certain and capable. Each time He turns to an external woman for guidance, remind Him to turn to Her. Outside feedback is important, but not when the tendency is to always turn outward. So, for a while, you must restrict Him. Otherwise, He will remain forever confused.

✳THE WISE MAN This thoroughly developed masculine will sometimes appear. He is strong and directed. His focus toward completion is remarkable and He knows how to accomplish things without effort or struggle. He is compassionate, loving, and protective of the feminine in a very healthy way. He is capable of accomplishing anything, but once again, He is limited if the feminine is not giving clear, strong visions. Nor can He compensate for Her distrust.

Wayne's masculine was strong and powerful. This Wise Man could be counted on to manifest anything, and yet He was held back by Wayne's feminine (he had two of them). He very much liked both of the feminines, even though He couldn't count on either one of Them. She appeared as either Crybaby or The Seductress. The masculine was very patient with both feminines, regardless of which one emerged.

Wayne was kind and gentle with an occasional tendency to have emotional outbursts, which cost him a great deal, both in business and in love affairs. These outbursts usually came from either feminine when They were rebelling. As we worked with these feminines They began to realize that neither one of Them was going to get what She wanted as long as They were at war with each other. Once They came to this conclusion, The Wise Man was able to guide the feminines into knowing one another better. He also began to give Them more boundaries so They could develop toward Their perfection. The masculine began to say no to unreasonable things that the feminines wanted. Eventually, Crybaby and The Seductress blended into one feminine, and She is now a fine match for The Wise Man.

Basically there is no need to change this masculine. He is already operating from His perfection. The work in this case is all with the feminine. You will find that The Wise Man is very flexible and can match Her easily.

Two or More Masculines   At first, work on getting to know each of Them. Help Them to overcome Their fear and distrust of one another, and to see the other's positive aspects. You will then do the same thing I suggested in the chapter on the feminine. You will eventually get Them to merge into one masculine.

The Collective Unconscious and You

Keep in mind that these various examples of the internal masculine and feminine are a product of many, many generations, as well as your own current family history and your unique psycho-spiritual development. You may have images and feelings that don't make sense to you and cannot be traced to any roots in your personal history. Let me give you an example.

I remember one client, Gina, who seemed at first glance the quintessential modern woman. She was a bright, talented, and successful graphic artist who had an active life filled with both male and female friends. However, this woman had not had a long-lasting romantic relationship for years and at thirty-nine she wanted marriage and children.

When Gina's internal masculine first emerged He was a warrior from another era whose sword was poised and ready to strike the enemy. Gina's masculine said that He enjoyed riding into battle and cutting off heads. His strength was reflected in Gina's ability to be successful. Gina's masculine was willing to work with her feminine in the work arena, which made her very successful professionally. In every other aspect of Gina's life her internal duo were not connected at all, even with her friendships with men. Her masculine was so strong that He wasn't allowing any intimacy in Gina's life. This elegant, soft-spoken woman had a relatively peaceful life, and was not an angry person, so it didn't seem likely that the image of her internal masculine was from her own life but rather from the memory patterns of generations past. These memories were very much alive in her cells. This is what I refer to as the "collective unconscious." These are ideas or memory that we possess, not as a result of our own life circumstances, but as a result of generations of thoughts and actions.

Through our work together we were able to go back in time and convince the warrior that His fierce approach to relationships was no longer necessary. We did this in a step-by-step way. I first had Gina's masculine view His internal feminine mate. He saw an image of a beautiful princess on the far side of the river.

I spoke to the feminine, who was a young Wise Woman. She loved and yearned for the masculine. In fact, She had long grieved His absence. As strong and courageous as She was, She desperately wanted to be His partner. He suddenly realized that He, too, yearned to be by Her side, although He had never before paid attention to these feelings. Gina immediately observed that her male friends were all very powerful personalities who were also without partners.

Gina's internal masculine decided that He wanted Her at all costs. She was on the far side of an impassable, raging river. He decided to build a bridge in order to reach Her. While He did this, He kept His armor on. The feminine stood waiting anxiously to see if He would be able to bridge the gap between Them. He managed this by aligning his decision processes with Her vision.

While the masculine built the bridge Gina's external life came to a temporary halt. She was incorporating newfound discoveries about herself, and this affected her ability to create and communicate with her friends. She couldn't paint anything that pleased her. She had some major arguments with her male friends, and everyone in her life found her behavior puzzling. Gina began to regret that she had begun this process.

The day finally came when Gina's masculine completed the bridge. He stood at one end readying Himself to make the crossing, but could not move forward. His armor, which no longer seemed to fit Him, impeded His movements. For a session or two I worked with Gina as her internal masculine battled with His conflicting need to take off the armor and His fear of His consequential vulnerability. During this time Gina's friends found her more impossible than ever to be with, and many began to avoid her. They never knew exactly how she would behave. Her work offers slowed down seriously. One or two offers came but Gina was unable to meet the deadlines.

Our job was to convince Gina's masculine that the war was truly over; He didn't need the armor anymore. Finally, the masculine began to peel off the many pieces of armor that bound Him, but He kept His sword. Gina became more open emotionally. The interactions between her masculine and feminine became more balanced, with occasional reversions to old behavior habits.

Her internal masculine had been understandably a little nervous about giving up a way of life to which He was passionately committed, but He started across the bridge. When He finally reached the other side They embraced passionately, beginning a new growth process together. As their relationship progressed the ferocious warrior transformed into a kind and gentle family man. Rather than seeking nations to conquer, He became an explorer. He ultimately transcended His violence and grew into an enormous, benevolent being who protected all humanity and loved only God through the internal feminine.

After a number of very intense sessions, Gina's masculine reluctantly laid down His sword. He did so only after we assured Him that He would be transformed into a glorious and courageous being. Gina was now much more authentic and available to people. She began to trust and follow Her intuition more often. She began to paint again but her style had changed drastically. Her paintings became stronger and more dramatic than her former whimsical drawings.

Even when Gina's masculine had laid down His sword, the healing process was still not finished. I still had to guide Him through a step-by-step transformation to bring Him into this century. This went quite rapidly. Over a year's time Gina had been through a tremendous healing. Now she experiences a growing love and acceptance for herself. As a result, Gina attracted a man who was very much like her new internal masculine. Some six months later they were happily married and their first child arrived two years after that.

If this sounds like a fairy tale ending, it is! The only difference between this and other fairy tales is that in order to live happily ever after, you must always continue to unfold in your awareness. Living happily ever after is a demanding journey filled with daily perils and pitfalls. The status of a well-balanced human being is an ongoing process requiring devotion and conscientious attention. Once you have your internal duo in a loving relationship, the real work has only just begun. Know that this is the beginning of a neverending story.

Our External World/Our Internal State

It is quite easy to see the masculine reflected in your life when you remember that He is the world of form. Therefore, your business activities and relationships will give you instant feedback about whether or not He is fulfilling His function. When I have problems, I don't get fixated on how everything is going wrong. Nor do I try to simply fix or change the behavior or actions of others. Instead, I turn inside to my own duo and determine what They are doing, what problems They are having, and how They are getting along. I know that breakdowns in my world of form are usually a reflection of trouble from His dynamic. I also know that when the men in my life become a problem, then it is because my own internal masculine is having a problem. I then correct my internal dynamic and almost always see a shift in my external reality.

I know that it is often easier to blame the outside world when things are amiss. What we are experiencing seems very real to us, and we genuinely believe that there is something wrong with others. There may be, but I cannot tell you how healing it is to realize that those very problems could not be facing you if they weren't also in your own cells. This is especially true in romantic relationships. We draw to us partners who will match our internal dynamic. Women will attract certain types of men who are a clear reflection of their internal masculine. Women, take a good look at men in your life. Did you ever notice how you seem to choose the same kind of men over and over? You may find, when you meet your own internal masculine, that He is reminiscent of the men with whom you've had previous relationships. Life is a mirror! The same holds true for men and the women in your lives.

How could this possibly be? Our view of reality arises from our innate knowledge as well as from knowledge we have gathered over the years. Some of this knowledge is conscious and some of it is unconscious. This causes a filter that limits our ability to see and know any truth but our own. Our minds, and even our vision and hearing, will selectively filter out anything that does not fit in with the model of knowledge that we have accepted. We then view our perceptions as the only truth. As we grow in consciousness, we expand our world and our knowing. Once we see other truths outside of us, we can see the part of us that is hidden from us and thereby correct it. Please understand that this doesn't mean that you create what happens outside of you. It does mean that if you respond strongly to something outside of you that response can only arise because it strikes a resonant chord inside of you.

If you can accept this profound view of life, you will gather valuable information for your personal transformation. Life itself then becomes your teacher, telling you exactly which corrections to make.

Ann was in a relationship with a man who acted as her business partner. He was very involved in every aspect of her life. As their relationship progressed they battled incessantly. Her partner was extraordinarily controlling and manipulating. Ann had worked on this issue of control and manipulation with her own masculine for quite a while. She thought she had transcended this behavior. However, there was still a shadow of the controlling masculine in her cells, or she wouldn't have been attracted to the kind of man her boyfriend was. Her relationship with this man brought to her the awareness that it was time for her to transform on a deeper level. Her partner didn't like the changes that took place and they eventually broke up.

As a result of the breakup, Ann found herself struggling to do everything that her ex-partner did, on top of her usual activities. Although she knew that she was actually working to develop a strong internal masculine, she didn't really see any way to replace the support of the external male. Within one week's time of the breakup, several people came into her life to work with her.

This same thing happened to me many years ago, but not with the same success. When my business partner/lover left, I expanded my business too rapidly and my back began aching. When I asked for clarification (see Chapter 8 on Building the Inner Relationship), I began to have disturbing dreams. In one such dream, I was on a long train. I had started out with a group of friends and left them to walk alone, down the swaying cars. As I looked out of the window at the countryside whizzing by, I didn't recognize anything. I wondered if I was on the wrong train. When I tried to return to my friends, I was unable to find them. I kept thinking that I saw them in the next car, but it was always an illusion. When I woke up, I felt that my masculine was confused and didn't feel confident about being able to withstand the new expansion and activity. But I still didn't feel that I could make my work load smaller.

A few nights later, I dreamed that my masculine had a gun and was trying to kill my feminine. She saw the gun, grabbed it, and blew Her own head off. Then a new head appeared and She said, "See, you can't destroy me. You'll have to try another way." When I awoke, I knew that She, as usual, was completely unaffected as my world grew increasingly turbulent. I also knew that He was getting angry enough to kill Her and it was time to listen to Him.

That morning I called a staff meeting. I said that we were doing too much, too soon and that I really had to honor His plight. When I postponed a couple of new projects, my neck and back began to relax. Things settled down in the office, and my usual relaxed state, not to mention my good humor, returned.

Your external world is indeed a reflection of your internal masculine, but He is just one-half of your dynamic. We must also look at how He is working in conjunction with your internal feminine. She is your guidance, your inner vision. If He doesn't follow that vision, He loses contact with the whole picture and becomes mercilessly focused on the particulars. He becomes overly focused. If someone has told you, "Maybe that is a good idea, but forget it. These are the rules," you can bet they have a masculine that doesn't follow a vision.

Your goal is always to keep your internal masculine and feminine in balance through constant sensitivity to both of them. I will talk about how you can develop this sensitivity later in the book. For now I want to show you what happens within your life when you allow Him to have total control.

Manifestation without Guidance

There are many people who have powerful abilities to manifest. They build their world with an intensity that is validated by their impressive results. Their view of the world is linear, practical, and tends to be narrowly defined. These people are extremely focused and know how to organize their world for success. Their ability to focus thrives on logic, order, and tenacity. Their left brain, which rules those functions, has a tendency to overrule any other mode of perception, especially if that mode includes the intuitive, which is perceived as illogical and unrealistic.

The more a person follows the path of the manifester, the more he demands clarity, logical thinking, and decisiveness. The diffused, nebulous, and often spiritual world of vision is extremely uncomfortable to him. The nebulousness creates a feeling of being on the verge of anarchy and chaos, which is the manifester's nightmare. Therefore, in following the path of the manifester, some people eventually shut off their visionary abilities and become driven toward a narrow focus. They usually lose their alignment with their original dream or purpose and definitely forget that there is a larger perspective from which to view life.

Alan Watts was one of the first people who addressed the issue of focused awareness versus diffuse awareness. He spoke of the way we look at one small aspect of life (focused), totally ignoring the context (diffused) from which that aspect arose. According to Watts, it is this tendency that has left humankind divorced from our inherent connection with our world and universe. Here is an excerpt from one of his talks:

> Often with a group I'll draw a circle on the blackboard and ask, "What have I drawn?" In the vast majority of cases people will say I have drawn a circle, or a ball, or something like that; very few will ever suggest that I have drawn a wall with a hole in it, because again we tend to notice a small figure enclosed and to ignore the background. While this gives us enormous power of description it also is a serious disadvantage for human survival in that it makes us blind to the environmental factors of all things and events. We regard what is inside the boundary of

one's skin as being much more important than what is outside . . . When human beings do not notice this they become
unaware of the solid fact that the earth around them is an
integral part of their own body.

He went on to suggest that this was a "masculine" way of
perceiving the world. I agree with him, and I also see this phenomenon as a functional by-product of our internal masculine's
capabilities to manifest, which often results in His desire to control.
This important ability to manifest will always become destructive
if He loses sight of the infinite.

Dane Rudhyar, astrologer and philosopher, also explored this
subject. In his book, *We Can Begin Again Together*, Rudhyar discusses the polarization of opposite functions within us and the
necessity to harmonize them. He addresses "mind" and "order"
versus "soul" or the spiritual realm. He mentions that throughout
the history of humankind we have vacillated between these two
functions. With the emergence of science and technology, we have
become even more focused on order, losing our emphasis on soul.
The result? We value logical reasoning and manifestation while we
denigrate intuition and following spirit. Rudhyar states, "Reason
and objectivity must always turn negative and lead to egocentric
pride and a sense of futility unless they are balanced by 'Love'
(Agape) and self-surrender in total dedication to the whole—to
humanity." Rudhyar discusses *order* while I use the terms *masculine
principle* or *manifestation*, because I feel order is the domain of our
internal masculine.

It Started Out with Such Good Intentions!

The manifester tendency is strongly imbedded within the memory
of our body's cells. So much so that even though people may follow
their inner voice in the beginning, the growing power behind manifesting the vision gathers force to the point where many of those
people eventually lose contact with Her and the original vision.
This doesn't just apply to businessmen. It can also apply to artists,

performers, and athletes, to name a few. In the beginning these people followed the purity of their vision, but now their drive to achieve becomes their destiny. Jim Bakker is a solid example of this. I fully believe that the feminine (what he would call the Holy Spirit) guided each step he initially took, but soon the form of his work became a demanding, overpowering structure. Whether deliberately, or through oversight, the entire structure became bigger than the holy vision and ultimately crashed, bringing devastating changes into many lives, including his own.

Terry Cole-Whittaker talks about this loss of inner vision in her book, *The Inner Path from Where You Are to Where You Want to Be*. She started as a young woman minister, feeling a special call to bring an important message to the world. However, she fell into the trap of trying to find recognition in a male-dominated world. She began to build a personal monument instead of following her original quest. In terms of my theory, Ms. Cole-Whittaker lost contact with her internal feminine, or vision. The loss of her personal vision led to a decline in which both Ms. Cole-Whittaker and her organization fell apart. It was the masculine's empire that fell apart. What He had built was not really in line with the feminine. As Ms. Cole-Whittaker's inner vision became her primary focus, she realized that she had been following the wrong path for some time. She was smart enough to know that since the structure of her life was offtrack, there was no way to fix it, so she allowed her external world to collapse. She went away and spent quiet time alone. Once she was recentered, she began to build a new foundation for a new life. This is a truly wise woman.

We are usually given many signs that we are offtrack long before our world collapses. These messages grow stronger and stronger until we wake up and take positive action. I am not speaking metaphorically. Our physical world will give us concrete messages, letting us know what corrections we need to make.

This is a process I know extremely well. In 1980, newly divorced and having just received my Ph.D. in transpersonal psychology, I decided to move back to San Francisco where I had been raised. I was full of unwarranted confidence and was enamored with following Her visions. At the same time, I had a low-level anxiety that had nothing to do with the sorrow of my separation from my husband.

The cost of houses was at an all-time high and interest rates were 13 percent. I turned down my recently separated husband's offer to give me the house we owned in Carmel, which had payments of $300 a month and had only two more years of financing before it was free and clear of debt. I really wanted a whole new life. My internal feminine found a Victorian home that She just had to have. It felt like the perfect thing to do until about ten months later when my variable interest loan climbed six points and the expenses of my life-style mounted. Suddenly I realized that it wasn't my internal structure that had made the money in my life; it was my ex-husband's. I was in a blind panic for several months and felt that I couldn't go on. The handwriting was on the wall—I was going to have to cut way back on my style of living.

I kept looking to see what my internal masculine could really back up and the more I looked, the more dismal my possibilities seemed. Two years after I had purchased the house, I sold it at a $100,000 loss, which is considered an absolute impossibility in San Francisco. Through another series of costly mistakes and several of what I called spiritual initiations, more of my money dwindled. There I was, with no notion of how to take care of myself. The world looked very frightening and I was furious with my internal feminine. After all, I had given my whole life to God. How could He/She/It let me make such a stupid mistake?

My financial state continued to deteriorate until I couldn't even afford to rent something nice by myself, let alone buy something. For the first time since I was twenty years old I had to share a house with another person. Fortunately, she was a friend I really loved, so at least we had fun together. Nonetheless, I had to work daily on forgiving myself for the mistakes that put me in the position in which I now found myself.

It was another year before I could buy a home. What I could afford was a far cry from what I was used to living in. This time, however, I knew I couldn't go past my internal masculine's abilities to manifest. My new home was in Novato, just north of San Francisco, in a neighborhood of beer-drinking, tattoo-covered motorcycle drivers. At first my new neighbors and I were rather appalled with one another. Our worlds were so different that we didn't know how to relate, but eventually we became friends. I actually learned a great deal about building my masculine structure from these people, because they were, despite the way they looked, hard-working family people who brought home weekly paychecks.

I was also confronted with my judgments about what I deserved in life. My masculine kicked and screamed for a long time, especially as I patched up the large holes in the walls, papered, painted, and replaced the shabby carpeting. My state of mind was a reflection of the anger my internal masculine felt as He saw the reflection of where He truly was. I told Him if He didn't like it, He had better build quickly and get us out of there.

I lived in Novato for two years. When I had learned to love my new life-style as much as I had loved my old one, when I could see that I had used my money to separate myself from unconditional love, I became happier. I felt my internal masculine and feminine join forces inside me. I was no longer a visionary without a matching manifester. I could tell, because by then my career was solidly established and I was happy with my personal life. However, just when everything was stable and successful, my spirit said, "Leave California." For ten months the messages grew stronger and stronger. My masculine liked it in Novato and didn't want to leave and rebuild. He had become content where He was. But ultimately the messages were so strong that they could not be ignored, and He finally saw the wisdom of them. I sold the house and left California.

I have witnessed many cases where, after years of building a successful empire, people were told by their inner guidance, "Walk away from this." Some of them heeded the message, others did not. Those who did went on to greater fulfillment and peace of mind. My leaving San Francisco in 1987 was due to a strong prompting from my message. As I watched the San Francisco earthquake on TV two years later, I was profoundly grateful that I was not there. In the immediate aftermath of the disaster, I worked with many who had suffered terrible losses and were grieving. Most of their grief centered around the fact that they hadn't followed Her. But as I told them, "Now you know the work that He has yet to do."

Most often, those who didn't listen to these initial messages continued to receive stronger and stronger messages until all was finally lost. The classic manifester can't just walk away. His attitude is, "Are you crazy? I've spent twenty years building this. What are you talking about?"

Such a person was John Delorean. I say "was" because through the total destruction of his world of form, he built a new foundation for himself. In order to keep his Delorean car business going, he began to deal drugs. But he was caught and his world collapsed. Through his tragedies, Mr. Delorean was able to take a good look at himself and decided that he needed to make major changes in his life. His way of doing that was to develop a closer relationship with God. On a national television show Delorean admitted that greed can take over the mind and heart of a person who is driven by the desire for financial success and power. An overwhelming drive to accomplish clouds one's judgment.

When following the true feminine, there is no loss. There are only corrections that must be made. Ms. Cole-Whittaker, instead of seeing the collapse of her structure as a failure, viewed it as a vital part of her spiritual process. This loss was necessary in regaining her inner vision. Loss of your old world of form is often essential if you are to build a new world that reflects your inner guidance. Loss then becomes a vehicle of spiritual initiation, and carries within it the seed that is a hologram of your future existence. The new form arises out of the field of the old, but is radically different, with its own force and direction.

Terry Cole-Whittaker did listen to the message that she was offtrack, and she collapsed her own empire. People like John Delorean did not heed the warnings, and their empires were collapsed for them. Theirs is an important lesson, reflecting the need to constantly keep our vision and manifestation in touch with each other—always listening to Her warnings and always making sure that He can back Her up. We must be ever alert to our feminine, noticing when She is taking a different course of action from the path we are currently traveling.

The internal masculine, whether balanced or out of control, is a powerful element in you. You can either use that power or be consumed by it. The more your internal manifester is out of balance with your inner vision, the more likely your external world will reflect this separation.

You will experience changes in your external reality when you work with your masculine. In order to do this process in a conscious way, you must allow the old structures to leave your life. If your world collapses, it is easier to bear it if you know that you are being guided in new directions and are ridding yourself of old limiting patterns. As your new form tries to emerge, there is literally a pressure that builds inside you, growing until the old form falls away. If you refuse to change, the response from your reality becomes harsher.

Letting go is often an uncomfortable process because your thought forms are usually filled with inertia, fear, and hesitation. It takes courage to go forward, to remain undefeated by the pressure of your past and by your mental image of yourself. If you can withstand this pressure, you will become a living process of unlimited potential.

By consciously committing to following Her, you start a deliberate quest for self-renewal through the unfolding of new structures. By consciously building your internal masculine to match your feminine's ever-changing vision, you develop compassion and live in a state of success and fulfillment.

SEVEN

Counseling a Troubled Marriage

People hope that love will transfigure their lives. All that's needed, they believe, is to meet the right person and everything will change. Discontents and insecurities will drop away. Life will take on a richer meaning. Everything will be better. . . . And people are afraid that love won't transfigure their lives.
—Daniel B. Wile, *After the Honeymoon*

*W*hen you came into this world you were small, vulnerable, and inept in your new environment. Yet you brought with you all the complexity of your humanness. Your internal feminine and masculine were born into this world as essential parts of you.

They lay in readiness from the time They first joined in the womb to start Their development toward full perfection. They were prepared to use your unfolding life as a laboratory for Their continued positive growth. They never really stood a chance, because as They grew with you in the womb, They were influenced by the genetic structure of the collective unconsciousness, your family patterns, and your past lives (if you believe in such). Chances are that during the course of your life, one or a series of events further arrested the development of your internal duo. In your attempts to transcend the events of your growing up, you most likely developed dysfunctional survival mechanisms that caused you to divorce the part of your internal masculine and feminine that were continually being hurt.

When we lose touch with our internal masculine/feminine, we also lose contact with an essential part of ourselves. The result is that our life isn't satisfying and we become aware of an internal emptiness. The most common reaction is to look outside ourselves to fill the gap created by this separation. We turn to material possessions, drugs, alcohol, sex, work, and even organized religion in our attempts to fill that empty feeling.

If we are lucky enough to realize that these physical things offer only temporary, if any, relief at all, we often decide to spend our lives on a journey of self-exploration and growth, sifting through many psychological and spiritual teachings searching for answers. Despite all the work we do and the many changes we may make, we rarely resolve our personal issue of inner emptiness.

One way you can alleviate this poverty of self is to heal your internal separation. Their inner love can and will transfigure your life. But that inner love will have to be nurtured, leading you into a lifelong journey, just as any relationship will. Anyone who's been in a relationship has experienced ups and downs, especially in the beginning when you are getting to know one another and communication techniques are still being learned. This chapter focuses on some of the internal marriage problems that you may encounter. Don't let the stories discourage you. In order to correct a problem you first have to know its extent.

You have now met your feminine and masculine, discovered what They are like, and how They feel about each other. Now it is time to learn how to work with Them to form a real partnership. It is important, if you want to work with your internal feminine and masculine, to understand the various types of relationships He and She may form, and to understand how your physical reality reflects Their dynamic. As you may have discovered, both your masculine and feminine can initially emerge in a variety of ages or abilities, and do not necessarily emerge in the same state as one another. Their capability level may also be vastly different. In fact, as you might have discovered, there is often a major discrepancy between the two when they first emerge, which will affect Their ability to work as the wondrous team They were designed to be. This discrepancy can last quite a while, even after you start working with your internal feminine and masculine.

When most people get in touch with their feminine and masculine, they usually experience two dysfunctional archetypal images at odds with each other. If you think of all the relationships you have seen in your life, and in movies or books, then you will have an idea of how many possibilities there are for the relationship dynamics inside you. One of Them can be overpowering while the other one will be weaker. For instance, a powerful, self-assured masculine will often have a young, insecure feminine. One may be harsh and judgmental while the other one will either be rebellious or filled with fear and be very, very hurt. Occasionally both will be powerful but at war with one another, rather than giving each other support. If your childhood was particularly horrifying, your masculine and feminine may both be weak and undeveloped or both may be angry and hostile.

Their relationship might not be that dreadful. In many cases the internal masculine or feminine may not know that the other exists. Each may suspect the existence of the other, but not know how to make contact. It is quite revealing when you discover that there is an entire aspect of yourself that you have ignored most of your life. It is not only revealing to you, but also to Them. When He and She first become aware of each other, They may have varying responses. However, once They meet each other, a very real connection is made between Them. Then, even if one of Them wants to forget about the other, it is impossible to shut off Their mutual awareness. Once you have all met each other, you will never be able to fall back on ignorance of each other.

When the internal feminine and masculine are not operating synergistically, either or both of Them will often try to deny the function of the other or strive to accomplish the other's tasks. As you know, They can't operate in Their full power without each other. She knows where She wants to go but doesn't know how to get there. He knows how to get there but doesn't know where to go. The internal war doesn't always manifest as a dramatic battle, but can instead be more of a Keystone Kop comedy where no one is able to solve a problem because they are falling all over each other. Unfortunately, the results of Their antics often aren't as humorous as those of the Keystone Kops.

Signs of Their Troubled Marriage in Your Life

Keeping in mind that the external reflects the internal, our environment gives us feedback as to what is going on with Him and Her. The clearest, most immediate signal that a problem exists with my internal feminine or masculine is the attitude and actions of the people around me. When I'm not listening to my internal feminine, the women in my life become demanding, emotional, and irrational. My female friends and staff people become upset with me and our communications become twisted and impossible.

When your feminine consistently acts up, you will usually find that you have too many irons in the fire and can't complete anything. The other possibility is that you never really know what to do, which direction to take to make your dreams come true. If this has been the case over a long period in your life, you will probably be able to look back over the years and see that you have never really accomplished anything. You can often tell when your masculine is acting up because your physical world starts to fall apart or the men in your life start behaving badly.

Although you can get quick feedback from your environment, it is wise to go inside to check on your internal duo and see what is happening. Your internal masculine and feminine can both be distressed and sometimes it is almost impossible to tell which one is out of sorts. In fact, when most people tell me they think one of their internal duo is acting up it often turns out to be the other. For instance, a lack of anything in your life may be a sign that He can't back up Her vision, but it can also be that She is not giving clear, manageable guidance.

Don came to me and said that his internal masculine was out of alignment because everything in his life was falling apart. When we checked, the masculine was just fine. He thought things were going along quite well and that He was doing what his feminine had told Him to do months ago. The feminine, on the other hand, was in a stony, cold outrage. She had given the masculine new directions but said that He hadn't followed them. Don's masculine had gone in a different direction from what the feminine had ex-

pected. He was following Her old vision. What had happened that
He wasn't doing it correctly? Don's feminine had been going too
fast for the masculine. She hadn't given Him clear directions, so
He was only doing his job half right. Don was shocked to discover
that the problem actually rested more in his feminine than in his
masculine. She expected Him to be as quick as She was, and He
wasn't. When we got Don's masculine to realize what had happened,
He turned around and soon They were back on track. Don had
lost some time but he did finally pull off his projects successfully.

Morgan had been married five times. Her strong Germanic
upbringing made her very intense and driving. Men loved her strong
energy—until it finally ran over them. Morgan was an exceptional
woman in many ways, yet her ability to be intimate and to give
and share was almost nonexistent. She only knew how to take
charge. Morgan was demanding and unyielding about how things
should be done. Her marriages always ended in divorce within three
years. She couldn't understand what was going wrong.

Morgan's masculine was Attila the Hun and her feminine was
The Crybaby, who was almost always curled up in a corner, very
frightened. The masculine had absolutely no use for "the whimpering child." He was used to having things His way and He wasn't
about to listen to Her. I asked Morgan's masculine if He would like
Morgan to have an intimate relationship. He said, "Yes, but the
men Morgan chooses are all wimps." I suggested that this was true
in contrast to Him, but that at least most of the men Morgan was
interested in weren't battering her like Attila battered her Crybaby
feminine. I asked the masculine how He felt about his Crybaby
partner. "What partner?" He asked. I responded, "The feminine,
your internal partner." The masculine was stunned with the realization that the frightened child was His mate. Part of our conversation follows:

> I: Morgan will never be able to be with a man until you
>   and the feminine heal your realtionship.
> HE: I don't like and I can't imagine ever being close to Her.
> I: What if She could grow into a beautiful, powerful
>   woman?
> HE: Well that might not be so bad.
> I: Are you willing to at least talk to her?

HE: Yes.

I: *(I directed Morgan to let Him go and we accessed the feminine.)* Hello.

SHE: *(Barely audible)* Hello.

I: I know that you are very, very frightened, but I am here to help you. Would you be willing to tell me what you would like most, if you could have anything you wanted?

SHE: *(Crying)* No one ever cares about what I want.

I: Well I do, and there is nothing that I would like more than to help you get what you want.

SHE: Well, I would like for Him to be nice to me. *(Struggling)* He is so frightening.

    (I got Morgan to focus her attention on a spot between her solar plexus and her backbone.)

I: Would the masculine please join us?

HE: You can't ask me to talk to this whining child!

I: Remember the possibilities of who She can become.

HE: *(Yelling loudly)* All right. What do you want, child?

SHE: *(Curling up)* Nothing. *(Looking at me)* I knew it wouldn't work.

HE: I'm trying. I know I'm loud but please stand up and talk to me.

SHE: *(Shaking as She did so.)* I want you to be nice to me.

HE: What does that mean?

SHE: I like to have fun sometimes and you are always too busy.

HE: You and I don't like the same things. What could we do that would be fun?

SHE: Could we go to the beach tomorrow and swim and play?

HE: Yes, we could swim, but what do you mean by play?

Morgan's feminine was so happy that She could barely talk. She went on to tell Him that She didn't know yet. When They got to the beach They played volleyball, built a sand castle, and met a wonderful woman with whom Morgan became fast friends. Everyone enjoyed the adventure. The next time Morgan came to see me her masculine had softened and was in modern clothes, and her feminine was now a shy, lovely young woman.

Then Morgan began to take her inner relationship for granted, feeling that They didn't need to do any more work. Her life slowly reverted to the old patterns. It wasn't until Morgan's life reflected separation that she wanted to resume the inner marriage process. Morgan had once felt the aliveness of working with the feminine, and longed to experience that vitality again.

When we resumed her work, Morgan's masculine and feminine had not gone back to Their original states but They were rather estranged. The young feminine was feeling somewhat sad and hopeless because He was ignoring Her again, and He was very upset with the calamities in Morgan's life. Morgan's renewed commitment brought quick and powerful changes in both her masculine and feminine. When our work terminated, Morgan's masculine and feminine were radiant, powerful beings who walked side by side. Sometime later I attended Morgan's wedding, and was touched by the sweetness of the bride.

Life Out of Balance

Both your internal feminine and masculine have Their strengths, but as you now know, these traits, when untempered or taken to an extreme, can cause you tremendous pain in your life. Until your feminine is fully developed, Her desire for change can be insatiable or can become focused on acquiring things. When She is out of control, She is unmanageable. The rush of energy that She uses to guide you can also flood you when She sees something like a hot car or an exotic outfit in a store window. She wants ten new cars, twenty lovers, and four new houses. The minute She gets one thing She wants something else. She is also ruthless in Her determination to acquire Her desires. When She is ruthless, She is far tougher than He could ever be.

When He is functioning in His highest ability, the masculine tempers Her chaotic nature with the boundaries He creates, allowing Her vision to unfold in a way that is for your highest good. Her spirit of desire is tempered by the internal masculine's structure. The feeling of fear that you experience when you are out of control is often Him saying, "This will come to no good." Your feeling of resistance or procrastination may be Him requesting more time to build his ability to match Her. If He is weak in any way, the feminine can run rampant.

Laurel is a perfect example of the feminine out of control, with no real guidance from the masculine. She began working with me because of a serious spending addiction. She would shop to the point where she was actually exhausted, but still she could not stop. Wherever she traveled, her first priority was to go shopping and buy all sorts of things. I love beautiful things and have expensive tastes, but I was stunned by Laurel's ability to spend money. If she saw a sweater she liked, she bought it in every color available. When at a sale she would even buy clothes she couldn't wear, just because she hated to pass up a good bargain. Her house was piled high with unopened boxes and her closets were bulging. Every nook and cranny was filled to overflowing. Laurel once said to me in a session, "My feminine thinks I need a larger house and I'm going out to look for one today." I asked Laurel not to do that until we built the masculine into His full strength and power. The desire for a new house could have been just another farfetched and addictive spending spree by the feminine.

Laurel agreed and told me that once she had just purchased a new Jaguar car, and as she was driving it out of the lot, someone drove by in an Excalibur. "Oh," she said, "I want that." She could hardly wait to get the Jaguar home so she could begin her search for an Excalibur. Even though she was still quite well off financially, she could see that if she didn't learn to control her spending she would soon be penniless.

Laurel also had trouble with intimate relationships. Her weak masculine was extremely undependable. She connected immediately with people, but in the long run none of her relationships lasted, because her masculine couldn't be counted on and her feminine was so wild that warmth, love, and caring were unable to survive in her relationships. People simply couldn't trust her.

Laurel's internal feminine was a Free Spirit, strong but irresponsible. Her internal masculine was Goody Two Shoes and He certainly couldn't do anything to stop Her spending. He said, "I can't do anything with Her. I try but She just runs over me." Because Laurel could afford her bad habits, it took us two years to build a masculine strong enough to temper the feminine. As her addiction subsided, Laurel returned to school where she received her psychology degree. Now she works primarily with others who suffer from addictions and have no boundaries (little masculine structure).

Another story of a weak masculine allowing addictive behavior is that of Jesse. Jesse was an actor and had many remarkable breaks over the years. Each time his career would take off he would either get drunk or have a tantrum. Twice he had been on the verge of success when his actions brought everything to a screeching halt. While living in New York, Jesse was given a number of very good parts on Broadway. Soon he was working hard but he was also playing hard. His feminine wanted more and more women as well as more and more fun. Soon Jesse's play began to outweigh his work. He began drinking too much and arriving late to rehearsal. His acting degenerated. He began to get a bad reputation in the industry and soon the phones stopped ringing. He stopped getting new parts.

Jesse then moved to L.A. and captured the hearts of many well-connected people. He landed parts in three very successful movies before the old cycle started again. Because he now had money, he was able to afford cocaine, which became his drug of choice. Soon the old trouble started up again and he was labeled difficult and undependable. Seven years went by without any movie offers. Jesse had become a full-scale alcoholic and addict. Finally his life became unbearable and he checked himself into an addiction center.

When Jesse was clean of his cocaine habit, he moved to a small town in the Southwest, where he waited tables in a popular tourist restaurant. Jesse's dreams were shattered and he was afraid to return to acting for fear he would be constantly tempted to renew his old addictions. His life was stable yet the longing to act continually haunted him. One day our paths crossed and Jesse waited on me. As we talked, I ended up telling him about the inner marriage process. Jesse told me later he felt a thrill in his soul as I described the work and he knew we had to work together.

Jesse worked with me every other day during my four-week stay in that town. His masculine was an old cowpoke who liked to sit out under the stars. He didn't like to make plans and he liked to be free. He was definitely a Peter Pan type but he was an aged, weathered, salty one. He was still very, very shaky from the cocaine addiction and thought that waiting tables was just fine. His fear was that if Jesse went back to acting, He wouldn't be able to hold up to Her "speed." He said, "She plumb tuckers me out, and I split. I go off on my horse and leave Her to Her chaos." Jesse's feminine was a Polynesian princess. She always wanted the best of everything. She loved to dance and celebrate and to be the center of attention.

I prepared each one to know that if They didn't pull together as a team, at the very best, They were destined to live an unfulfilled existence. At the worst, Jesse might wind up dead. It was apparent that under pressure He would again act up. We worked diligently to teach Jesse's masculine and feminine to operate together, even in the high-paced world of theater. As They integrated, Jesse's masculine became the owner of a horse ranch, and his feminine became the masculine's loving mate who also sang and danced. Soon the masculine was a highly polished businessman who knew exactly how to take care of the feminine. In fact, He became Her business manager and He was strong enough to temper Her. She became a highly skilled artist who took Herself and Her career very seriously.

One of the indications that Jesse had created positive changes was the reaction of his Hollywood friends when they visited him. They were amazed at the differences in him. They could see that he was now solid and stable. Gone was the raucous behavior and the wild guy they had loved, yet hated being around. Word got around Hollywood and one day a producer offered Jesse a chance to audition for a role. He got the part, moved to L.A., and we kept working by phone. That was many years ago. Jesse is now quite well known. He still calls when he senses that some of the old pattern is reappearing.

When your feminine doesn't listen to your masculine, you can see the results in your finances, your stability, and your life-style. Your checks will bounce, you'll lose your job, and so on. Nothing will work out right. She must not only learn to listen to Him, She must also slow Her pace so that He can develop and gain strength.

When your masculine deliberately ignores your feminine, She becomes quite angry. The longer it takes for Him to hear the message, the stronger the messages will get. If He avoids Her long enough She will begin to destroy the structure that imprisons Her. This means that many parts of your life may fall apart.

Turner, a very fine traditional doctor whom I worked with in San Francisco, began to practice a more holistic approach. His feminine was The Seductress and his masculine was His Majesty. The feminine became intrigued with holistic medicine and during

the next year Turner increasingly moved his practice toward hol-
istically oriented medicine. Suddenly Turner began to get messages
from his feminine to quit practicing traditional medicine altogether,
or to quit going so far into holistic medicine, or to start something
totally new. His Majesty loved being a doctor, so Turner doggedly
tried to go the straight and narrow but he just couldn't. Turner was
torn so his actions were erratic. By the time the masculine was
willing to hear the message it was too late. Turner was faced with
two malpractice suits, and he was bitterly disappointed.

Even though he was now terribly unnerved, Turner began to
work in earnest with his internal duo. She slowed down and looked
at each step required to direct the masculine. His Majesty scru-
pulously followed Her in every way that He could. One day, for
no apparent reason, he started to think about how nice it would
be to live in the country and own a bed and breakfast. The thought
wouldn't go away. Turner realized She was offering him a way out
of practicing medicine. The masculine was in full agreement with
Her. So, with the little money he had left, Turner bought a farm
in Vermont. The farm needed a lot of work, but as a young man
his father had taught him to be a skilled handyman. For almost a
year he sweated and toiled. He cleared the land and planted vegetables. He undertook a major restoration of the farm and the barn.

By the way, the malpractice suits were eventually settled in his
favor. I went to visit Turner a couple of years later, and he told
me, "When I was a doctor, I was always frantic and overworked.
I never had time to live or be peaceful. She led me right to the
peace I longed for."

You Can Act as a Marriage Counselor

Many have said to me, "My internal feminine and masculine are
so far apart, how can They ever learn to cherish one another and
learn to work together?" This is where the services of a good marriage counselor are needed. That counselor can be you. I've taught
others to do this successfully.

A client of mine named Samuel had a masculine that was a

Scoundrel and was very powerful. His feminine was Mrs. Nice who went along with everything He said. Samuel was a very good businessman, but he was operating in the old-world form. He controlled, manipulated, and dominated. As a result, His feminine had no real voice. As you can imagine, Samuel's marriage, being very much a reflection of his internal marriage, was difficult. Samuel's masculine and feminine had to get to know each other and spend time together. The hard part for the masculine was actually having to listen to Her and pay attention to what She wanted. The hard part for Her was knowing what She wanted.

As soon as we sensed a little opening between Them, I convinced Samuel's masculine and feminine to spend fifteen minutes a day in communication with each other. The purpose was to build Her visionary capacity and to build His trust in Her. She would give Her vision and He would follow Her direction. Even this short time was unnerving for both of Them. He stated that She wanted to do too many things that were contrary to everything He knew to be right. She was afraid to tell Him what She really wanted. "He will just get angry at me, and I don't really know what I want very often." But in a few months the masculine discovered the excitement of following Her. His feminine had come up with some very creative solutions for some of Samuel's problems.

Then I stretched the time They worked together to one hour. Things went along quite smoothly, with only an occasional mishap, until I asked Samuel to spend at least one day a week following his feminine. Samuel's inner masculine panicked but was somewhat willing. We picked a Sunday when Samuel didn't work, so it wouldn't be too threatening to the masculine. Samuel spent the entire day trying to stay in contact with his feminine. She never appeared. In the early afternoon the masculine became quite disgusted. He said, "If you don't start speaking up, We are going to stop this. It is a waste of time." She didn't and the masculine quit for the day.

During our appointment the next week, I discovered that Samuel's feminine was absolutely frightened of being responsible for the vision all day long. She felt too weak and inferior. We worked on strengthening Her. As She grew stronger and more responsible, the masculine softened a great deal. Business was better than ever and so was Samuel's marriage.

For a while that worked very well, but then Samuel's masculine began to understand the enormity of what was happening. The feminine was gaining in power and force. The masculine knew that His rigid structure was being threatened. He went on a rampage and wouldn't listen to Her for weeks. But it became apparent that the masculine could no longer rely on His old structure. Samuel's sales figures were going down for the first time, and his marriage was getting worse again. Reluctantly, the inner masculine turned back to following the feminine. As She blossomed into Her full power, He had to build new, flexible ways of thinking.

If you play the role of marital counselor, you can help your internal masculine and feminine stay on the right track toward a successful partnership. It is as if you have two friends since childhood but they are estranged from one another. You know that They belong together and can have a beautiful marriage. With all of you, want them to fall in love, marry, and have this marriage work.

You don't have to experience major trauma to get Them aligned. You just have to pay attention to the warnings when they happen. If you let those signals go unheeded, the messages will get louder and louder.

Justine was a client who had once had a feminine who was very wild and powerful and a masculine who was weak. She was an alcoholic and a codependent. After several months of work on her inner marriage, Justine's masculine had developed into a strong figure and both her masculine and feminine were doing quite well together. Justine had not had a drink for two months.

Then Justine hired Crystal, a woman who was skillful at public relations and marketing. Soon after Crystal's arrival there was a new flurry of activity around Justine's home, which also housed her office. The two of them developed an immediate rapport, and Crystal was looking for a place to live. Her need to find a place to live and the need for more office space triggered Justine's feminine into wanting a larger house. She then started spending a great deal of time looking through real estate ads, talking to real estate agents, and looking at homes. She even got her office manager involved in the search. Justine's entire work flow was disrupted, as all this activity took a great deal of time. Justine's back started acting up but she was in such a flurry that she barely noticed. She did notice, however, that she wanted a drink badly.

As we worked, Justine's internal masculine said, "I just can't do all of this. I can't expand the business, finish all the projects we have, and move to a new house." He also couldn't bear the extra financial burden. Justine's feminine said She would slow down, but I knew She wasn't yet convinced that They were in trouble. Justine started lamely saying to everyone, "We have to stop this; it is disrupting everything." No one seemed to believe her. Everyone continued to look at homes.

Then strange dreams began. Justine dreamed she was caught in the middle of a war with Russian and German soldiers (the old masculine). Crystal had dreams of her brother (who loved her dearly) beating her to a pulp. Still the two women were the intrepid house hunters. The dreams were a signal that the masculines were enraged at all this activity. Justine finally woke up one day with her jaws aching from rage. That very day she said, "I don't want to see or talk about another house. My masculine can't back it up and we have to get back on track and get our work done." And that's just what they did. Eleven months later they found a larger house and the entire process was effortless.

You may be wondering, "If the feminine can get so out of control, how can the masculine ever trust Her guidance?" Or else you may be asking, "If He can become a brute so easily, how can anyone trust Him?" Trust has to be built and developed. People are often frightened of their internal powers, fearing that they will be led astray if they follow a wrong lead. This fear can paralyze the growth of your feminine or masculine. You can learn how to work with your internal marriage so that your masculine and feminine grow harmoniously, instead of leading you astray.

Don't think that because you start working on your masculine and feminine that your life will fall apart. Remember that your life's events are merely feedback. You will have all kinds of trauma and stress befall you, whether or not you work with your inner relationship. Most likely you can change the direction of those events more quickly if you work on your internal duo than if you don't. If your inner marriage has been more of an internal war, you are bound to see some dramatic effects in your life. As you work on your inner marriage, your internal duo will malfunction less and less over time, and then you will see the fruits of Their love. Also remember that once They are in harmony, She will continue until the day you die to take leaps, and He will always have to rebuild to match Her. Once you are fully integrated, They will leap and match simultaneously. But until then, be very aware of Their continual integration process.

One day when my client Leo was overcommitted and moving too fast, he received a jolting sign that something was going on with his masculine. He discovered that his checking account was extremely overdrawn, or so it seemed by his calculations. Because he knew that this was a sign of some problem with his internal relationship, he stopped everything and checked with Them. His masculine was furious with his feminine. She had worked Herself into a frenzy, and the masculine was letting Leo know that He couldn't back everything the feminine wanted. In fact, He let Leo know that He desperately needed a vacation.

Leo and I worked together for about an hour on this issue. Just as we finished the internal marital counseling session, Leo's accountant called to say that there was a bookkeeping error and that he still had $500 in his account. Why would such a thing happen? It was a wake-up warning, making Leo aware that something was out of line between Them. When his internal feminine realized the masculine's inability to back Her up, She immediately backed off. She knew better than to go past Him on this. Three months later Leo was vacationing in Hawaii.

The Courtship

In order to be a good relationship counselor, you can create an atmosphere where He and She can have an internal dialogue and begin to work with each other. That way you can walk Them through the exciting stages of falling in love. For this reason I call it a courtship. Once you create a dialogue between your internal masculine and feminine, tremendous changes in Their archetypal images will occur. Those images will develop and change in direct reflection of Their growing capabilities, as They slowly transform into Their full power. As a result of all this internal change, you will experience tremendous shifts in your response to life.

As your masculine becomes aware of the tremendous impact these changes have on what He views as His security, He may become despondent, angry, and more controlling and manipulative. He usually doesn't like change at first, especially when He discovers that She is totally uninterested in the impact that these changes are making in the material plane. You can see the impact of His fear, anger, and resistance on many levels.

I remember a TV program about the struggle between environmentalists who wanted to save an endangered owl and a large lumber mill that cut trees from the forests in which this owl lived. The environmentalists had been successful in preventing the lumber mill from cutting down the forest. As a result the mill had to lay off a great number of people. With no means of financial support, many of these people, descendants of generations of mill workers, were forced to move away, leaving family and friends. This absolutely destroyed the towns whose populations worked at the mill.

The battle between environmentalists and the lumber industry is a good example of the struggle created when there is an attempt to restore imbalance in any system. There is a great deal of pain as the masculine fights to maintain the previous structure. It is not that the masculine energy that created the lumber mill didn't want to save the owl. It just didn't know how to do that and still take care of the needs of employees and business.

This same kind of battle happens in individuals. We create family and friendship dynamics that affirm our internal malfunctions. When anyone in the system changes then all must change. As you begin to follow Her, people in your life will either flexibly change with you and create new systems, or they will leave your life. Things cannot stay as they were. As you grow healthier, those around you will be challenged to do the same or they will leave you to find someone who will support the structure they are holding on to. Others will be touched by the changes in you and will want to work with their own internal masculine and feminine.

A man came to me who had been a law officer for twenty-five years. In the line of duty he had killed a man and was completely shattered by this experience. Until that time he had been a somewhat difficult man who controlled his family with an iron fist. The family didn't argue, they just did as he said. Now he questioned everything about his life—what he was doing and why he was doing it.

After the shooting there were dramatic changes in his personality and the value he placed on life. He loosened his tight rein on the family and tried to show more love toward them. Interestingly enough, even though his behavior toward his family was previously abusive, they didn't like this new man. He and his family had constant arguments, something that had never happened before. He came to me because he felt like he was going crazy. Nothing seemed to work anymore. I made him aware that for the first time in his life he was trying to follow the feminine. As he tried to repair his damaged internal marriage, his outer relationships would reflect that process. His family was formerly dysfunctional and was now trying to reach a new healthier state of equilibrium. Seen in this manner his disturbed family relations began to make sense.

He began to build a new internal masculine who matched his feminine. Soon he found a good career in the computer field and was personally quite happy, except with his family. The family was unable to make the adjustment to the new person he had become. Now that he was really himself, his wife didn't particularly like him. This made her start thinking about what she wanted for her life. They came to couple's counseling for quite a while. Eventually he and his wife divorced, and it was the best thing for both of them. Once they had only themselves to count on, they blossomed individually. They even liked what happened to one another, but they still didn't want to be together. The children had difficulty at first accepting either one of them. Over time they too began to see things about their "new" mom and dad that they genuinely liked. They grew to love and respect each other, and a healing for the whole family took place.

It is fascinating how rapidly the environment mirrors back your changing and growing internal alignment. As your masculine builds to match your feminine, your reality will radically change and the lacks in your life will begin to disappear. On a personal level, when I listen to Her subtle signals and follow through with Him, my world operates miraculously. People around me are efficient, impossible schedules fall into place, and the men and women around me are loving and supportive.

Introducing . . . Them

Now you have met your internal masculine and feminine. As you have been contacting Them, it's probable that They know about each other by now. However, They haven't been formally introduced. You will get more information as to how your internal duo are functioning and exactly how They feel about each other by doing this. They will get a chance to interact with each other and hear each other's responses. Take on the role of the marriage counselor, seeing your internal masculine and feminine as a couple who have come to you for help. I will discuss the various possibilities of Their interactions and give you hints as to how you can intercede.

In order to start the introduction, do exactly as you did when you first contacted your masculine and feminine individually. Get yourself into a relaxed state and contact Her first. Initiate an extended conversation with Her as you did before, asking Her somewhat the same questions. You will discover how She has changed as you hear the difference in Her answers. Find out if She is willing to meet and work with Him. If She isn't willing to work with Him, you will have to find out why not and coax Her into the relationship. You might even want to strongly remind Her that it is Her divine *duty* to work with Him.

When She is willing to meet Him, ask Him to appear on stage. You then can start talking to the two of Them, asking first the feminine and then the masculine if They know each other. If They don't then introduce Them. If They do, ask each how He or She feels about the other.

Let's go through a first meeting session by using Ben as an example. Ben's feminine was strong and peaceful. When we first talked She didn't know about the masculine. He had been mostly unavailable. During the second session, They talked:

I: (*Addressing Ben's feminine*) Have you talked with the masculine yet?
SHE: No, but I have seen Him. He doesn't seem to be there for me.

I: Are you there for yourself? In other words, do you have
      a right to have your visions and do you speak them clearly
      to Him?

SHE: I don't think of my needs much.

I: Well, that is a big part of the problem. We'll do some
      work on that next week. If you could communicate your
      visions, do you believe He could learn to back you up?

SHE: I don't know, but I would like to talk to Him.

I: All right. Let me see if He is willing to do that. Thank
      you for coming. *(Once She leaves, I then call Him forth.)*
      How are you today?

HE: All right, but it certainly seems hopeless with Her.

I: Why?

HE: Well, we lead two very different lives and I can't imagine
      blending them together. I like to do my own thing.

I: Could you back up Her visions if they were aligned with
      yours?

HE: I think so, but I don't know if I want to.

I: Would you at least try to talk to Her, with my help, and
      see if it's possible?

HE: All right. But I won't promise to work with Her.

I: That's fine. I appreciate that. *(Then I keep Him present
      and ask Her to join us, although I still primarily talk to one
      at a time. You would be using your observer self to mediate
      Their conversation. Then I speak to Her)* 'I would like to
      formally introduce you to your internal masculine.

SHE: *(Speaking softly)* Hello. I don't know what to say to you.

HE: Well, that makes two of us.

I: *(To Her)* What do you think of Him?

SHE: Well, He is very handsome, but He looks a little harsh.

I: *(Turning to Him)* What do you think of Her?

HE: Wow, She is really something. I wouldn't mind following
      something that looked like that.

I: *(To Her)* Would you be willing to tell Him what you
      want in the next month?

SHE: This feels very unnerving to me. *(She take a number of
      deep breaths and her voice is quivering)* I want to see some
      cooperation in Ben's marriage.

I: What would that look like? You know how practical He is.

SHE: Well, I want Ben and his wife to start working as a team.

I: Anything else?

SHE: It seems too much to ask, but I want his wife to get a job so that they don't have to sell their house.

I: Well, He can't make someone else do something, but if the two of you were working as a team, the wife would have to change or they would separate. *(To Him)* What do you think, could you two get together?

HE: I'd be willing to try. I really like it when She speaks so clearly. I now know exactly what She wants. And you know what? We both want the same thing.

I: Isn't that marvelous? I am very pleased about this initial meeting. I would like the two of you to have frequent conversations together. *(They both nod Their heads and Ben then comes out of his meditation.)*

Ben suddenly had a whole new understanding of the dynamic between him and his wife. He could see that they just kept going through the same old game and nothing ever changed. I saw Ben three more times and observed a marked difference in his behavior. He no longer seemed beaten and hopeless. His wife agreed to see me as well. After several sessions with each of them alone and then the two of them together, both Ben and his wife were able to find ways to work together. At the time of this writing, we are still working on their relationships with their internal duo and with each other.

Tuning Your Internal Partnership

After your internal masculine and feminine initially get together, you will want to meet with Them regularly and slowly work toward setting up a courtship between Them. It's best if you meet with Them as often as possible. It is up to you how much time you want to spend doing this. Do whatever feels comfortable to you, but spend some time with Them each day. As in any relationship, the more time and attention you give it, the stronger the relationship will be. This is the period of courtship.

Through this courtship They can grow to the point where She says, "Jump off a cliff," and He says "Great." He will be able to do this when He is sure of Himself and when He knows that following Her will not harm Him. He will know that He is safe and that She will protect him. She will leap out into space with unfolding passion as She knows that He is there with Her. She will become more and more sure of Her visions.

Miracles will occur when the two of Them start working together. Try to never ignore either one of Them, because as soon as you do They will go into some kind of disruption. Out of that internal disruption will come external disruption in your life. When He says that He can't back Her up, He is letting you know that He sees no way to honor Her vision at that moment. It is a matter of Her waiting for Him to match Her dream. If He says, "I'll take care of it," He'll take care of it and you can count on it happening. When She won't listen to Him or give Him clear instructions, She is letting you know that She is afraid to trust Him or that She is confused. Sometimes She may not know what She wants to do yet. Try to never act out of deadness. She is probably building toward a direction, but it is not yet known. Once She gains confidence, you can depend upon Her guidance when it is there, and will learn to wait when it is not.

Below are the responses you might get from Them and suggestions on how you can work with those responses:

HONORING THE FEMININE

She feels She knows where to go and She can get there Herself. She is fooling herself. Let Her know this immediately. Work with Her until She is open to the possibility of cocreating with Him. You might tell Her that you know She is an Amazon, and that while She can do many things by Herself, She is not really accomplishing what She could. Let Her know that He can grow to match Her and that They will be unbeatable if They work together.

She feels He is a bully and She hates Him. First you will have to calm Her, so She can muster the strength to talk to Him. You will also have to calm Him. You might tell Him that while He likes being in charge, it is not serving you for Him to be out of balance. Point out to Him how unsatisfying His life is and how few people seem to like Him. Your approach should be to convince Him how happy His life could be if He would work as Her partner.

At the same time you are molding Him into a more supportive role, get Her to see the positive things about Him. This should be a lovely round-robin. Each of them doing better in response to a growing awareness of how much They like being together.

She feels too small to give Him Her vision. Usually He is quite strong and willing to be with Her. He can help Her find the courage to speak up by giving Her positive feedback. With just a little encouragement She will begin to blossom and grow up. She must be corrected very gently. If He has tried to make Her small then lead Him toward encouraging Her.

She likes Him but cannot trust Him. You may be able to convince Her that He can be trusted if given manageable tasks, but basically He is going to have to work to prove Himself to Her. Ask Him if He's willing to consider backing up Her vision. If He's not willing, coax Him as you did with Her. You will find that He usually has a strong reason why He doesn't want to work with Her. Ask Him if He would be willing to support Her if His complaint was rectified. If so, then you can discuss the complaint with the feminine.

She thinks He is a jerk and She doesn't want His help. Here there is a basic disrespect for the functions of the masculine. Work on misandry from the beginning, discovering the roots of this hatred of men. Over time She will grow to forgive Him for not being perfect and allow Him to make mistakes. She will need to know that He is not just like all the men She has ever known and that He wants to love and support Her. If He really is a jerk then He will also have corrections to make.

HONORING THE MASCULINE

The most common reactions I hear from the masculine when I am working with clients are as follows:

He feels burdened by Her requests. He makes statements like, "I just can't do this." When this happens, facilitate by asking Her to slow down. Mediate by saying something like, "He can't back your requests right now so we're going to ask you (the internal female)

to wait or cut back on your demands." It is the internal masculine
who takes the action. The feminine must rely on His focused awareness to fulfill Her dreams. Without Him She cannot manifest Her
vision. Because of this, She must listen to His perceptions, taking
into consideration what He can and can't do. She functions at her
highest level when She gives clear, concise visions and does not
go beyond His ability to manifest.

He has no use for Her. If He says, "I wouldn't dream of following
Her; She's not trustworthy," then you must remind Him of the
essential nature of Their union. Convince Him to try backing Her
up in small ways. Don't unnerve Him or Her by asking for too
much. It may be for just a few minutes at first, then possibly longer.
You want to learn to wait until They are both comfortable working
with each other. One way to do this in the beginning is to give
Them small tasks to do together. If She is really untrustworthy, it
usually means that She wants too much too fast. Work with Her
to slow down.

*He is unwilling to back Her simply because the notion seems ridiculous
to Him.* In this case, He's usually the reflection of an old-world,
patriarchal male. He may be really taken aback by being asked to
follow Her. Once again, act as intermediary and convince Him to
cooperate. Start with small things in your everyday life. It's too
threatening to try to have Him back up anything extremely important or to ask Her to tell Him what She wants in a critical
situation. He will have to let go slowly. Try asking for something
to this effect: "I want you to listen to Her while we do our errands
today. Find out what She wants to do first. Check each step along
the way. There may be some things that She doesn't want to do
today. If She wants to go to the cleaners, go. If She feels like calling
someone, call that person. If some big decision must be made,
revert to your normal way of doing things." She will want to grow
until She feels very capable and confident and knows that He listens
to Her.

If all goes well, They will begin to gain confidence in each
other. They will get a chance to see that the other might actually
make life easier. As He learns to trust Her, Her trust of Him will
increase and vice versa. With this growing trust, Their signals to
one another will become increasingly stronger.

Then take it a step further, begin to increase the stakes and see if He's ready to follow Her in bigger ways. Let's say you're to go out of town but at the last minute the "juice" dies. See if He's willing to cancel, even if it is a business trip. If She doesn't want to be with someone with whom you have a dinner date, see if He's willing to cancel the date. He may be very frightened or angry before taking such steps, but this is really what is required of Him. It will be easier for your masculine to carry out Her visions each time He takes that leap to support Her.

He is really outraged with the internal feminine and He's quit trying to back Her up. If your internal masculine said, "She never pays attention to me, She never puts any value on what I do, let Her do it Herself," then He is very angry at Her. The first thing you want to do is let Her know the dilemma. Talk to Her until She sees that She is turning away valuable support. She will need to regain His trust because She has been so abusive in the past. He will usually move off of his stance in a relatively short time.

He totally denies Her. He pretends He is both the vision and the manifester. He often despises her and devalues Her guidance. He expects Her to follow Him. He is controlling, dominating, and usually somewhat brutal. If She dares to make a mistake, He is on Her immediately. This is a clear case of misogyny. The feminine found with this type of masculine is usually an internally abused wife. I usually start out by inspiring Him to agree to have conversations with Her daily. He gets to know Her and to see what She wants in life. Often She is not nearly as bad as He thinks She is. If She makes a mistake, patience is required.

DIALOGUE

You can use this exercise to engage in dialogue between Him and Her. Plan on doing this every day for about three months. They will grow and change and may turn into archetypes I haven't even mentioned. Always analyze these characters and keep working on Their relationship. The minute you get cocky about Their ability to communicate, Their relationship will begin to fall apart, just like a marriage does without good communication.

1. When you first begin you may want to place two chairs facing each other.
2. Sit in one chair and take a few deep breaths to relax and open yourself to the energy of your masculine and fem-

inine. When you feel at peace, simply state the issues you hope to resolve in your life.

3. Access your feminine. Explore the issue you stated above through Her eyes. Let Her speak through you, to Him. Have Her tell your masculine how She feels about the specific problems needing to be addressed.

4. Now sit in the other chair and access your masculine. Have Him tell your feminine how He feels about what She explored. Have Him discuss whether or not He can back up what She desires. See if He has any ideas for resolution of those issues.

5. If there was a problem with Their working together, then go into your quiet space and become a mediator for your feminine and masculine. Work with each of Them until you reach some kind of resolve.

If you work with your internal duo in this way He and She will grow in their ability to communicate with each other. The more your masculine and feminine get to know and understand each other, the more successful you will be in living your life with Them.

If you find that you can easily access Him and Her you may work without the chairs. You can merely go back and forth inside. I check in with my masculine and feminine all during the day. Remember to establish contact with your solar plexus before speaking with Her and establish contact with your backbone before contacting Him.

Whenever it becomes apparent that the two of Them are not cooperating in one of my clients, I give the client a simple affirmation to work with. I tell my client to simply say, "I have a body that matches my vision now" or "I have a masculine that matches my feminine now."

The Happy Ending

As you work with your inner couple and they get to know each other, you will experience greater and greater passion between Them. It is very exciting. Most clients experience the kind of tremendous elation that they feel when they are falling in love with an external partner. I wish I could tell you that getting Them to this stage is the end of the story, but unfortunately the work continues long after the honeymoon. I can promise you one thing. If you work on your internal relationship, you will always find yourself in a new, exciting phase of your own life. You will never again see anything that happens to you as an event over which you have no power. You can learn to control your response to life, because that control comes from within. You will not see something leaving your life as loss; rather, you will experience that something new is in the birthing process. Your life will have a happy ending again and again and again. When it doesn't, turn to your internal duo.

You will be able to regain control by going inside and talking to Her and Him. Once you understand the messages They are giving you, you will be able to get yourself on the right track. You will not spend precious time and emotional energy haphazardly trying to find the solutions to your everday problems. You will learn to ask for a body that matches your vision or a masculine that pursues only the feminine.

You will realize that the actions of other people are related to you. You will know that the actions and words of those around you are a reflection of some pattern that is buried in your cells or a reflection of what is going on between Him and Her. When you fully realize this, you will no longer experience angry words and actions from others as an attack from the outside. You are more likely then to want to explore the other person's behavior as feedback for you, rather than feeling that you must counterattack. You will want to first talk to your own internal duo and then gather information by having a conversation with the actual person in question. Most importantly, feelings of self-acceptance and love will grow in you. You will begin to live in the condition of love, and that will draw the love of others toward you. Love is the basis of true success in every area of life.

EIGHT

Building the Inner Relationship

> The unblocked flow of male and female energy is the base for all creation and opens up the secrets of the universe.
> —Shirley Gehrke Luthman, *Energy—The Essence of Male and Female*

*H*ave you ever experienced or overheard an argument that seemed unresolvable, with both parties contradicting each other's interpretation of the same incident? Heated words flash back and forth. Each party feels that they are right in their interpretation. The argument could go something like this:

"Well, you said . . ."

"No, I didn't, I said . . ."

"I distinctly heard you say . . ."

"I never said any such thing . . ."

"Yes, you did . . ."

The arguers usually become frustrated and leave the interaction with unresolved feelings. They suppress their hurt and anger in order to get along. These painful emotions of hurt and anger rarely dissipate fully, and the negative feelings inevitably come out at another time during another argument. The result? The arguers now have a history of hurt and injustice that affects their ability to communicate and work with each other. After a series of arguments, the partners begin to close down to each other, eventually shutting off all communication. They then coexist in a dysfunctional relationship.

The same dynamic can happen with your internal duo. Your internal masculine and feminine may have Their own history of hurtful interactions that keeps Them in a dysfunctional pattern, if They interact at all. Even if your masculine and feminine want to work with each other, you might have to act as a marriage counselor, or as an objective observer, to help Them resolve Their differences.

As an internal marriage counselor, you will want to develop your feminine into a strong intuitive so that She keeps Her loving qualities, yet becomes precise in Her directions to the masculine. You will also want to develop your masculine (logic) to be strong and unthreatened by Her as She grows in Her power, so that He can lovingly support Her. If you spend the time and energy that is needed to bring Him into union with Her, He will steadily become more balanced and more in love with Her. At the same time, She will grow in Her love for Him.

You have now met your masculine and feminine and have introduced them to each other. By now you might know enough about Them to start building Their relationship. As your internal masculine and feminine really get into the swing of Their togetherness, your feminine will learn to operate more out of infinite knowledge, and your masculine will begin to harmonize with Her and become more adept with His abilities. Every time He matches Her, He gets stronger and clearer. Every time She gives a clear message and He follows through, She too becomes stronger and clearer. This process can be very exciting, especially as you experience the growing power of your internal marriage and begin to master situations that were once difficult for you. Your self-esteem and self-worth will grow. Your relationships will improve. You'll experience giving and receiving more love. Your friendships will take on a new and powerful meaning as a reflection of your own growth.

Helping Your Dysfunctional Archetypes

Chances are that when you first met your internal feminine and masculine, you discovered two inner personalities that badly needed work. I will discuss the most common dynamics that can occur, and will then show you how to work with them. While it is impossible to discuss every possible situation that could occur in your inner marriage (it would be like trying to catalog every interaction that has ever occurred since the beginning of the human race), you will find that the examples below are of great help to you. These exercises will help you understand how to work with your own inner marriage dynamic. Remember that in your internal work, you are the objective observer and will want to learn how to solve problems when there is a conflict or an impasse. Let's begin with the child archetypes.

✳THE CHILD ARCHETYPES   The Inner Child has become a major focus with many therapists, counselors, and teachers. In your own internal work you might wonder if there is a difference between the child version of your inner masculine and feminine and the Inner Child you might have heard about. Although there are many behavioral similarities between the child archetypes I discuss and the Inner Child, the Inner Child is *always* a childhood version of yourself. The child I discuss in this work is not you as you were when you were young, but is an archetype and may appear as either masculine or feminine. Aside from that, the inner masculine/feminine work further defines the child as either your intuitive or your logical function. Both the inner masculine child and the inner feminine child can be meek and helpless, or terrified, or angry and spiteful. They can also be happy or sad. Depending upon whether the child is your masculine or your feminine, you will experience problems in either your ability to create and lead your life (your feminine) or your ability to manifest (your masculine).

Working with the archetypal child in the inner marriage is complex because the child is not an isolated phenomenon. It is an active part of the inner relationship. Nothing is worse than being coupled with a child when you are trying to function in the adult world. The child, being expected to act and function as an adult, can become increasingly dysfunctional as It continues to fail in its responsibilities. On the other hand, you will discover an extremely problematic child if It has been completely ignored.

Examining this from the viewpoint of the other member of the internal marriage, you can imagine how frustrating it is to rely on a child to fulfill the responsibility of adult duties. The archetypal child's partner will be outraged, disgusted, will have given up, or will appear thousands of years old.

In your inner marriage work you will elicit help from the stronger archetype in working with the child archetype. It is through Their relationship that the child can blossom and grow. While you can do exercises that individually support the growth of your internal feminine or masculine, it is more helpful to work simultaneously with both of Them. For example, trying to get an internal feminine child to give stronger, clearer directions is rarely possible if the masculine is unwilling to encourage Her by acting on Her directions. He does become the positive reinforcement for Her initial attempts at growing up. The same is true if the roles are reversed and He is childish and She is the strong one.

Working with Your Child Archetype

You will want to do the same exercises for either a masculine or feminine child archetype. Whether it was your masculine or feminine that emerged as a child, your first goal is to make that child feel safe so that healing can occur rapidly. If both the feminine and masculine appear as children there will be a lot more work to do but this rarely happens except in the most extreme cases of psychological abuse during childhood. If your archetypal child is in really terrible shape, please seek a competent counselor or therapist to work with. Do not try to diagnose and heal yourself. You will need professional support.

To make communication easier I will refer to both of these feminine and masculine archetypes as the child. Do not confuse this with the Inner Child work described elsewhere by other people. I will also refer to this archetype as "It" so that you won't have to belabor constantly reading "She or He."

Earlier I mentioned that if you have a child archetype, it is because there was an incident or several incidents in your childhood that made your masculine or feminine withdraw. What you do with the child archetype depends on which version it is. If your archetypal child is frightened or sad, the next technique, adapted from one created by Dr. Nathaniel Branden, is helpful in reliving the incident or incidents that caused you to disown this internal aspect. Before you start this exercise, get some paper and a pencil and place it beside you. In fact, you might consider keeping a journal of your inner marriage work in a notebook.

GREETING
Imagine yourself as you are now, sitting comfortably under a very beautiful tree, far out in the country. Ahead of you is a quiet, winding road. Let yourself become very still, relaxed, and peaceful. Soon you see the figure of a child coming toward you. As the child comes into view, you see that It is either your inner masculine or feminine child. Notice how you feel about the child. Describe It out loud. Now ask the child how It feels about you. See if It trusts and loves you. If It doesn't, try to create a safe feeling for the child and convince It to sit down beside you. Talk to the child and establish a rapport.

Now write down what you experienced in this exercise. If you weren't able to create an air of trust and love with this child, then continue your attempts to make friends with It. This child is very precious. In order to establish trust and love between you and the child, spend some time doing fun things together. I would suggest that you do things with this child just like you would if you were trying to reassure and build a truly loving relationship with a real child. This means getting together with your archetypal child two or three times a week. Keep a journal of your interactions.

When you make a date with your archetypal child, make sure that you ask the child what It would like to do. Some children want to go shopping. Some want a day off to read. Some want to spend time with a friend. The main point of this exercise is to make a date and keep it, and to be true to the promise you make. If you disappoint the child too often It will stop trusting you. This is true for your external children as well as your inner child.

Terry was an only child, born to older parents who were insensitive to the needs of a growing child. Nothing he did ever seemed to be good enough for them. Terry feels that he never had much play time in his childhood; he was always trying to be a grown-up. Now that Terry is an adult, he is always too busy to spend any time doing the things he likes to do. When I first met him it had been ten years since Terry had taken a vacation, and he had no time at all for a relationship.

When Terry first met his masculine, he began to cry. Terry had

a very young masculine. He was touched by the boy's sweet in-
nocence. Terry's child masculine didn't trust him because he was
an adult. This child masculine felt that Terry had abused Him but
He did admit that He wanted to believe and trust in Terry. Terry
made a date with Him the following Saturday to go hiking in the
woods.

Terry's inner boy was ecstatic to finally have time to play. Terry
and his child masculine talked and played during their first date,
rapidly becoming friends. In no time at all the young boy opened
up. He was so willing to love Terry that it was easy for Him. Terry,
of course, was completely enamored with the child. This was the
beginning of many happy times together. Because of this loving
attention the child grew rapidly.

If your archetypal child still feels unsafe after you've had a few
outings, or if It doesn't trust you at all, do the following exercise.
You will find this particularly useful if you had a traumatic childhood.

REMEMBERING THE WISE PARENTS

Get into a very deep, relaxed state. Let your every breath take
you into deeper and deeper states of relaxation.

Imagine yourself as a young child again. You are standing
in a very beautiful place, somewhere out in nature.

Now imagine that from your right, walking toward you, is
a beautiful, loving, wise woman. She stops directly in front of
you. Notice everything about this woman, what she feels like,
smells like, and looks like. Have her turn and notice you, the
child. She is the perfect mother that you never had and always
wanted. Have this woman take your right hand. She has absolutely nothing to do but love and care for you. Notice how
you feel about her. Do you feel safe and happy? Are you deeply
touched by her love? Are you too distrustful and frightened to
believe her? Simply make a note to remember how you, as the
archetypal child, responded to her.

Now from the left see a handsome, loving, wise man walk
toward you. Notice everything about him—what he looks, feels,
and smells like. He is the perfect father you always wanted and
never had. Have the divine father take your left hand. He has
nothing in the world to do but love and protect you. Notice
how you feel as he holds your small hand. Do you feel safe and

happy now? Or do you feel nervous and untrusting? Make a
mental note of your feelings right now.

Let the perfect parents work with the child until It feels
comfortable. Now allow yourself to step out of the picture and
into yourself. As if you are watching a movie, envision that the
child and the perfect parents are walking off together until they
dissolve. Know that the child will be safe from harm's way and
that it will be much calmer now. Become yourself, become
aware of your surroundings and open your eyes.

Whenever your child gets frightened in the future, you can call
forth these caring parents for comfort. It may take a while before
the child trusts the perfect mother and father. Be patient.

✳THE BRAT/THE MONSTER   If your child feminine or masculine
is angry, chances are that It will act out. These archetypes learned
to act out instead of retreating in order to cope. The Brat/Monster
is actually easier to deal with than any of the other child archetypes
because at least this type communicates, even though the communication is hostile. If you have an inner child that acts out, then
the perfect parents must give firm guidance and teach the child not
to be destructive.

Helen was a successful businesswoman who had trouble with
her personal relationships. When people first met her, they were
very drawn to her. She seemed wise, funny, and entertaining.
However, very shortly thereafter, Helen's angry feminine would
appear and She would begin to make trouble in the relationship.
Helen would become very demanding and insist on having everything her own way. When Helen's friends balked at this, her Brat
would become exceedingly angry and have screaming fits. Most
people simply felt that enjoying Helen's intermittent joviality wasn't
worth dealing with her temper tantrums, and they would walk off.
Finally, Helen grew tired of losing people she loved and decided
to do some work on herself. When Helen came to me, we found
that she had a masculine who was a cross between the Wise Man
and Attila the Hun, and the Brat for a feminine. Her masculine
was very controlling of the Brat feminine but felt He had to be so
forceful because She was so impossible. Between Helen's extremely
controlling masculine and The Brat's flare-ups, it was no wonder
Helen was unable to maintain relationships.

Our work was to get Helen's masculine to be firm in not following the feminine when She was outrageous. This meant He needed to appear to quietly withdraw. As Helen's masculine loosened His control of the feminine, the feminine began to calm down. Her flare-ups were no fun now that He no longer tried to boss Her around. After She really relaxed, we discovered that She didn't know how to get Her way except by being bratty. The Wise Man told Her that if She were willing to listen to Him, He would try to back her up if She asked for anything. He further told Her this meant that He might tell Her something was not good for Her, or that He couldn't do what She wanted at that time, and She would have to listen to Him. The Brat liked the Wise Man and her anger eventually subsided. Now Helen's feminine has grown into a lovely young woman who is highly creative. Helen no longer works as hard, and her friends can see the changes in her. She's a great deal more fun to be around as well as more loving.

✻SHRINKING VIOLET/FEARFUL FREDDY These poor child archetypes are afraid of Their own shadows. They spend most of Their time hiding from life and perceiving everything as a danger. Their fear may come from either the fact that Their childhood was a nightmare or the inner masculine is brutal. This type of child archetype generally wants to be cooperative and would love to live life more fully, but the fear is too great. It is not unusual for this archetype to reveal itself only in unusual circumstances.

No one would have dreamed that Chris's feminine was a Shrinking Violet. He was a large, strong man, a construction worker. People counted on him and knew that if there was a problem they could turn to him. Chris almost always appeared to be strong and fearless. Then he became very seriously involved with a woman. As his relationship with this woman grew more intimate, Chris began to experience a growing, free-floating fear. The longer Chris went with this woman, the stronger this free-floating fear became. Chris hardly knew what to make of it. He was frightened all of the time, except when he was at work. Eventually Chris even became afraid of doing things he used to do freely at work. For instance, he could no longer work on a roof without becoming absolutely terrified.

His girlfriend started to have second thoughts about him because of his extraordinary fears. Things swiftly came to a head for Chris.

One day he was forced to go on the roof of a new building because of a problem that had developed. Stiff with fear, Chris climbed up toward the roof. He missed a step and fell. Although not badly hurt, he realized that he had to do something. He and his lover came to see me together.

It was decided that Chris and his girlfriend would take a two-week vacation from one another so that we all could sort out what was really going on. Each day he was away from her, he grew stronger. It was apparent that he loved her, but that he was immobilized with her. Chris told me this had happened once before. (He had only been in two relationships.) He also told me he loved this woman and wanted to be with her.

On the third visit Chris and his girlfriend came together and we coaxed Shrinking Violet to come out and talk to the woman. She was painfully shy and couldn't look her in the eyes. After about fifteen minutes, She looked up at the woman once in a while. We asked Shrinking Violet what She needed in order to feel safe. She said that She needed to spend time with the woman alone. Chris's masculine, Mr. Nice, would just confuse their time together. She and the girlfriend made a date to go to the zoo.

This was an excruciating process for Chris. He said, "You really want me to go to the zoo as Shrinking Violet? I can't." I told him he didn't have to be obvious; just let himself feel his fear, not pretend to be strong, and let the woman take care of him. He was a courageous fellow, and the next Saturday, off they went. The next week Chris excitedly told me that he felt very happy and encouraged. It had been a tremendous relief to just surrender to his fear. Shrinking Violet was beginning to trust the woman.

Not everyone is lucky enough to have a friend like Chris did, but you can do this same thing alone. Try to take Shrinking Violet and Fearful Freddy on small adventures. Spend time with Them, help Them feel safe and secure. It is critical to remember that this is only a child. Don't try to make It do grown-up things.

If Chris had been alone we could have done this same work utilizing Mr. Nice. Mr. Nice is usually very willing to change. If this is your dilemma, get yourself in the role of your observer self. Work with Them by having Her tell you what She wants, then tell Mr. Nice in great detail exactly what to do. Tell Him where She wants to go. Pick the time and the date. Make sure He knows how to get there. Make sure that until the actual event, Mr. Nice doesn't get sidetracked and make other plans. Since He gets confused by others' needs, He could wander away and forget.

✳CRYBABY/SAD SACK   Crybaby and Sad Sack are very remorseful child archetypes. They, like the other child archetypes, are usually the products of an especially sad early life. The sadness both of the archetypes feel stems mostly from a sense of hopelessness and lack of self-worth.

Anyone with these archetypes will want to delve into the source of this sadness in order to release it. Quite often, just reassuring Crybaby and Sad Sack and then allowing these archetypes to totally experience Their sadness will be enough to free Them into becoming much more mature. There are several exercises below that will help you do this.

The following exercise works well with all of the archetypes, but is especially helpful with Shrinking Violet, Fearful Freddy, Crybaby, and Sad Sack. This exercise was created by a friend and cohort, Tim Heath, who is a remarkable teacher.

THE HEALING ROOM

Put on some soft music and get into a relaxed state. Prepare to enter a very safe space inside of yourself.

Focus upon the center of your chest and solar plexus area. See a small you, about four inches high. Now see the child/you entering into this special place near your heart. As you enter, you see that you are in a beautiful room lined with quartz crystal.

Now ask any figures of loving power that you feel safe with to join you in the room so that they can protect you. You can envision a Buddha or Christ, a Native American power object, a powerful warrior, a mentor, or someone you love. You can envision a guardian angel or make up your own protective beings. You may even want to choose the business people you admire the most.

Now imagine that there is a throne in the center of the room. Recall someone who hurt you very much, and see the true negativity of that person sitting on the throne. Let that negativity take on a personality. Have it appear as a monster, a color, a shape, anything that represents the pain you've experienced from that person. Ask the negativity what it was trying to do. How did it think that was helpful? (Negative patterns are often forms of protection that have outlived their usefulness.) Now tell the negativity all about the pain it has caused you and let it know that you will not allow it to be in your life anymore.

Repeat these words: "I now dismiss you from my life—in the past, the present, and the future. You are no longer a part of me and I remove you from every part of my being: mind, body, and spirit."

See all of the loving beings you envisioned in the crystal room escorting the negativity to a vehicle, any kind of vehicle you want, that travels at a high speed.

Say to the departing monster, "I send you far, far away so you are no longer a part of my life and my world." See the vehicle being driven swiftly out, and escorted to a faraway place. Now build a barrier around it, and encase it in a very thick coat of steel. If it is in a cave, simply seal the opening.

Now go through the same process with all of the people who have hurt you, one at a time. Bring up any experience that has caused you pain or suffering, or anyone who has harmed you in any way. Be sure to take each of them to a different place and to seal each one off with a steel barrier.

Notice that where once your mind and heart were filled with monsters, now you are filled with sunshine and the goodness of your own nature. See your protectors gathered around you and thank them. Say good-bye to them and walk out of the inner sanctuary.

At this point, your internal masculine or feminine child should feel a great deal safer. Now call on the perfect parents and have them escort the child to a beautiful, safe place. You can then contact the next layer of your internal feminine or masculine.

You will usually find that once your child archetype feels safe, It will emerge as a more mature feminine or masculine. During times of great stress, however, you can count on the child archetype to reemerge until It becomes very, very secure. The child may not show up exactly as It once was, but It will more than likely reappear in a similar angry, hurt state. Each time this happens, help the child feel safe again. Do not grow impatient if your temperamental child occasionally emerges. Eventually you will find that your inner child will completely heal and transform.

The following technique is one that you can use on the spur of the moment when your archetypal child emerges at a critical point. At such times you will want your internal child to feel safe, so that your adult can function well.

SECURITY

Remember a place where you felt safe as a child. Take your internal child there, tell It why you must leave for a while and that you will soon return. This will help keep the child from acting out.

Check to see if It wants someone to stay with It. If It does, see that the person is there before you leave. If It wants another child, however, be sure to leave the wise mother and father with It so the two children don't get into trouble.

If you never felt safe as a child and have no image of a magical place, then ask the child archetype what kind of a place It would like you to build so that It feels safe.

Go on about your business and when you're finished, check in with the child in the playroom. Perhaps you could take the child for a walk or spend a few minutes playing with It. That way the child will feel safe when you leave It for brief periods of time in the future.

Never take your child into situations where It will feel unprotected or unsafe.

*Sugar and Spice/Goody Two Shoes These two child archetypes are simply too good and too nice. They survived in Their life by always being the perfect child always doing what adults wanted Them to do. As a result, They are generally not adventurous and they rarely take unique actions. They are not accustomed to thinking for Themselves but rather to following external guidance. These child archetypes need to develop the courage to break through Their programming and to decipher what it is *They* really want to do. Their programming is so deeply embedded and constantly reinforced by society that you will want to begin Their healing process in small ways.

The most effective way of working with Them is to make a list of what They were told to do and not to do by parental/authoritarian figures. Try the following exercise.

RELEASING

1. Go quietly inside and talk to your child archetype. Help the child to feel very, very safe by talking soothingly and

comfortingly. Encourage the child to tell you about the things that have made Him or Her unhappy or fearful.

2. Ask the child to list all of the things They have been told to do. Make a list. Do the same with all the things they were told not to do.

3. Address each issue on both lists and give the child another view of how these dictates might be perceived differently and offer the child your more mature perspective.

4. Bring in the divine parents to be with the child and bring yourself back fully into reality.

Spend a week or so talking to others about your rules list. Many of them will have been given the same rules. Be open to your friends' input about how they handled the voice of the parental figures.

Then have another session with your child. This time, write new rules together. Review those rules regularly. Make sure the rules are loose and flexible, such as, "I will listen to my own inner guidance" or "Always ask yourself who is saying this" or "I am free to live my own life." You might even hang those new rules somewhere you can see every day.

Once you feel like you have developed some new ways of dealing with this old, limiting behavior, then continue to talk to your child each time It tries to be a good little girl or boy at your expense. When the child is able to think and feel somewhat by Him or Herself embellish the exercise in the following way:
Ask your child to tell you what It would like to do or have happen. This will really be hidden in the deepest part of Its heart. Encourage your child archetype to believe in Its dreams and help It to figure out how to accomplish those dreams. Once your child archetype has this sense of fulfillment, the voice of external authoritarianism will be greatly diminished.

This completes our discussion of the child archetype. I think you will find that these exercises are very helpful to you. I want to now discuss the different archetypes I've presented to you in this and earlier chapters, and give you exercises to work with those archetypes. First, let's discuss the feminine.

Working with Your Internal Feminine

✳THE FREE SPIRIT   If your feminine is a young, unpredictable Free Spirit, teach Her to make an attempt to give small visions that are not too outlandish. You cannot expect this feminine to be fully responsible at first because She doesn't know how.

This type of feminine can result in compulsive behavior. I give more in-depth information about this in Chapter 9. For now, look to see if you are in any way excessive in your life. It may be any of the habits of physical addiction (drugs, alcohol), eating, talking, continually overbooking your time, always being late, or spending excessive amounts of money. Determine to work on your compulsive behavior by seeing what kind of controls you can initiate that might be bearable to the Free Spirit. You can enlist your masculine, if He functions well, to help you decide what measures would be most effective. For instance, one of the first things I do with compulsive spenders is ask them to put away their credit cards and operate on a cash-only basis. If this is too tough, then we agree that they can keep one credit card for six months only and stay well within a spending limit.

Marge was constantly in trouble about paying her bills and had filed bankruptcy twice. When I first started working with her, she had become totally irresponsible and had left two states owing a great deal of money. She had written many bad checks and ended up, in effect, stealing a car. She knew that she was totally out of hand, but couldn't seem to stop herself. At first, Marge's feminine didn't want to deal with the issue at all. She was having a wonderful time with things as they were. Finally, after several sessions, Marge's feminine was willing to listen and to make some changes, realizing that Her irresponsibility was not going to lead to a productive end. The masculine was greatly relieved. He was actually in fairly good shape. He was strong and willing to work with the feminine, but She had been so out of control that He had practically given up.

The next time Marge came to me she had prepared a list of her creditors (including the owner of the car) and all of her bad checks. We decided to write to just two of the creditors. She couldn't really face anymore. Writing these letters terrified Marge, but after she had written them she felt calmer than she had in a long time. As positive responses came back from the creditors, Marge's youthful inner feminine actually began to be more responsible.

The next time we got together, we wrote the same letter to the rest of the creditors, except for the car owner. Marge found this stack of letters easier to do. By the third session I pressed forward and asked Marge if she was willing to talk to the man from whom she had essentially stolen the car. Marge began crying at the thought of doing this, but she really felt an urgency to get this off her shoulders. It was a good thing, too, because the man to whom Marge owed the car payments had discovered Marge's other financial transgressions and was preparing to file a report with the F.B.I. Once Marge contacted him, he was quite willing to work with her and not press charges.

Marge became less compulsive. Her spending slowed and she began to pay off her charge cards. Her internal feminine began to trust the internal masculine and He became very capable. Marge no longer uses charge cards, never buys clothes and presents with money needed for other things, and she always makes her car payment on time. Marge still struggles with her Free Spirit feminine occasionally, but for the most part, She is very cooperative and becoming much more responsible.

An effective way to contain the flighty tendencies of The Free Spirit is to narrow Her visions so She can get results quickly. This will let Her become excited about the possibilities of working with Him. If you attempt to give Her too much responsibility, then this Free Spirit will just throw up Her hands and wander happily away. So, cut Her visions down to a manageable size and keep Her down to two or three at a time. For example, She might want to go to Tahiti, explore a new career direction, expand Her current job, stay in Her current relationship, and meet someone new. In order for Her to learn Her lesson about too much desire, you could do the following: first talk to the masculine and see what He is willing to do. It may be that He can take Her away for only three days, somewhere closer to home. He may say She has to keep Her current job for now and take the next three months to look into what She would really like to do careerwise. In the meantime, tell her that She should look for some way to make Her current job more exciting. Find out if She no longer likes Her boyfriend or if She is just a little bored and trying to stir up trouble. If things really aren't too bad with the boyfriend, the internal masculine may ask Her to just sit quietly for a while.

＊Mrs. Nice This feminine must learn to be more assertive and less focused on the internal masculine. She will need to grow in Her trust of Her ability to really be the visionary. This will upset Her and it will upset the masculine. After all, She will be taking away some of his absolute authority, and He will have to learn to let Her take the lead. She will have difficulty doing this because She has always followed Him. *Never* do anything too dramatic at first or They will both be far more upset than you will ever want to see Them. It will be important for you to follow the exercises on spending an hour and then a day following only Her (See Chapter 4). Then you should move rapidly into following Her as much as possible. Be prepared to have your observer self strongly involved in this process. The observer will be alert to encourage Her. The observer will also calm the masculine, reminding Him of why you are doing this. When He balks too badly at something She wants to do, then let Him briefly take charge.

＊The Amazon When working with the Amazon, you must get Her to allow the internal masculine to develop. The main issue with an Amazon is to create an opening for Her to see the value of the masculine. Convince Her that the masculine has merit and that She is basically overpowering Him. It is very helpful to get Her to slowly set down Her weapons and allow the masculine to protect Her. Have the feminine give the masculine small, even almost meaningless tasks until She learns to trust Him. Let me give you an example.

Doug had an Amazon feminine who was extremely powerful and wasn't the least bit interested in working with the masculine, no matter how hard we tried to persuade Her. After several sessions of working on this Amazon, we asked Her if She was tired of fighting. She reluctantly said, "Yes." At this point I asked The Amazon how She would feed Herself if She put down Her weapons and couldn't hunt for Her food. The Amazon said that She would gather fruit and would plant vegetables. I then asked The Amazon to sit down quietly for a moment, and allow Her mind to take Her to another time and place.

The Amazon suddenly saw Herself in frontier America. She was very excited at what She saw, and said She would like to stay

there. I asked Her why. She said that in this place She could use
Her tremendous strength to nurture the land, instead of dominating
the masculine. After a month or so, She realized that in Her new
life as a pioneer it would be nice to have a husband and children.

The feminine then began working with Her masculine and soon
got to know Him. He first appeared as a farmer but soon transformed
into a city slicker from the early 1930s wearing a wild suit. The
feminine responded by transforming to match Him and put on a
dazzling red dancing dress. We had finally transformed Doug's feminine enough to start working on His masculine. His progress from
this point was rapid.

*THE BANSHEE   This feminine archetype can be the most difficult
to transform. She is usually furious with the masculine and wants
to figuratively wipe Him off the face of the earth. She usually feels
that the masculine has repeatedly deserted or ignored Her in the
past, or that He is too much of a wimp to back Her up. She has
built a history of absolute hate and distrust of Him. Regardless of
whether or not His past interactions with the feminine were jus-
tifiable, the masculine's present efforts to rectify Their dynamic are
almost futile because of Her built-up fury. The thing that will calm
this feminine the most is the reassurance that He is willing to work
with Her and is capable of backing Her up.

DISSOLVE

Either literally or figuratively go to one of your favorite places.
Be sure that you feel safe and are alone. Quite a number of my
clients go to the ocean or the forest. Take some bells or a cassette
player and your favorite tape.

Begin your ceremony by ringing the bells or listening to
music. Now do some ritual that has special meaning to you. I
usually meditate for a while and then ask that the spirit of peace
come and that God's healing presence be with me. The point
is to get very, very centered. You may want to meditate a few
minutes. TAKE YOUR TIME because your internal state is the
key to the success of this exercise.

Now imagine a building that you find pleasing and safe. See
yourself walking into a unique room with shelves of audio or
video tapes. Each tape has the name of someone whom you
have known and loved. These tapes are your history of interactions and feelings toward all those who have touched your

life. You know that you automatically replay these tapes in your mind whenever you interact with these people. If you are to have new beginnings many of these tapes need to be destroyed.

You also see a large, comfortable chair. In front of it is a beautiful table. There are only two objects on the table: a very large crystal bowl, filled with a clear, golden liquid, and a VCR. Beyond the table is a very large TV screen.

Go to the chair and sit quietly for a while. Allow images of various people to drift in and out of your mind. As a person appears, go to the shelf and find the tape with his name on it. Put the tape in the VCR and watch it as if you are watching a movie. You may become emotional. Allow that to happen and release the emotions because you are watching this tape for the last time.

When you finish watching the tape, imagine placing it in the bowl with the golden liquid. As you put the tape in the bowl, the liquid dissolves the tape so its contents can be released from your consciousness. As the tape dissolves, say to yourself, "I am ready to let go of this tape." If you feel heavyhearted, just remind yourself that you are letting go and forgiving both yourself and the others.

Then take another tape and repeat the same procedure. Do this until you feel satisfied that you are clear of your resentments with all the people whose tapes you played. Process only as many tapes as you can comfortably and plan to do some more next week. You may find that you can finish all of them at once.

Leave the room and the building and walk right back into your chair.

PUNCH OUT

If you have a place where you can hang a punching bag, it would be worth the investment to get one. Find photos of people who make you angry and photocopy them. If you don't have pictures, draw a face representing that person. Make a number of copies. Then whenever you are angry, tape a picture up on the bag and punch away. You can also do this kneeling by the bed or sofa, but I find that standing and moving into the punches helps the most. This method is used in many Japanese factories where all of the bosses' pictures are available. The Japanese find that this practice has cut down on both illness and absenteeism.

✳THE CRONE This feminine usually has a Peter Pan masculine who, like The Free Spirit, is completely irresponsible. This feminine has had to do the masculine's job for so long that She is completely worn out. She usually loves the masculine and is kind to Him, but has definitely given up on Their working together. The only way to help get this feminine to feel young again is to get the masculine to share the burden. Normally a person with this feminine is seriously overcommitted with projects. The Crone is usually longing for some fun in Her life, so I start there. If you have this kind of feminine, plan a couple of small outings of Her choosing. Cut way back on the number of projects you are doing. With fewer commitments to burden Her, your feminine can now relax a little and turn things over to Him.

Therman had a Crone for a feminine when he first started working with his inner marriage in 1980. His feminine was at least 10,000 years old. She loved Her young, ferocious warrior masculine, even though He had no time for Her because He was always playing war games.

At first Therman's masculine was outraged to even have to talk to the feminine. The feminine barely had enough energy to stand firm with the masculine and insist that He listen to Her. When the masculine did finally listen, He found merit in what the feminine had to say. Slowly, He began to take small steps toward Her. He was very clumsy when He tried to follow the feminine's lead but They both kept trying. She didn't dare ask for anything more than going to a movie with friends, planting flowers in the garden, or reading. Otherwise the masculine would become enraged and storm off.

One day Therman's feminine suddenly turned into a Free Spirit and his masculine became more cooperative, but became The Scoundrel. Briefly, Therman's life looked like a disaster. He almost lost his wife and his job, and he didn't know what to expect from himself. I told Therman to use his observer self to oversee both of Them carefully. He found himself in almost constant conversation with Them.

Then his feminine shifted into The Wise Woman and the masculine shifted into The Wise Man. For quite a while Therman would shift from the wise beings to some of his less-developed archetypes. But he worked diligently, and now he operates most of the time from The Wise Woman and The Wise Man. Therman has became a profoundly wise and caring teacher in the field of motivation and now teaches and lectures all over the world.

✳HER ROYAL HIGHNESS   This feminine can be like a benevolent ruling power, but somewhat officious. She is usually quite reasonable and can be convinced that She needs a mate of equal power. Some people wonder whether or not this is possible. The answer is yes, but it means that She will have to step down off Her throne and become quite ordinary. It can be difficult to convince Her that being a "commoner" is preferable to the royal "we." Show Her the most delightful things about life at first. Do not burden Her too much with the suffering often attached to ordinary life. Realize that She needs to be special in something. That may mean extra training or some new focus that is aligned with her hidden talents. She will reveal Her desires to you if you ask.

✳THE SEDUCTRESS   In order to heal this feminine keep an eye on Her flirtatious nature. Teach Her to relate to people in a clean, straightforward manner, particularly the opposite sex. She must learn to value people as something other than a conquest or a means to an end.

The use of seduction is a hard habit to break. Each time the feminine starts to flirt, call Her on it. Ask Her to take a deep breath, recenter, and focus on something else. Then ask Her to reevaluate the person with whom She is flirting and see if She sees another way to relate to that person. Another good technique for this feminine is to have Her keep Her visions simple and direct; nothing fancy until She learns what it means to be straightforward and to turn to Her own inner masculine for manifestation.

✳THE WISE WOMAN   This feminine really is in a state of perfection, except that She may not have given any energy toward encouraging the masculine to grow up. (She is often paired with a child masculine, although She can be found with any of the masculines.) She thinks She can take care of everything and She often can. Convince Her to sit back and give Him only one or two tasks at a time, so that He can grow. Remember that She is masterful in Her function, so you should have no trouble getting Her to cooperate.

✳MISS MOUSEY   She actually knows what she wants but she is afraid to trust Her visions. This lack of self-trust causes Miss Mousey to keep changing Her mind. While Miss Mousey's incessant change of mind is annoying, She actually can be retrained more easily than most of the other feminines. Basically Her issues are building trust in both Herself and in Her masculine counterpart in whom She has no faith. The most difficult part of Miss Mousey's transformation will be to help Her feel safe so she can come out of hiding. So while you are working on building Her self-confidence, you will want the masculine to cooperate. Otherwise, He can undermine Her efforts in taking a stand.

As Miss Mousey becomes more self-assured, you might discover that She has suppressed a great deal of anger that will probably begin to surface. You will want to guide Her anger so that it is expressed as nondestructively as possible. One of the first things angry people want to do is blame someone else for their hurt and angry feelings. They often lash out uncontrollably at the target of their anger, causing more damage than good. Their anger release might feel good initially but there are usually deeper repercussions. It is one thing to assertively express your needs and feelings and another to attack someone else.

Miss Mousey responds well to assertiveness training classes and becomes empowered when she learns to speak up. Before you go too far in working with Miss Mousey, you might want to do the punching bag exercise that I gave you under The Banshee. Even if Miss Mousey has to pretend to be angry during this exercise, the release will start to happen. Then, have Miss Mousey begin telling people when they hurt Her, or insult Her, or treat Her badly. Do not begin with highly charged situations such as your relationship with your mother or father. Instead, speak up when someone cuts in front of you in line or pushes you. Step-by-step assertiveness is the best way for Miss Mousey to develop strength. Otherwise, She might make someone very angry, and that anger might frighten Her back into hiding.

∗A Symbolic Archetype   If your feminine (or your masculine) doesn't emerge as a person, don't worry. Often archetypes appear as colors, symbols, or as simply a feeling. If a color or a symbol appears, then it is the essence of the archetype that you are experiencing. You will have to interpret what your are seeing, feeling, or hearing. Ask yourself what a particular color or symbol means to you. How do you feel about it? Does it have a feeling or a vibration that you can identify? If you get no response from the symbol, and can't figure out anything about it, then let it rest for a few days. Ask for clarification in your dreams. Then come back to the symbol, and you will find that you are now much clearer. That symbol or image may change into a person if you ask it to.

One of my clients had a feminine who appeared as a bubble of rainbow colors. At first she could receive no information from the symbol. I asked her what the qualities of the bubble were and what her response to it was. She said, "It seems light and loving and I like it." I asked her to go deeper into the bubble and really examine its qualities. She said, "It likes to move and it seems to be exploring everything it sees. The bubble wants to embrace everyone it is with." Over the weeks we went deeper into the qualities of the bubble, monitoring how it changed or responded to certain questions. The bubble would never cease its movement. It would, however, change colors. Once when we asked how it liked the internal masculine, it became a fiery red and zoomed around very rapidly. Then the lovely bubble turned into a fairylike creature who was in constant motion. We were both entranced with the bubble feminine until we realized that it could not land. Still, the mere mention of the masculine would cause Her to flee, but at least we could hold a conversation with Her and go about setting Her down and healing the separation. The masculine in this case was always reaching for the feminine, but was exhausted from trying to make contact with Her.

❋MULTIPLE ARCHETYPES THAT APPEAR SIMULTANEOUSLY   If multiple feminines (or masculines) appear, then you will have to have conversations with each one of Them. Find out how They feel about each other. Find out what They like about each other and what They don't like. Keep talking to Them until They see each other's merit. Then ask if They are willing to merge into one. If They won't do this, work with Them until They realize that life works more easily if They are merged.

Once the archetypes are prepared to merge, find out which one is willing to dissolve into the other. You may discover that one or the other fears They will be giving up Their essential nature if They merge. Again, mediate with Them until They have chosen who will merge into whom. They also might merge and become a completely different image.

Max had an internal feminine who appeared as both a sorceress dressed in black and as a voluptuous blonde who was light and happy. Initially, neither one wanted anything to do with the other. We worked on getting both feminines to accept and love each other's great qualities. Max's two feminines came to respect each other's attributes and agreed to merge. The blonde feminine was more than willing to merge with the sorceress. When They merged, a tall, voluptuous yet trim brunette, physically resembling Max's wife, appeared. She was youthful, sparkling, and wise beyond Her years. Max was ecstatic at the merging. Days later, he called to tell me how much better he felt. Max said, "I have always felt torn inside. That feeling just disappeared."

When Your Internal Masculine or Feminine Resembles Someone You Know

If your feminine or masculine looks very much like your real-life mate or someone else you know, try to find out what that image is telling you. It may be pointing out how much you have confused the external world with your feminine or masculine. It may also tell you that some qualities of that person are admirable or authentic to you, and that he or she is a mirror of your own internal state. After you are sure of what that image is telling you, ask it to step aside for a moment so your true feminine or masculine can emerge. If nothing changes, then you can be sure that this is an archetype, and that you have pulled someone into your life who is a clear reflection of this archetype to you. In every area of life, it is useful to see what is being mirrored to you.

Working with the Masculine Archetypes

✳PETER PAN   This masculine is like the Free Spirit feminine. He would rather be out riding His horse or painting than bother with making a living. He is so charming and captivating that He often gets away with this kind of irresponsibility. She, His internal feminine, is often enticed to let Him get away with these things, so one of the cures for this masculine is for Her to hold firm in Her desires. He, like the Free Spirit, must learn to live up to His commitments. Challenge Him to reach beyond what He thinks He can do, but don't overload this masculine with too many visions. If you do, He will seriously malfunction.

Just as with the Free Spirit, I would have the Peter Pan clean up His life, like paying back taxes and cleaning out the garage. This will help Him build structure. This masculine grows rapidly when He can easily see His results. He responds well to tasks like chopping wood or working on a ranch. He most often likes helping others, like taking on the responsibility of being a Big Brother/Big Sister or doing volunteer work with the elderly or the dying.

Tommie was a very creative artist. He loved people, and people loved him. He had many outrageous ideas for sculptures, and easily sold his designs to excited clients. The problem was that even though he had been paid to do a sculpture, he would often take seven or eight years before he even got around to starting the project. By that time the person who had ordered the sculpture would be thoroughly disgusted. His feminine was an outrageously strong, very creative Amazon. She was constantly coming up with new projects. The masculine only wanted to work on each project while it was new. That usually meant that He seldom completed any of the projects.

Tommie's feminine, The Amazon, didn't like the sound of cutting back on Her creativity. For a week She went on a rampage and didn't do anything but ride Her horse over the sand dunes, fast and furious. Then She calmed down and admitted that She and the masculine loved to play too much. She was very tired of being broke all of the time and of dealing with Tommie's unhappy customers. Once She really accepted the fact that too many desires were a major problem for Her masculine, She backed off. She agreed that She would only give the masculine three visions at once and that for a while, at least, She would curtail Her zest for play.

I worked with Tommie's Peter Pan masculine until He could promise that, even though He was excited about many things the feminine wanted, He would not go running off in too many directions at once. The masculine agreed but He didn't know if He could really accomplish this. He wasn't sure exactly how to do it. When I asked Her what the first project was, She said, "Clean out the studio." Just as He started to work on the studio, She wanted to go to the beach or take a cruise or make a new dress. Tommie's masculine mustered the courage to say, "No!" and He then finished cleaning the studio. As soon as this was accomplished, She wanted the fence repaired.

Next, she wanted a half-done sculpture to be completed. I noticed at this point that both the masculine and the feminine were growing restless. I knew that Tommie had to do something creative in the moment, or we were going to lose the tiny gains in stability that we had made. It was obvious that He needed to experience what He called freedom. I said we could take a break. Tommie went off on a tangent and took two weeks to build a float for the Fourth of July parade. Once that was done, we returned to the work of accomplishing small, simple tasks again.

One of the most helpful exercises that I gave Tommie was to take on a new project only when He had completed two old ones. In this way, he began to work himself out of the dilemmas that had burdened him for so long. Also, through this process the masculine began to grow and develop stronger boundaries. Sometimes Tommie's feminine forgot about limiting Her visions but the masculine developed the ability to say to Her, "No, you said you wanted this done and I am going to finish this." Less and less they ran off to play at the drop of a hat, as they had once done. Today Tom's Peter Pan is a grown, handsome, and reliable masculine and his feminine is flexible and not too demanding. Tom is still highly creative and more successful than ever.

✳Mr. Nice Guy   Since the feminine rarely knows that Mr. Nice Guy exists, the key to His growth can be as simple as introducing Them to each other. If the feminine does know about the masculine, but has no respect for Him, you will have to work on building His personal power. In either case, this masculine has been taking a back seat in your life. He is capable, which means that your life is probably pretty stable. Yet because He doesn't work well with the feminine, He isn't used to His full potential. This means that although your life is probably very stable some dreams are falling by the wayside. This masculine will have to learn to take more risks in order to follow Her direction. Risk is a word He probably doesn't have in His vocabulary. This means that you will need to live out some of your fantasies so that He can grow. When encouraging Him to take risks, start with small ones at first, then larger ones as He becomes more confident.

When Marlene came to me, she had been at the same job for twenty-five years and was terribly bored with her life. She was forty-five and still single. Her feminine wanted to travel to exotic places, which was very unnerving to Marlene because she had never been anywhere alone in her life. She feared that something awful would happen to her while she was in a foreign country. We worked on getting Marlene to fulfill her travel fantasy, so she started by planning a trip. I encouraged her to go alone, in order to allow her masculine a chance to build. At first, her inner masculine tried to get family or friends to go with her. But the feminine wanted to go alone and have an adventure. Six months later, Marlene left on a guided tour of the Far East, without any family or friends. She met people on her tour and had a fabulous time discovering how well she did by herself. She learned to find directions when she needed them and what to do if she was lost. She learned to shop and barter. Once her masculine began to take chances, there was no containing Him. It seemed as if Marlene was off to some exotic, new place every few months. When she was home, life was very different from what it once was. She had many exciting new friends and held a variety of jobs. She would only stay long enough to earn enough money to go somewhere else. As her life continued to develop, she began to meet interesting men and began to explore relationships with two of them. They both loved to travel and so she had frequent adventures with them. I attended her wedding the following year.

✳THE SCOUNDREL   This masculine needs to learn about kindness. He also needs a feminine He can look up to. She will have to tell Him when He is treating Her badly. As She grows stronger, it will help Him soften greatly.

Never let this masculine seek the easy way out. Every time you catch Him lying, talk to Him until He admits the truth. Scoundrels have a deep desire to be in control but are often covert about it.

People who associate with them will almost always feel subtly controlled and manipulated. Don't let Him bend the truth. Allowing reality to be as it is is very important for this masculine.

The Scoundrel often wishes to be more straightforward and honest but easily slides into the old pattern. If you keep a watchful eye on Him, you will see that He likes the new changes that develop.
ATTILA THE HUN This masculine is as wrathful as the The Banshee and as tough as The Amazon. He runs over everyone and everything in his path. He can create empires, but he has to learn not to destroy others or the planet in the process. The feminine will be willing to tell Attila when He is out of line. In order for Him to be receptive to this, constantly guide Him to stop driving ahead so relentlessly. First of all, ask your Attila if He would be willing to give up any of His projects. If He says yes, then ask your feminine which ones She would like Him to drop. Once that is determined, find out if He is willing to let go of those projects. If He says yes, then determine with Him how best to do this. If your masculine says no, then ask Him if He would consider it in the future. Then ask Him if would at least be willing to slow down. If Attila is completely disagreeable to all of this, make Him aware of how alone He is and that if He were willing to work with the feminine, He could have a great deal of love in His life. Often this masculine has been so brutal that He has not been open to love for many years. The most important part of His change will come when the feminine is willing to speak up.

Jacqueline's masculine was so forceful that He insisted on doing everything by Himself. He couldn't be bothered with the feminine. Jacqueline had decided that she wanted a man in her life, but as long as her own internal masculine was so strong there was no room for another man. He would blow other men away. While Jacqueline was working with me, she met a man her feminine loved, but her masculine didn't care for him. Her masculine agreed to follow the feminine with this man. The relationship was very trying and He began losing patience and confidence in Her. Over and over again, He threatened to walk off and forget the whole thing. The feminine continued to have the juice to stay. The relationship lasted a year, longer than most she had had, and in that time Jackie softened. She became much more receptive and open to Her internal guidance. She began wearing softer, frilly clothes and seemed happier. As the feminine became stronger, the masculine also got gentler and less aggressive, yet more self-confident.

✱LOVER BOY   This type of masculine may get a great deal done, but more by seducing than straightforward work. He's a lover through and through and has used this technique to get what He wants most of His life. He's very much like The Seductress in that He really believes He is a great lover and a gift to everyone. This routine works for a while but people grow tired of His game rather rapidly. This doesn't bother Lover Boy, however, because there is always another person just around the corner waiting to be seduced. To make matters worse, He has little regard for His own feminine and you can count on His seducing Her more than He does anyone else. She will also, at some point, grow tired of the game. Lover Boy's communications are often covert and couched in sexuality. He hurts a lot of people but He is not really a mean person.

If you have this type of masculine and you work in an office, rather than simply telling the secretaries what you need and when you need it, you will seduce them. For instance, if you are a man, you may sit on the desk and tell them how wonderful they are. You may lower your voice and tell them you have been thinking about them a lot, and hope that soon you can have a drink together. Then you may add, "I'd really love to have a drink with you tonight, but I have this report to do." Nine times out of ten the secretary will drop everything to help you. Lover Boy is quite limited by His inability to do anything but seduce. He preys on people, particularly the opposite sex. The first thing you will have to do with this masculine is convince Him to listen to the feminine's directives.

When working with Lover Boy, remember that seducing any-one, even His own feminine, is quite dangerous and very destructive both to Himself and to others. Without the voice of the feminine giving Him visions, He will not really accomplish much in life. He is too busy seducing. When He finally gets the message He will be quite taken aback. He never dreamed of being in this position and for a while He feels emasculated. The safest way to deal with this manipulator is to get Him to avoid "quick deals," and keep out of shady situations. In this way He will be forced to walk the straight and narrow, and do things in an honest, straightforward way. When

He is first beginning to listen to the feminine, He may make a lot of false promises, since the only thing He really knows how to do well is to seduce other people into doing things for Him. You will have to keep after Him, and never allow Him to backslide or take shortcuts.

I had a client, Jan, who called her manipulator masculine "The Weasel." Over and over again, Jan's masculine would tell her feminine that He was right there for Her and that He could manifest whatever She wanted. Yet, in the final analysis, everything would fall apart, whether it was with Jan's profession or with her relationship. Jan's feminine would go along, believing the false promises that The Weasel made. As He repeatedly let Her down, She became quite furious. The Weasel was very seductive.

Jan's boyfriend lived back East and every time he came to visit her The Weasel would really act up. He would become overly involved with the boyfriend's needs while pretending He was taking care of Jan's business. The Weasel was very codependent. (I will discuss my theory on codependency in Chapter 9.) The destructive aspect of the Lover Boy is that He is very adept at pretending that He is focusing on His feminine rather than elsewhere. This is a very unhealthy and destructive dynamic.

In Jan's case, her masculine felt compelled to focus on anyone else's business needs rather than His own. Jan had been working with marketing oil essences for her massage work when her boyfriend appeared with his own line of products. Jan dropped everything she'd been doing with her business and immediately got to work on a catalog for her boyfriend. She helped organize his product line and started on a marketing campaign. Finally, one day She realized that her own business had come to a dead halt. Jan said, "Enough!" She told her boyfriend to take care of his company, and she would take care of her own.

If you have an internal masculine who is a Lover Boy, never let Him get away with anything. He's often quite likable and you will be very tempted to take Him at His word, but you can't afford to. Keep your eye on Him. He loves to pretend to take care of the inner feminine while He is busy giving in to external demands.

Jan had to break up with her boyfriend for a while until The Weasel could consistently follow the messages of His own feminine, The Crone. She could no longer afford to be with her lover and fall into "The Weasel" routine. As Jan's masculine became strong enough to withstand external charm, Jan learned to maintain her boundaries and sense of direction. Her boyfriend began to show more devotion to Jan. He was more attentive than ever and rarely asked Jan to run his business.

Another tack that we took was to get The Weasel to focus on Jan's career. The Crone wanted very much to go in new directions. She was tired of everything but still felt life would be worth living if She could become involved in something new and exciting. She beseeched Jan's masculine to back Her up.

The Weasel then turned into a competent but fairly shy teenager before finally turning into Mr. Dependable. Jan's feminine ultimately became young and exciting, and even though the masculine still occasionally behaved like a weasel, He was infinitely more dependable. The change signaled to Jan that her masculine was opening up to His evolutionary process. Things were going to be different and indeed they were! Right now Jan's relationship is very successful and her business (oil essences for personal change) is now marketed nationally. The Weasel exists no more (or at least hardly ever).

✱METHUSELAH He is worn out handling everything Himself. He is usually found with The Banshee, The Free Spirit, or one of the child feminines. He is in this condition partially because of the feminine's childishness, irresponsibility, or rage. He is accustomed to doing everything Himself and longs for Her to become His equal partner. This is definitely a case where it is necessary to work with both the feminine and masculine simultaneously. If He has a Banshee for a mate, it will take some effort to get Her to the point where She doesn't hate Him and is willing to have something to do with Him. If He has a child feminine, help Her to become more responsible.

Teach your Methuselah to let go of the reins and wait for Her to give Him a vision. This may cause Him to worry and fret, but there is no choice. He must also be quite strong in saying no to some of Her requests for play and youthful adventure. A child feminine has no problems with giving directives for play. Get Her to start with small, more responsible directives. This may mean weeks of sitting and waiting for Her to come up with the vision, but it will be worth it. Each time you feel Him starting to take over, just take a deep breath, relax, and tell Methuselah to back off. He will need to be reminded that the vision is not His function. Every time He refuses to take over the function of the vision, He will get younger and She will mature, becoming stronger and more capable of actually being the visionary.

Another way to rejuvenate Methuselah is to take three to six months and do as little as possible, particularly new planning. This will give you the space to "hear" Her messages and teach Her how to work with Him.

✱THE WIMP   This masculine is simply too weak to do His job. Some of my clients have not even been able to find Him because He's so fragile. When this happens I take the client through an exercise of holding the left nostril and breathing in and out through the right. This stimulates left-brain activity and facilitates building a stronger masculine. When the masculine finally does appear, He may be very meek. The feminine, usually The Amazon, The Banshee, or The Brat, has been discounting Him for years. Sometimes He can't talk to us for a couple of sessions. We encourage Her to keep quiet and coax Him to come forward.

At some time, probably quite young, He made some mistakes and She has never forgiven Him. I tell clients with this masculine to back off of all important decisions for at least four weeks while He begins to build Himself. The exercise is to have Him say whether or not He can fulfill Her visions at the moment She gives them. This can be done through either an inner conversation or through feeling the energy in your back and neck. You can also look at the unaccomplished dreams or projects in your life to see if you still want to follow through with them. If you do, discover what needs to be done, encourage Him to do it, and see if He can make a step-by-step plan to accomplish your goals.

Whatever your Wimp masculine says, He cannot change His mind. He may be quite frightened to move ahead, but He really has no choice. In a very short time He will get very clear about His abilities, and He will see those abilities rapidly increase. This masculine responds very well to some of the martial arts. The martial arts make Him more aware of his powers. He will also grow stronger whenever He follows Her.

Each time the feminine wants to do something, The Wimp will

be asked if He can follow through. This is a perfect exercise for developing Him. Focus on meticulously checking with Him. For one day, check in with your masculine every time you want to do something. Expand that to one week. Your objective is to find out whether or not He can back Her up. Whenever He is cautious or says He can't do something, halt the feminine movement and go no further. This will build your masculine until His messages get stronger and clearer.

Giles worked for me as a handyman, and we had a number of conversations about my inner marriage work. He decided one day that he wanted to do some work on himself. He had a business background but was ineffective in that arena. His relationships were always short term. Women were attracted at first to his niceness, but he was so unsure of himself and so unable to make decisions that they soon tired of his uncertainty.

No matter what we suggested to Gile's Wimp, He would say, "I'm thinking about doing that." Finally I told The Wimp to quit thinking and see what He could really do. We began with the one-day exercise I described above. For the one day, The Wimp agreed to take action on everything She wanted, even if it terrified him. It was a long, slow process but eventually Giles got the hang of it and he learned to make decisions and stand up for himself.

Durant first came to me right after his alcoholic wife had left him. His children didn't talk to him anymore. His work history was sporadic. When we first tried to contact Durant's masculine, Durant was unable to connect with his back and spine. He simply felt nothing there. When He called his masculine onto the stage, nothing appeared. On the other hand, Durant's feminine was clear and very powerful. I told Durant to just keep focusing his attention on his backbone over the next week. He began to notice a pain there. By the second session, his masculine appeared, but He had no legs. We gave Him artificial legs so that He could experience moving and taking action. After the third time He backed Her up, the legs solidified immediately and He wanted to dance and play with Her. He changed so rapidly that Durant went right out and got a good paying job. In fact, as I write this, Durant is dating his boss's daughter and he has begun to repair his relationship with his children.

The Wimp often needs a great deal more coaching than this to become strong. Durant was an unusual case. The masculine may often return to hiding. When that happens, ask Her to calm down and slow down so that He can reappear.

*BEWILDERED BENNY This masculine can be a real nice guy, but He never knows what His own internal feminine wants to do. He's afraid to trust Her so He always looks outside of Himself to see what He could do. He can be lovable but very undependable. Always listening to everyone outside of Himself, He is thoroughly confused. The problem with this masculine is that at some time in life, He decided following Her was too risky. He decided He just didn't want to put Himself on the line for fear that She would criticize Him. People with this masculine were almost never allowed to follow Their own direction when They were growing up. They may even have been badly abused physically or emotionally on the rare occasions when they did make a decision, and it turned out badly. In working with Bewildered Benny, once again, start with small things so that He will not run away to the outside world again. Most of all, it is important to get Her to stop picking on Him because He is very sensitive to criticism. He can be found with any of the feminines. If His feminine is childish or doesn't give clear messages, it is important to work with Her until She can do so. Just follow any of the exercises in this book for building Her.

When Larry came to me for therapy, I could see why people found him frustrating. Larry could never make up his own mind about even the simplest things. He just did what people told him to do. It was almost impossible for him to make a decision by himself. I began by having Larry make two decisions a week and then follow through with them. Our agreement was that he wouldn't call anyone for an opinion. The feminine had agreed that it was all right with Her if He made some mistakes. For the first week Larry used choosing his lunch from a menu. He was to take no longer than ten minutes. Sometimes Larry liked what he ordered and sometimes he didn't. I told Larry that right or wrong, he was at least making decisions for himself.

Our next step with the internal masculine was to have Him back Her up instantly two or three time a day. This was very difficult at first but after about three weeks He could easily do it. One day

He was floored when She said, "I want to get a new car and I want it to be flashy!" Much to everyone's surprise Larry went out one lunch hour and purchased a used red sports car. He was as pleased as He could be. What a change for Larry. He was becoming assertive and clear about what he did and didn't want. His masculine was really getting into the swing of things. Now Larry is manager of his company and is a rising star there. He has a wife and three children and many friends.

✳His Majesty He, like Her Royal Highness, feels that everything is beneath Him. He expects to be served. The very best exercise for this masculine is to perform menial tasks that serve others. Just as with Her Royal Highness, until He learns that scrubbing the toilet is the same thing as ruling His kingdom, He will not learn humility. When working with this masculine, I do nothing to encourage His haughty behavior. It is only after He has experienced menial labor for a while that I ask Him to really mingle with "the people."

✳The Wise Man He, like The Wise Woman, is in a remarkable state of evolution. He cooperatively relinquishes the reins and allows the feminine to grow, if She is an undeveloped archetype. Rather than being so strong and capable, He will gently and kindly let Her give visions that He backs up. If the visions are not productive once they are actualized, He will let Her learn from Her mistakes and go forth again. In this way She learns and grows. She may get unnerved when things don't go well and want to withdraw. He should, however, do nothing until She is willing to give Him a vision.

Let the Dance Begin

As you continue to work on your masculine and feminine, Their images will change, sometimes drastically within a few hours' time. This is a signal that They are moving toward Their perfection. Because Their image is the manifestation of your cellular memory, Their changes are a direct signal of the transformation occurring within you. Their growth into perfection occurs through your becoming more and more observant of Her shifts of vision and of His flexibility or resistance. I am not suggesting that you live your life by stilted exercises, but I am suggesting that in the beginning, the exercises will help you understand more keenly how to continue to build Their relationship. These exercises put you in touch with an aspect of yourself that when tapped allows you to experience your full capabilities.

Building Her: Your Inner Guidance

If you feel fully out of touch with your intuition, it's very important for you to start using it in small ways. Don't expect to immediately receive blaring messages on critical aspects of your life. I am sure that you have experienced Her messages as little gnawings in your gut or maybe a quick warning flash not to trust someone or to walk away from a situation. That is your intuitive speaking to you. When you haven't listened to these flashes, you have often suffered the consequences and have then dealt with the regret.

Start paying attention to those gut feelings. Let's say that you need to take your clothes to the same cleaner that you've been going to for years. You walk in the door of the shop and all of a sudden your gut tightens up, the energy drains out of you, or you hear a voice saying, "No, stop." Even though you may feel a little foolish because the owner has already seen you coming with your clothing in hand, turn around and walk out. You don't need to know why. The point is She doesn't want you there. That ability to back Her intuition without knowing why is the very essence of developing trust in Her. Every single time you follow Her in the small ways, She gets stronger. Conversely, He becomes stronger every time He backs Her up.

REMEMBERING
Here's a four-part exercise that will help you understand how you feel about your intuitive process and then prepare you for following Her.

Part I
Put on some relaxing music. Choose a room where the light is not too bright.

Get into a very comfortable position and focus on your breathing for a bit. Now relax all of the muscles in your body.

Imagine that you are lying on the grass in a nice comfortable spot. As you stare up at the crystal blue sky you watch big, fat, fluffy clouds float by. The more that float by, the more relaxed you become. The more relaxed you become, the more easily you can remember events from your past.

Now reach back into your memory and recall several times when you acted on pure inspiration, without thought or consideration of consequences. Vividly recall each of these times, one at a time, and reenact the actions and outcome with each one.

Where were you? Who else was there? What were you wearing? What did you do? How did it feel when you were doing it? What was the result of your action? Now, in retrospect, how do you feel about each of the events?

Write down these feelings for your reference.

It is important for you to vividly recall the outcome of incidents when you acted on pure inspiration, because this will let you know how you felt when you followed your feminine. If you have been primarily unconscious about Her guidance, you may not be aware that it was Her vision you were following. Each time you followed Her visions, things either did or didn't work out. You most likely developed unconscious feelings toward your intuition based on these outcomes. If, for instance, you felt that it never worked out when you followed your impulses, i.e., Her vision, you may have developed a distrust of Her. At some point you might have made the conclusion that She only gets you into trouble.

There are several possible reasons why you didn't succeed when you acted on an impulse. She may have communicated Her vision in terms that were too general, so that the masculine wasn't sure of how to manifest Her guidance. It is possible that your masculine actually created the lack of success because of His inability to manifest Her vision, and it is He who needs to be more fully developed. Ask Her to break up the visions into smaller components. In any case, you will change your attitude toward your intuition if there is a lack of trust, so that healing the prejudice you have developed against your intuition can take place. This trust will have to be built over time. One can be educated to let go of prejudice, and to build a sense of mutual trust.

In most cases you can look back at failed attempts to follow your impulses. You will probably find that if you had done something differently, things might have turned out well. If your memories of those incidents cause you any discomfort or aggravation, you are carrying anger and regret, which will affect your ability to trust and work with your intuition. Healing those memories will allow you to start fresh.

Part II

Please get into the same relaxed state you did in the first part of this exercise. Play soft music and breathe deeply before starting.

Now you are going to go back through the same vision of when you acted inspirationally. Imagine how things might have worked out if you had moved a little slower or a little faster. Ask yourself what would have happened if you had used your logical masculine as well as your intuitive feminine to come to a decision about acting on your impulse.

Imagine that you feel the intuitive messages but this time relive the outcomes so that the outcome is more productive. Notice the difference in your attitude and feelings about the impulsive action you took.

Part III

Now let your mind wander back in time. Do you recall times when you received a clear message and wanted to follow through but couldn't act upon the message for one reason or another? Take these occasions one at a time and see if you can tell what kept you from going ahead in following the message. These are excuses your masculine used for not following through.

Do you recall a time when you had a strong message to do something or not do something and you deliberately ignored it? Look back at the outcome of ignoring that message. What happened? How do you now feel about having ignored that message? Once again, it was your masculine that ignored the message.

Relive these same moments, but this time see yourself following through on Her guidance. Envision how it might have turned out if Her visions had been manifested. Notice how you now feel about the many changes that have come about. Remember as many other incidents as you can.

Simply make a mental note of these occasions or speak them into a tape recorder.

Part IV
Decide that you are willing to let go of all of the above situations. Forgive yourself for what looked like failures on your part and never look back again.

Now go back to each incident that you recalled in Parts I, II, and III. When they are clear in your mind, see each situation enclosed in a pink balloon filled with helium. Each balloon is attached to a long string. Let go of the string and watch every single incident sail away until it disappears. Then say, "I am now free of you."

If you are unable to complete this exercise all at once, then go through past incidents one or two at a time. Do not stop until you have let go of all of them.

Now write down your impressions. By reliving the incidents in a positive manner you can dissolve your feelings of failure and regret. Your mind is like a computer; whatever you program into it is the way it will respond. If you program yourself with positive outcomes, your mind and body will react as if that outcome really occurred. By reliving the past and mentally changing outcomes, you can let go of limiting thought forms and be free of them.

Intensification

Let's start working on building your intuition. Almost everyone can learn to read the feminine's messages, regardless of how those messages come. You will gain confidence in your feminine by following Her. First take notice and have faith in those fleeting, subtle notions. This will actually give you a deep sense of Her. Over time your internal feminine will build to where you will receive clear, clean guidance. When you get repeated messages and don't know what they mean, ask for intensification. I usually say "Truth intensify. I don't know what you're telling me." When you ask for intensification, things literally become clearer.

IMMEDIATE TRUTH
1. This practice is slightly different than the Truth Intensify practice. It is done right in the midst of chaos, regardless of where you may be.
2. Let go of all thought regarding the confusing messages.
3. Focus on your solar plexus, but be sure to stay alert.
4. Now, say something such as, "Feminine, I don't understand what you are telling me. Please intensify." Say "please intensify" several more times.
5. Then just stay alert and watchful. Notice any sudden signs you see or messages on cars, or something someone says to you. Be especially watchful of those fleeting thoughts.
6. Tell the feminine, "I just had this thought. If I am on the right track, please intensify the message."
7. Stay alert for the intensified message or for other messages.
8. The more you deal with repeated problems in this way, the clearer the messages will become and the more you will know what corrections to make.

Messages may come to you from phone conversations, from a moment of watching television, or from a book you are reading. Messages may be given to you through an incident that is repeated several times over. Like the client who kept attracting alcoholic men who needed to be taken care of. It was a signal that it was time to build her masculine, who was compulsive and quite weak. Most of the time a sense of inner knowing will click into place for you. The intensification message may be from the internal masculine or the internal feminine.

I'll give you a humorous example of what can happen when you ask for intensification. Several years ago, I was overcommitted on several projects and was rushing around from one appointment to another. My back was aching, yet I absolutely knew that She wanted me to go in this direction, so I was frantically trying to do everything.

One day as I raced to be on time for an appointment, cars and trucks were constantly pulling in front of me or nearly sideswiping me. I couldn't seem to get out of harm's way. I finally said to my feminine, "I don't understand what's going on. You told me to go to the meeting, but life is reflecting serious warnings. What is it? Please intensify the message." Just at that moment a big two-trailer truck drove up beside me. There on the side of the truck was an enormous cartoon character and three giant words: SLOW DOWN STUPID. My masculine had been racing around and had quit listening to my feminine's messages. She wanted Him to move in a new direction and to drop a couple of the old projects, but He was so busy speeding around, He didn't hear Her. As a result, I was trying to balance too many projects and my masculine was starting to buckle under the stress. When the truck passed me, I finally got the message. As soon as I could get off the freeway, I got to a phone and delayed two of my projects. There were no more close calls.

When you are first trying to follow Her messages, don't ever act when the message isn't clear, and don't assume that the message remains the same. Keep checking in with Her. If you are not getting a clear answer, wait until you do. She may be building up to go in a direction you're not aware of, but may not have enough juice built up to let you know. Remember that the message is rarely verbal. More than likely it is an energy, a feeling, a color, or a symbol.

DECISIONS

The next exercise is for checking out Her directions in the moment. I would like you to find a quiet spot where you won't be disturbed. Get in a relaxed position and breathe in and out deeply and slowly.

Think of a decision you've been trying to make.

Come up with two or more statements regarding possible solutions for that decision. (For instance, "I am going to move," "I am not going to move," or "I'm going to move but not right now.")

Now deepen your sense of relaxation and concentrate on your solar plexus. Close your eyes so you are able to really move into Her.

Make the first statement (I am going to move).

Pay attention to the reaction you feel in your solar plexus or anywhere else in your body when you make this statement. Was there a lifting of energy? Was there a falling of energy? Did you feel a pinching in the heart or solar plexus or a relaxation? Did you feel a tightness or a freeing feeling somewhere else? Did you get a sense of a warning or a go ahead? Did She say yes, or no, or whatever you want, or nothing?

Then make the second statement (I am not going to move). Now what did you feel?

Go through all of the statements until you have finished.

Write down your responses.

Now repeat the process with your masculine. Restate each statement. Look for a tightness in your neck or back. Notice if there is a tension there or a tiredness. In this way you find out what He wants and if He is actually able or willing to back up Her choice.

Generally a rising of energy and an open feeling mean that the feminine is saying yes. A pinching in the solor plexus area or a deadening of the energy is a sign that She is saying no. Sometimes you will get a yes on both questions. She's telling you that you can do either one. You can also get a no on both questions. It may be that She doesn't like either choice or She may not know yet in what direction She wants to go. If you really can't tell the difference between either the yes or no response, do absolutely nothing. You can check with Her again a little later. Think about what other alternatives there might be. Perhaps your questions need to be more precise, or broken down into smaller parts. Check again in a few hours. If you still find no juice in one direction or another, then wait and check again in a few days or a week. In the meantime, you might find other alternatives. Or by then She may have built enough to choose one of the original ones. Wait until She tells you what steps to take. Until then, please do nothing. Wait and keep rechecking with Her until She has built in the new direction.

If you receive the message that you are to act in some way, then you will probably want to check out the next step. When I began checking on my move from California, I asked Her about each city. I said, "I am going to move to Boston, etc." Then I began to check the route I was to take.

Practice this decision-making process and attempt to act as soon as you can. You can also do this with a partner when you are both trying to make decisions. Simply help each other figure out what the real questions are. Form these questions into simple statements. One of you then contacts Her and the other says the statements. Then reverse roles.

FOLLOWING
Now you are going to learn to follow the feminine in the course of your daily life. After all, this is where it really counts.

1. Start by picking one hour when you are committed to absolutely following Her, *regardless* of any excuses you might have for not doing so. Of course, if something unnerving comes up, you may want to ease off. But my recommendation is that you really stretch yourself to take risks.
2. Then pick out one day each week in which you will spend the entire day following the guidance of the internal feminine and backing it up with your internal masculine.
3. When you feel comfortable with doing this, then go for a week of following Her. It may be unnerving but you will learn how to really follow Her and trust Her. REMEMBER, YOU WANT TO LIVE YOUR LIFE THIS WAY.

Why do so many people have trouble reading their intuitive messages? Emotions play a part here. Remember that your cells contain all the programming of your entire family history and all of your life experience. Let's say that fear around survival issues runs in your family, and that as far back as anyone can remember everyone had worked hard, done the right thing, and lived a life just like all of their neighbors. You, however, are more adventurous but every time you took a risk your family may have told you that you were doing things the wrong way. Later in life, when you even think of following your feminine, fear comes up. You think She is telling you not to be impulsive when it is actually your own family program of fear. For many of you, the fear response has nothing to do with Her. The best thing to do for this condition is to work on the fear. Begin by becoming aware of what triggers it. Notice who you are with and what you are doing. Notice what you are thinking or planning. Write down the incident right after it happens. The pattern that generates the fear will become apparent. Then you will want to do some Branden-like sentence completions:

When I tried to take risks as a child my mother would _____ .
When I tried to take risks as a child my father would _____ .
When I was a child I was frightened of _____ .
One of the things that frightens me now is _____ .
The good thing about fear is _____ .
The bad thing about fear is _____ .
If I were willing to give up my fear I would _____ .

Also, each time the fear comes up, please try to remember to stop and do the "Truth Intensify" exercise. If your real problem is emotional fear, then as time passes this fear will reduce as you learn to follow Her visions and He begins to enjoy taking risks. Don't try to force the issue, as you will only create greater fear.

Building Him: Your Manifesting/ Logical Powers

When your back or neck feel constricted in any way, it is His signal that He can't or won't back Her up. You cannot afford to ignore His signals. You see there is really no way to get past Him when it comes to manifestation. What you want to do instead is build His strength until He can back up anything She asks for. He may not support every request, but if He is strong He will be able to communicate with Her about why this is so.

When the masculine is weak, He will either fear the feminine, or will not have the vaguest idea of how to do the things She wants. In either case, a weak masculine is not accustomed to being included in any plans, which is what has made Him weak. The help of the feminine is needed when working with a weak masculine. She can slow down enough to let Him build. Each time He can back Her up, He gains strength. The more He sees how well things work out from the sheer power of Their dance, the more confidence He gains. You will have to start off slowly.

A "stretching" exercise for Him usually helps. Suppose that He says He can back up two of Her ideas. Ask Him to really stretch and see if He can back up three. If He says no, then ask the feminine if there is another small thing that She wants. The purpose of this is to keep stretching His abilities to manifest. Your feminine can usually think of something, and He usually can do it.

Be sure that He can really do what He claims He can do, especially at first. He will rapidly grow to like the feeling of accomplishment, but will be prone to pretend at times. Don't delude yourself. If He says He can back something up, and He can't, then He will rapidly fall apart and so will your life. The simplest way to resolve this is to give incremental directions that can be accomplished by a certain deadline. It is through your monitoring of Him over time that you will begin to know when he can do what He says He can.

My client Dean had a remarkably weak masculine and an irresponsible feminine. It showed not only in his finances and relationships, but also in his posture and facial expressions. He looked lost and beaten. He was in one of the worst relationships I had ever seen. His health was degenerating and he had very little income with few possibilities of better employment. After working with Dean for about six months I saw few changes. His masculine and feminine refused to work together. I had to admit that Dean's situation was worsening each day, but I had a hunch that if we kept going things would eventually shift.

Dean's life grew progressively worse until he bottomed out. It was only then that Dean experienced a breakthrough, and his masculine and feminine decided They had better get together quickly before all was lost. Dean's breakthrough occurred because everything in his life blew up at once. His girlfriend left, he lost his job, and he wound up in bed with pneumonia. Although these were dreadful circumstances, they offered Dean an opportunity to completely rebuild his life, utilizing both his inner masculine and his inner feminine. He was so shattered that he didn't even waste any

time getting caught up in fear, anger, or regret. He used each terrible
or sad incident that happened to him or around him to build the
masculine. Even though Dean was desperate, he decided that he
wouldn't take the first job he was offered. He would only go to
interviews that he got a strong yes on and he wouldn't take any
job until the masculine and the feminine agreed. This meant that
She had to take Herself seriously and give very clear messages. It
meant the inner masculine had to pull Himself up by the bootstraps
and not lose heart.

At first She guided Him into taking odd jobs. From Dean's old
weakness he was tempted not to ask for his money if his employer
didn't offer it. But he had made an agreement that he wouldn't let
himself fall into his weakness, so he asked for a deposit before he
did a job, and asked for the rest of the money upon completion.
It turned out that Dean's internal feminine had been waiting for
this moment. As Dean's old images of himself were shattered, She
became very strong with Her visions and each vision was one that
would help him move steadily forward from the last vision. He
worked his way to a fine job and a lovely home. It took almost two
years but he was victorious. Now Dean is ready to have a good,
productive relationship.

You can avoid such drastic change by constantly intervening
in your internal relationship, so you can create compromises. When
I was doing a workshop, a participant, Blake, stood up and said,
"I'm wondering if I should take another week vacation. My female
says, 'Go for it, enjoy it.' My male says, 'Get your rear back to
work.' How do I get the two together? I'd really like another week
vacation, but I don't want to cause problems at work." I talked to
Blake's internal masculine and asked Him if He was willing to take
at least another half-week vacation. He wasn't. We began to work
toward a compromise between his internal masculine and feminine,
just as I would with any two people. I first negotiated with the
masculine. I asked Him if He could back up staying another four
days. I then asked the feminine if She would be willing to honor
three more days instead of an entire week. She said that would be
fine with Her. When They are working together as a team, They
usually can come to an agreement with a minimum of intervention.

Blake was happy with the agreement. I told him, "Remember,

Their process is a living, vital force, constantly moving and changing. Things can change suddenly, so check in with Him throughout the afternoon. He may originally agree on three days and somewhere before the end of those three days, the internal masculine may say, 'Oh, what the heck, I can handle three more.' After the workshop, Blake continued to negotiate with Them until They were at least going in the same direction and He was able to truly follow Her. Blake ended up staying four days after the workshop and having a wonderful time.

Building your masculine may also mean teaching Him how to be willing rather than just capable of following the feminine. Strength does not lie simply in being powerful and capable. It is also a matter of being able to work with others and honor their strengths. Although masculines such as Attila the Hun are strong and even successful in manifesting, they are not in Their full perfection because They abuse the feminine and ignore Her direction. The general direction for working with these masculines is to temper the ruthlessness of Their power and redirect Their attention and activity to Her. This is not easy because They are usually rampant with hard-line decisions and abilities, incapable of following Her directions. They have to realize that They will actually be much happier when They honor the feminine and Her guidance.

I try not to give too simplistic an assignment to these masculines because They initially resent following the feminine, and tasks that are too simple only make Them more resentful. We find out some real issues facing the feminine and present those to Him. For instance, Nancy's Mrs. Nice feminine had tried not to bother Him in the past. What She most wanted was to go out dancing. She told Him that She wanted to see the world. She was bored with just working. She told Him that She wanted to wear frilly clothes. We asked Attila to really listen to Her, and then tell us what He thought. He liked the thought of dancing and said that any time She wanted to She should tell Him and They would go. He saw the excitement in Her eyes and His interest in Her began to grow. He felt empowered by Her enthusiasm. He thought Her urge to travel the world was foolish and He didn't even want to discuss it. At first He was furious that She wanted frilly clothes. How would He look at work? He did finally agree that She should have one glamorous outfit to go dancing in. We encouraged Her to speak up more. She became stronger, He mellowed, and They became a very cooperative couple.

One last bit of advice when working with your internal marriage: be sure to have fun with it too. Allow your masculine and feminine to date and play. You can set up your practices more playfully, if you wish. I often have clients arrange a date between their internal masculine and feminine right after They first meet. I had a client, Sandy, who went through all the motions of Her feminine getting ready for a date. She bought a bottle of wine, cheese, and crackers for her guest. She took a candle-lit bath with soft music, and dressed up as if to go out. When it came time for the date her feminine became very nervous. By the time the masculine came to the door to pick up the feminine, Sandy's feminine became frightened and slammed the door in His face. Sandy found this hilarious. Instead of getting upset, Sandy enjoyed the opportunity to feel vulnerable and a little shy. Nor was the masculine upset although He was quite surprised and embarrassed. He knocked again. By this time the feminine had calmed down and invited Him in. Sandy enjoyed the fact that the masculine was patient enough to try again.

Others who have had their masculine and feminine go on a date have shared wonderful romantic stories of Their inner court-ship. Martin saw his feminine opening the door. The internal mas-culine and feminine were quite open to one another. They spent the whole evening talking. When He left He kissed Her gently. Over the weeks They fell hopelessly in love.

Bring an attitude of adventure into your first attempts at building your inner marriage. I can't repeat myself enough: start small. If your feminine or masculine can't meet Her or His goal, so what? Trust that They eventually will. Give Them a break. Remind each of Them to give each other a break. No one has ever succeeded in this world without a few setbacks, especially in the beginning stages of a major project. They are just like any two people who must come to know each other. Allow love to grow at its own pace.

I asked you to start a journal logging your feelings during some of the exercises. This is to help you see the progress you're making. We often advance and don't realize the transformation we have experienced, because we quickly become accustomed to the new us. The journal will also help you to review insights you have experienced and perhaps forgotten. You might become stumped somewhere in your journey, and that forgotten insight will be the key to your continued growth. Keep working on your inner marriage as you finish this book. I will describe how to work on specific areas in your life in the next few chapters, so that you will understand how to use your inner marriage to effect the change that you desire.

NINE

Transcending Addiction and Codependency through the Internal Marriage

Now that my barn has burned to the ground,
I can see the moon.
—Japanese haiku

Are you aware of the primitive method of catching monkeys that uses a pretty bauble in a jar that is fastened to a tree? The fascinated monkey reaches inside the jar to grab the bauble. Once he has grasped the bauble the monkey will hang on to it and refuse to let go, even as his captors converge upon him. We do the same thing when we hang on to conditions, people, circumstances, or behavioral patterns that no longer serve us.

In psychological terms this is usually referred to as an addiction. I define an addiction as a person's inability to stop doing something even when that activity is destroying her life. The word *addiction* has been traditionally linked with substances such as drugs or alcohol. We are now beginning to realize that we can be addicted to many other things as well, such as people, sensations, and behaviors.

How many of us have watched friends or even ourselves, like the monkey I mentioned, continue to live out a devastating pattern rather than go through the pain of letting go? Have you ever taken back a lover with whom you have had a very painful relationship, had another glass of wine when you knew it was bad for you, or eaten a box of chocolate candies even though you knew you shouldn't? At times like these you couldn't seem to stop yourself, even though you knew the harmful consequences. Addicted people have no boundaries. Boundaries establish the mental and physical limits that we need to live happily and healthily. Without boundaries we are incapable of saying no to anyone or anything that intrudes upon us. We also are not capable of saying yes to a healthier life-style. When the feminine is out of control, and She is coupled with a weak or ineffective masculine who has no boundaries, then addictions are sure to follow. Most of us with strong feminines are saved from addiction by having at least a moderately well-operating masculine who does not want the body harmed. It is your masculine who establishes the boundaries you need to overcome addictive tendencies. Through His strength, you can gain enough courage to heal your attachments and control addictive behaviors.

Let me give you an example of a lack of boundaries. A young woman from the West Coast came to me to talk about a very painful relationship. For a number of years she had dated a man much younger than herself who was an alcoholic and was emotionally abusive to her. Five months before she had come to see me she had successfully ended the relationship—she thought. A month before our first session, her old boyfriend called from somewhere on the East Coast and begged her to take him back. After much pleading on his part she finally agreed to try again, but she told him that she would not help him financially, and was especially emphatic that she would not pay for his cross-country trip back to her. About a third of the way across the United States he called and talked her into sending him money. By the time she came to see me, she was back into the same codependent, abusive situation with him as before. He had gone back to drinking, was living on her income, and was once again abusing her.

Since she did not drink, take drugs, or overeat, my client had never seen herself as an addictive personality. However, in looking back at all her relationships with men, she realized that she was addicted to saving weak, insecure men. This was her feminine, out of control in its need to both give and receive love, regardless of the situation and regardless of the effect on her life. Her undisciplined feminine could have been brought under control if her masculine had been well developed. Unfortunately, this was not the case. As we worked together, my client realized that she would have to give up this destructive relationship in order to be able to have the mature and fulfilling relationship she desired. This happened as her internal masculine developed and began to take charge.

The problem was that her self-image was tied up in being a savior. If she wasn't a savior, what worth did she have? As she developed a balance between her internal masculine and feminine she developed a new concept of self-worth, and found many new ways of having a rewarding life.

The Dynamic of Addiction

Addictions usually arise when the internal masculine is incapable of matching the internal feminine. There is a difference between unwillingness and inability. When your masculine is *unwilling* to follow your feminine, you can become very attached to things or situations that you have created. Remember that the old masculine builds monuments and doesn't want to see them destroyed, so He usually holds onto them for dear life. He can often become fixated in some way, and refuse to let go. This is not addiction.

Since your feminine is the spirit of evolution, She is often not focused on the creations He manifests, but instead wants to move on toward the next step. You may often experience powerful resistance and defensiveness coming from Him at such times. Have you ever heard it said of someone that he is being "stiff necked"? This aptly describes the masculine when He is rigidly holding on to something that He is unwilling to change.

In contrast, your feminine can be so detached from results and from the need to complete projects that She can often get into uncontrolled consumption. If your masculine is *incapable* of matching your feminine, He will be too weak to temper Her drive to continually move forward. The resultant behavior is often addictive. You could easily be left to Her mercy and feel consumed by Her desires. The weaker your masculine and the more imbalanced your inner relationship is, the more likely you are to have an addictive behavior pattern.

Addiction and Relationships

Addiction goes hand in hand with codependency. A person can be codependent without being an addict per se, but codependency usually takes on the behaviors of addiction. The codependent person lives her life for someone else. All sense of self is lost in order to maintain the relationship. In codependent relationships, where one of the partners is an addict (e.g., an alcoholic), the person who is not an alcoholic will often lie to herself about what's really happening and will do all sorts of things to cover up for her addict partner. She needs this self-deception to survive in the relationship with the addict.

If you are with a partner who has severe problems (emotional, addiction, uncontrolled anger, sexual promiscuity, or any kind of disabling difficulty) it's important to know that person's problem can't help but become yours if you are codependent. Let me give you an example.

I knew a young woman named Hannah who had a wonderful job counseling at a junior college. She was well loved and respected by her cohorts and the students. Hannah had a sweet and loving feminine who wasn't highly creative, but She did have some unique ideas. Her masculine was strong, capable, and kind. Hannah met a well-known artist whose name and work were nationally known. She was very excited at meeting Randall because he was very handsome, dashing, and fun. Hannah was immediately swept up in their relationship and before she knew it Randall had moved in with her.

He was a wonderful artist with few boundaries, who painted from his whimsical feminine aspect. It didn't take long after they had moved in together for Hannah to find out that Randall had a drinking problem. Randall's feminine loved the swirling feeling that alcohol gave Her body. His masculine just sat there, resigned. Randall would stay up late at night, drink, and paint. The problems really began when Randall started to awaken Hannah at around three each morning to show her what he had done and to tell her he loved her. When she told him to let her sleep, he would get irate and often call an old girlfriend to show Hannah that somebody cared for his work. It didn't seem to matter that Hannah had to be at work fresh and alert early that day. Those middle-of-the-night awakenings were destroying her sleep, and Hannah started calling in late to work. She also started getting sick frequently.

Another problem was that Randall turned out to be exceedingly insecure and jealous. He started accusing Hannah of having affairs with her coworkers and even with her supervisor. Hannah was absolutely dumbfounded. "How could you think such a thing?" she would ask Randall. "I'd rather tell you if I wanted to sleep with someone else than live with a lie. In any case, I love you too much to do that." Her reassurances didn't help. Randall soon became so intensely jealous that he would leave a party if Hannah talked to a man for more than a few seconds. Hannah believed that the only thing wrong with Randall was that he had never experienced a good, loving relationship. She hoped that once he realized that she truly loved him and was honest that he would calm down.

Hannah was about to learn one of the biggest lessons in her life. Randall never changed as a result of her love. She experienced nightmarish arguments with Randall and began living in fear of his behavior during his drinking bouts. Hannah became frantic. She knew that she had to separate from Randall, but she couldn't seem to get him out of her house. Things progressed to the point where one night Randall threw a lighted cigarette at Hannah, hitting her in the eye. She was rushed to the hospital and spent months recuperating after emergency surgery. It was only after such a horrible tragedy that Hannah was able to force Randall to leave.

Codependent relationships are unhealthy attachments. If you are codependent and in a relationship with someone who is quite needy, you will become so absorbed in that person's needs that you will function less productively in your own. By and by you will lose your boundaries. You may think you are experiencing more intimacy, but true intimacy is not possible when you are consumed by another person's issues. In fact, undue focus on another's issues prevents you from listening to your own guidance and actually prevents intimacy. Over time your attachment to your partner will drain your energy and creativity. Your relationship can't help but become distorted and unhappy.

Whenever we meet someone whom we have a strong interaction with, we form an emotional cord that attaches us to that person. The Hawaiians call these cords *Aka* threads. We become attached to people throughout our life: our family, friends, lovers, and partners. The more we associate with a person, the stronger the attachment becomes. When we think of that person or that person thinks of us, the *Aka* thread vibrates. The Hawaiians believe the other person can feel the vibration of the *Aka* thread.

Here's an exercise that will give you a personal experience of how the *Aka* threads affect all of us.

AKA THREADS

This is a lighthearted exercise with strong impact. Unfortunately, this is not an exercise you can do alone. You will need at least three people to get the full effect. You can do this exercise any time you are with others.

Using a spool of string, cut enough strings so that each member in the group has two to three strings. Each string should be six to eight feet long. The larger the area that you plan to use for this exercise, the longer the strings can be.

Have everyone in the group stand in a circle whose diameter equals the length of the strings you cut. Each member of the circle should hold one end of the strings and give the other ends to anyone in the circle he feels a strong pull to give the string to. Some people may wind up with more strings than others.

Now space yourselves out evenly around the circle and back up slowly until all the strings are stretched taut. Imagine that each string is an *Aka* thread between the two of you. Tug at any of your strings when you feel compelled. When you are thinking of your friend, pull the string and vice versa. When you are thinking of someone or something else, let the string go slack. Feel the pulls coming from the other persons with whom you share a string.

Now everyone should close their eyes and continue to hold the strings tight. Continue to play with the strings, loosening them and then tightening. What did you experience?

The above exercise gives you an idea of how your life and relationships can become sticky. You are constantly getting tugged at or are tugging at someone to whom you are corded. We become imbalanced if we are cocooned by the cords of others who are attached to us. In the most severe codependent relationships you will often see partners so entwined in each other's lives that they barely have a life of their own. In this case they are corded to a very unhealthy degree. It is important to clear yourself of all *Aka* cords occasionally so that you can operate unencumbered by other people's needs and expectations. I cut my cords with others on a regular basis. This is how I do it:

EXERCISE:
Imagine a cord running from you to anyone with whom you have had a connection, even if only a brief one. See yourself holding something you can use to cut that cord, like scissors. Now imagine yourself cutting the cord, in loving release of that person. Watch your half of the cord roll up into your solar plexus and the other half roll up into the other person's solar plexus. As this happens, say to the person you are envisioning: "I, (say your name) in this moment in time do willingly and joyfully cut, lift, heal, forgive, and let go of all ties to (name the person you want to release). I know that only love bonds can and will remain between us. I close off my body and emotions to all but my own self."

This exercise does not create a void between you and the other person; quite the contrary, it gives you a fresh, healthy link with which you can now have more balanced interactions with that person. However, you will continually develop new cords and become reattached to people, so the real work is to notice when an attachment is becoming unhealthy. When that happens, cut the cord and recenter upon your inner marriage.

You don't have to break off a codependent relationship in order to change your codependent tendencies. You and your partner can learn how to love and exist on an independent level, in which you support each other without one of you living your life for the other. In the case of Hannah and Randall this wasn't possible. Randall was so trapped in his addiction that he was not able to change, at least not within a reasonable time or without doing more damage to Hannah.

Kate and Hank, another couple who came to me for therapy, had a much different outcome to their struggle with codependency. Kate had once had a very outrageous feminine, until she was eighteen and became an unwed mother. Then her masculine took over and became rigidly controlling. When this happened, her feminine had no rights at all. The feminine became more and more angry, but couldn't express it because her masculine wouldn't allow it. Hank's feminine, on the other hand, just wanted to take care of the world. Hank could never say no to anyone, except Kate, and he did this indirectly. He didn't realize that by refusing to give Kate what she wanted he was actually saying no to her.

Hank was an easygoing person who liked to help people. He gave his time freely both to needy individuals and to organizations. He frequently found himself devoted to a number of charitable causes, spending many evenings and weekends away from home. Kate felt neglected and unappreciated. But she didn't know how to talk to Hank about her feelings, because she was afraid that he would tell her she was being childish. With this dynamic it was imperative for Kate's feminine to keep Her visions silent.

Hank, on the other hand, was a caretaker and had boundary issues. He needed to help other people in order to feel good about himself and he did it to excess. At first Hank was unwilling to understand that there was a problem in his relationship with Kate. He really did believe that Kate was simply being demanding and childish. Hank learned through our counseling sessions that, once in a while, his promises to Kate had to take priority over his charitable work in order for their relationship to survive. Kate learned that she no longer had to scream and yell to be acknowledged, as she had all during her childhood. The outcome was that Hank continued with the same activities, except now he listened to Kate and gave her the attention she occasionally needed. When Kate developed a sense of security, both within herself and in the relationship, she learned to give Hank the freedom to pursue his charitable activities. She no longer felt neglected.

Another client, Vicki, managed to shift the dynamics in her codependent relationship, but it wasn't easy. She had held a highly responsible position in marketing with a very successful children's television program. Vicki made the program quite famous throughout the country. She began to feel a strong urge to move to the West Coast, but stayed on for another six months. One day Vicki received an offer from a show that was produced in Los Angeles. She decided to quit her job and make her move.

Things went very badly for Vickie after her move to Los Angeles and she felt demoralized. Then she met a television producer who helped her begin a new program that quickly became a success. As they worked together to make this show happen Vicki became emotionally involved with this man.

While quite a marvelous man, the television producer was older than Vicki and his health was deteriorating. Her relationship with him was very loving, but Vicki kept getting pulled into his health dilemmas. Over and over again she wound up going through bouts of unhappiness because she had to do both of their jobs on the show and also nurse her older companion. She didn't have any life of her own. Vicki came to me to get help with her increasing depression.

I told Vicki that her depression was coming from the fact that her feminine's vision was being ignored as Vicki's masculine accommodated her external partner's needs. Vicki's masculine, while strong enough to manifest her feminine's vision, was an enabler. He focused on the needs of others rather than on Vicki's. It was easy for Him to lose his own boundaries and adopt those of Vicki's external mate. Whenever this happened, Vicki would become overstressed by having to oversee too many projects. Unfortunately, she began to act more like Him and less like herself. We immediately worked on Vicki's masculine so He could develop the courage to create strong boundaries for her. We did this by having Vicki and her mate sit down and discuss the reality of his illness. Then they looked at what Vicki could and couldn't do. In the end, he took a sabbatical from his work and served as her advisor. They hired someone to take care of his daily needs. Both of them were satisfied with this arrangement, and Vicki became a great deal stronger in the process.

It takes time to heal an inner masculine such as Vicki's, because He will tend to have regular relapses. You will find yourself in a never-ending circle of losing yourself and then recovering yourself until your masculine is able to maintain your boundaries. For this reason, I usually tell people with an enabling masculine or feminine that they can't afford to be involved with needy people. At least not until they have developed very strong boundaries within themselves.

Another problem that sometimes arises is that the enabler will often make commitments and will then have difficulty fulfilling them because of the partner's needs. Toby is a perfect example of this problem. He and his wife, Amanda, each had his and her own business. She was very successful, but had the kind of business that frequently involved last-minute emergencies. Whenever Amanda had an emergency Toby tended to drop his deadlines for hers. The result was that he had developed a poor reputation within the business community. When we checked Toby's internal feminine She was outraged that the masculine cared more about the wife than Her. Toby's masculine loved the wife's feminine and wanted to help Her whenever She asked.

His wife, Amanda, on the other hand, had a very strong feminine who always wanted to do everything. Her masculine would function quite well until they hit a deadline. Then He would fall apart at the seams and Amanda would turn to Toby. The tragedy was that Toby, like many other codependents, would hang in there and hang in there until the quality of his life was destroyed. This led to further self-defeat and self-criticism.

We devised a plan wherein Amanda would spend one week without reaching out for help from Toby. Toby agreed to pare down his commitments and to always make these few commitments his first priority. We then stretched the week to two weeks, then three weeks, and then a month. Then Toby and Amanda were on their own. We set up a schedule for them to report in to me each week. Just knowing that they were going to check in with me gave Toby and Amanda the support they needed to stay strong. Now they are both successful and are doing remarkably well together. If you have a similar problem, you can set up such a system with a friend or therapist.

Codependents aren't just people who are incapable of saying no to another person. Another kind of codependency concerns someone who is overly controlling, seemingly unable to honor the boundaries of the other person. Pamela was such a person. She flew in to see me regularly. She is highly successful in her profession, but had been hurt a great deal in her personal life, especially in her childhood. Pamela's feminine was strong and creative but also sensible. She didn't go running off on tangents unless she was in a relationship. Her masculine was Attila the Hun. His boundaries were inflexible and had nothing to do with the vision of the feminine. The result was that Pamela tried to control those around her. Any man except the most passive and weak would leave her because of this. Pamela found it difficult to let others have the freedom to do as they wished. She had to learn not to control others. Once we had her duo working in harmony that all changed.

Many of these controlling types of codependents have a manipulator masculine, and use very subtle and subversive means of control. One tactic used by such a person is to help others, but this help rarely comes from warmth and altruism. Rather, controlling codependents continually use their help as a means to emotionally blackmail those they've saved, and thus control them. The controller will make sure the person he helps feels obligated to him, often for the rest of that person's life.

An example of this is a woman I know who is a professional entertainer. She had lots of money and would help people out who were in dire financial difficulty. She was a very strong, controlling woman and expected a great deal in return for her help. The people she helped would then be continually asked to do her favors, most of which were time consuming. If these people refused, she would strongly remind them of her financial aid and would threaten to make life miserable for them.

There is another form of control that is even more insidious. You see it in people who are continually down and out and having severe emergencies from which they need rescuing. They can barely function and are so needy that they use everyone they encounter to get what they want. This type of person has a highly developed radar system (the feminine) for tracking down people whom they can prey upon. They are extremely adept at taking care of themselves in this perverted manner. They have a very strong masculine, who is also usually the manipulator. However, His abilities to manifest are parasitic and based on preying upon the success of someone else's masculine.

Control and manipulation can also occur with a person who has a seducing feminine. Often She will be coupled with a strong masculine, but will prefer that others do the work for Her. This person is overtly sexual and uses sexuality to control other people regardless of their gender.

They play the game of black widow spider, enticing their mates and then killing them when they have had their way with them. Wilma was such a woman. She pouted and flirted her way through man after man, letting them see how much she "needed" them. She played at loving them, getting them to do everything that she wanted, and then left them when she had gotten what she needed from them. This dynamic could only be corrected by stopping Wilma's tendency to reach outside for help. After working with me awhile, Wilma agreed to rely only on her own internal masculine. When she changed her reasons for being with her men friends, Wilma stopped being so magical and adoring of them. The men liked her as she had been before. They didn't realize that she was using them and crippling herself. She finally worked up the courage to tell her male companions the truth about her tactics in using them. None of them liked her much after that.

There is usually some loss on the way to having what you really desire. For some time, Wilma felt as if she had ruined her life. True, she did have financial problems because, even though her masculine was strong, He was rusty at manifesting. Eventually, she began to pull in men who wouldn't let her manipulate them and she liked this very, very much.

Why Is It So Hard to Transcend Addiction?

Do you remember the addiction studies of Drs. Stein and Belluzzi from the University of California at Irvine that I referred to in Chapter 2. Let me refresh your memory. Their research has shown that a brain cell can learn that it will receive dopamine or cocaine each time it registers an electrical discharge. The brain cell will become addicted to the drug and will deliberately increase its electrical discharges in order to get more of the drug. This gives us a new clue to addictive behavior. I hypothesize that as our cells cluster in certain patterns of addiction, it appears that we are "stuck" with the addiction. From Stein and Belluzzi's research, it appears that the cells can be retrained. If this is true, then we must look at the enormity of what faces us in cellular tranformation. We must address all seventy-six trillion cells in our body before we can be completely free of the addiction. This may explain why it is so difficult to overcome addictions and make lasting changes in our personalities.

Until recently, approaches to addiction have dealt with recovery but not with deep and abiding change that transforms an addict into a fully functioning person. In the traditional treatment of addictions, people usually begin an almost impossible process of trying to force themselves to conquer addictions through physical withdrawal along with the rehabilitation of unproductive behavior. It is generally accepted that addicts will always be haunted by the desire for their addiction, rather than transcending this urge. The twelve-step programs, for instance, make it quite clear that you are always an alcoholic or a drug addict and must be in a lifelong recovery process.

If we store memories of our life experiences in our cells, which means that our cells collectively react to external stimuli in particular learned patterns, then we had better start looking at transcending addictions on a cellular level as well as cognitively and physically addressing this problem. Otherwise, you will just continually shift one addictive behavior for another. While I do believe in working systematically to teach others a recovery process, I know that once the addiction is released from your cells, you are no longer an addict. Cellular release is a remarkable technique that allows us to move from despair and hopelessness into awareness and ultimately into freedom.

How can you create cellular release? As I mentioned earlier in this book, the transformation of your internal masculine and feminine is part of the process of cellular release. As you work with your inner marriage, you release the cellular pattern of your addiction. You essentially become a new person with a newly emerged construct, and will no longer be attracted to the object of your addiction. When you change a particular cellular pattern, you cannot go back to your former way of behaving because this kind of behavior will no longer be natural for you. The people around you who interact with and feed your addictive patterns will also change or else will leave your life. They cannot stay the same and remain around you.

The most powerful way to break addictions is to develop your masculine so that He develops strong boundaries. It is His strong structure that will enable you to break your addictions. If you concentrate on building your masculine, you will quickly shatter old patterns and reinforce the new structure that is trying to emerge in you. An evolving masculine constantly lets go of old limiting boundaries and continually creates new, more appropriate ones.

Unfortunately, He can be tenacious and will try to hold on to the old, even though He wants the new to emerge. Your masculine can't hold onto His old structure and move forward at the same time. There is usually a tremendous tension between His new structure that is forming and His old structure that is leaving. The two forms pull us in two directions simultaneously. The result is a feeling similar to flooring the accelerator of your car while simultaneously slamming on the brake.

While you are going through this process you may experience setbacks and many cravings. This can't be helped. You must get those seventy-six trillion cells to transform. Only your internal masculine can maintain your resolve to go through the pain of withdrawal from your addictions and to make full use of the extraordinary healing power you have within yourself. It is a matter of making the commitment to give up judgments, self-flagellation, and regret over past failures and losses. You learn to release the anger you feel at the way life has turned out and to forego any fear of the future.

When you first start this journey, I suggest you get help. This is where Alcoholics Anonymous, Co-dependents Anonymous, or any of the other twelve-step programs can get you started. I can also give you some quick exercises to help you resist the cravings, like the ones that follow:

LIBERATION
MEDITATION

If you don't already know how to meditate, then learn how. Daily meditation can be one of the most powerful tools to help you transcend addiction. Meditation allows you to become detached from your habit and from the worry, guilt, and fear that currently govern your life.

A three-year research program involving Harvard University, the University of Maryland, and the Maharishi International University proved that elderly people who did daily transcendental meditation had far greater physical and mental acuity than others tested who did not meditate. The elderly people who meditated felt younger, had more energy, had better health, and lived longer.

There were several forms of meditation used in this study. Transcendental Meditation was one of them. TM, as it is called, is a form of meditation that involves concentrating on a "source of thought," and freeing the mind from disruptive thoughts through the use of a Sanskrit mantra (repeated word). Another form, guided meditation, includes a form of self-hypnosis and positive input. (Some of the exercises in this book are guided meditations.) A third group in the study used mental relaxation in which any word was used rather than the Sanskrit words used by Transcendental Meditation. Interestingly enough, at the end of this three-year study on the elderly all of the Transcendental Meditation subjects were still alive. More than one-third using the simple relaxation technique had died, as had one out of eight in the group that used guided meditation. This study would suggest that meditation provides access to an inner healing power we all possess. It also accelerates creative thinking and integration.

SUGGESTIONS

I would recommend that you follow the concept of Transcendental Meditation, and repeat a mantra to yourself. If you can take a course offered by TM instructors, I highly recommend it. If you cannot, then the mantra should either be a Sanskrit word such as OM, or a holy word that has meaning for you. You can use the name of Christ, if you are a Christian or repeat a verse from the Bible over and over.

The traditional meditation posture is to sit in what is called the lotus. In the lotus position, you sit on the floor and bend your legs, so that your right foot rests on the top of your left thigh and vice-versa. You can see an illustration of this position in almost any meditation book. This posture; however, is not the definitive meditation posture. I've been told that the Japanese originally meditated sitting in chairs. This is certainly the most comfortable for Westerners.

If you meditate by sitting in a chair, put both of your feet flat on the floor and your hands loosely in your lap. Do not lie down. You run the risk of sleeping through your meditation and thinking that you are still alert and absorbing details, while you are not.

Whatever form of meditation you choose, close your eyes and concentrate on your breath. This will help you to clear the chatter going on in your mind. Begin to silently repeat your mantra. Thoughts and images will arise as you do this. Simply observe the thoughts that arise and then release them. Be willing to let each rising thought pass through your mind.

You will find that whenever your mind touches on some form of addictive thinking, it will then go off on a discourse about the subject. When this happens, simply refocus on your breath, let the disruptive thoughts flow away from you, and begin your mantra again.

This is a very simple exercise. Just as with releasing the physical aspects of an addiction, you can keep letting go of thought patterns that are associated with the addiction. When a thought or desire comes up say "Spirit, come strengthen me now."

Every one of us has our own very personal meaning for the concept of Spirit, God, or Higher Consciousness. For some people it is the idea of God, of external forces beyond human understanding. For others it is the concept of all within us that is pure and holy. Try to think of Spirit as that part of the universe that is benevolently powerful, the force and guidance that comes to us in time of need.

The impulse toward the addiction will usually begin to subside right away when you repeat these words. If it doesn't, then do the "Truth Intensify" exercise that I discuss in Chapter 8.

Detaching from Addictions

The first step in achieving freedom from your addictions is the desire to change. You want to experience change in yourself because some aspect of yourself has outlived its former usefulness. That's important enough to say again. We experience the desire to change because some aspect of ourselves has outlived its former usefulness. This concept is critical and has far-reaching implications. Let me explain.

We usually think of change in terms of something being ripped from our lives. As we change there is always a period when we live in a void created by the absence of the old pattern. In this nebulous place the old has dissolved and the new has not yet formed. Nobody likes the feeling of a void; therefore, we are often fearful of change. We can release that fear and progress more rapidly by knowing that the void is actually a space where the creative force is building with an emerging new structure.

What do I mean by structure? If you recall, I have stated that permanent change can occur only when we release the cellular structure that binds us to old patterns. Your addictive, attached pattern is in your cellular memory. But with the internal masculine and feminine working together you begin to build new structures that push out the old limiting structure. *New structures do not appear because old ones disappear. But rather it is new emerging forms that push out the old forms.*

The more attached or addicted you are to something, the more life threatening it feels as the addiction dissolves. It is helpful to remember that when you feel your worst, as if you really can't survive any longer, it is a signal that you are going through some rite of passage. So don't give up! It is not unusual for you to feel at times as if you can't go on with your process of change. When you are forced by circumstances to really let go of your addictions, you may very well be so frightened that you wish you could die. Regardless of how change comes, it is wise to remember that old sayings like "It's always darkest just before the dawn" are actually true.

It's far easier to become actively involved in change than to have it just happen to you. Viewing change in this light, you will be more motivated in your transition. I am not downplaying the fact that at times this may seem like grueling work. People experience physical and emotional withdrawal as their old structures break down, but by simply being aware of the dynamic of addiction, one can make the process more rapid.

Addiction and Spirituality

Addiction is always the result of having an internal feminine that is out of control and an internal masculine that has never learned to take charge when appropriate. Unless we work with an addiction on a cellular level we will only substitute one addiction for another. This includes relying so heavily upon a belief system, or religion, whether it is Christianity, Buddhism, or New Age spirituality, that it becomes an addiction in itself. Many spiritually sincere students become fanatically pure in their diet and life-style. Turning to these belief systems are helpful in making a positive transition, but these people merely substitute one addiction for another, and never really address the underlying issue of their addictive behavior. The result is invariably that these people are not successful in creating an intimate and healthy relationship with God, themselves, or others. They simply become driven and imprisoned in another aspect of their being. This is called spiritual materialism, and it is just as deadly as any other addiction, perhaps more so. Why? Because this addiction masquerades as a higher state of consciousness or a holy state.

Spiritual materialism is deceptive because it can feel like one thing when it is the opposite of what is occurring. People believe they are following God, but this can be an illusion. For example, I see a rise in the popularity of metaphysical beliefs, but the expression of those beliefs are often just another form of addiction. These people are focused on only one aspect of life, dismissing all else. They become consumed by their desire to join with the divine. They often spend thousands of dollars and endless hours in their quest for expressing certain spiritual abilities. This metaphysical emphasis on supersensory powers is extremely limiting, and runs the risk of substituting phenomena for true spirituality. All phenomena are by-products of devotion. They are not something we have to experience in order to be spiritual. Don't feel that any of us are exempt from this form of addiction. As long as we are in the human form and possess an ego we are susceptible to this trap.

Ordinary Attachments

We do not need to be a codependent person or an addict in order to be attached to people and things in our lives. We have a natural tendency as humans to hold on to things around us. We become attached to life-styles, our family, our career. We become attached to having new things and to the image we have of ourselves. While these attachments do not leave us dysfunctional, they do limit us from progressing further in our internal development. Learn not to hold on to people and things in your life so tightly. Your feminine may have wonderful new options in store for you. In order to detach, you will find my "thought hands" practice useful. Any time you experience yourself holding on to any person or object, do the following exercise:

THOUGHT HANDS
Imagine a set of hands reaching out from the center of your body, near your solar plexus. See them holding onto something or someone to which you are attached. See those hands as a color that seems appropriate to your interpretation of holding on. Many people see attachment as red or orange.

Now imagine these colored hands letting go of the person or situation to which you are attached. See the hands draw back into your solar plexus. See the person or circumstance to which you are attached dissolving in front of you.

The Promise of New Structure

As your new internal structure emerges, you will find that your perceptions of external reality change. Life will come to have more meaning and you will feel more empowered. You begin to really know that uncomfortable experiences are a means of release, and you will find that fear and regret are no longer part of your journey toward change. Life's vicissitudes will become more of an adventure. Your life will be like reading an exciting novel, with you as the main character. You will become an Indiana Jones in search of the Holy Grail.

You will find in this process that bliss will come and go, depending upon how facile you are at following Her juice. Your feminine will devise many situations as an opportunity for cellular release. Your masculine will want to become adept at following Her juice so that He can use the opportunities to release structure. You will go through many cycles of releasing attachment, and will find that you often encounter people and situations that operate as triggers for cellular release. You can continue doing this until you are fully detached from your addictions, which we know won't happen next week.

While it is possible to reach full integration in this lifetime, it is unlikely for most. This is true only because few people will apply themselves consistently, moment by moment, to the process of clearing. However, you can count on changing a great deal. You will also find that the process becomes increasingly enjoyable and exciting over time.

Declare your commitment to your personal aliveness. Your aliveness and its unique expression are precious gifts to all that you come in contact with. Take an oath with yourself and say, "I will no longer sacrifice my aliveness for anyone or anything. I will commit myself to following my aliveness. I will not look back, and I will not devalue myself or others with destructive self-criticism."

TEN

Business Success with the Internal Marriage

By identifying the forces pushing the future, rather than those that have contained the past, you possess the power to engage with your reality.
—John Naisbitt and Patricia Aburdene,
Megatrends 2000

What is the secret to becoming a highly successful business person? There is a thriving industry based on answering that question for you. You can walk into any bookstore and find a myriad of books addressing the "How To" of success. There are video and audio tapes that will teach you what to say and what to do to make yourself a master at sales. You can learn "How to Swim with the Sharks," as one book calls the experience. If you're really intent upon becoming a success, you can attend any one of a multitude of workshops that will show you how you, too, can actualize your dreams.

My concern is that we first ask ourselves just what success is in our eyes. Is it being financially secure? Is it receiving acclaim for what we do? Is it being respected by peers? Is it having personal happiness? Is it all of these things? Here are a few questions for you to ask yourself. Keep your attention on your solar plexus and watch your internal feminine's responses to these questions:

Are you excited about your career?

Do you wake up each morning feeling alive and looking forward to your activities for the day?

Are you content with your financial situation?

If so, are you satisfied with the way you achieved your success?

Do you have a rewarding personal life, full of loving friends and family?

If you answered yes to all of these questions, congratulations! You don't need to read this chapter! If you answered no to any one of these questions, I would like to help you achieve a balance between financial success and personal happiness. Let's examine success a little further before we do.

There are two kinds of success. One is success based on results, which involves such activities as your professional projects and daily job routines. The other is having a sense of personal fulfillment. When we talk about success, we usually focus only on the results-oriented aspect. I insist on focusing on both. Financial success certainly doesn't assure you of happiness; and having personal happiness is essential to your well-being.

In order to achieve both aspects of success, you will have to start relying upon both your internal feminine and masculine. Success in all areas of your life will then come more easily. Once They know how to work together, each seeking to balance your life, you will also find yourself happier and more excited than you have been in years and more able to meet your goals for greater satisfaction.

There is a pattern to success, but that pattern may not be what you think. Until recently most business success has been achieved by following a standard pattern. Classic examples of success through standard procedure are found in banks and most large corporations. There is little room for creative self-expression or individuality in this kind of enterprise. "Follow the rules" has been the corporate code since the fifties. This is not surprising, as a great majority of our country's retired military officers became corporate executives after the wars. If there is any group that is inner masculine dominated, it is the military.

The business world, since it runs mostly on standard procedure, operates primarily in the domain of the internal masculine. You can often become highly successful in this inner masculine-dominated arena, even if you don't listen to your feminine. This is because your success relies on following someone else's vision or surrounding yourself with visionaries.

All the major advances in civilization, including those in our business world, have been based on following a vision. The people who saw that vision followed a different set of rules than you probably follow to perform your daily job tasks. They are often highly creative and follow hunches, even though they may not label those hunches as intuition. They have to follow hunches in order to be successful. Most business success stories concern people who go beyond the status quo to create a higher level of achievement. In *Personality and Growth*, James Fadiman and Robert Frager comment on psychologist Abraham Maslow's study of highly successful people. Maslow classified a good percentage of them as possessing two prominent characteristics. The first was creativity; the second was self-sufficiency. Let us look at Maslow's notions on creativity. Dr. Maslow found that highly successful people were creative, not necessarily in the usual sense of creating paintings or writing poetry, but in the sense of being "original, novel, ingenious, unexpected, and inventive." Where does this creativity come from? From your feminine/intuitive.

Intuition/vision is not a hocus-pocus phenomenon, pursued only by sages or people on the outer fringes of society. I am not referring to voices talking to us in the middle of the night or specters appearing at the foot of our bed. Many members of the Fortune 500 Club talk about how their success came from their ability to "follow their gut" and to have faith that their hunches could lead to success. These people tell me that when they are trying to make a decision, they first notice their gut reaction. Then they will intelligently gather information, have planning sessions, and do all of the left-brain organizational work that is needed to substantiate or disprove their gut reaction. These people are an example of manifestation with guidance.

In following their gut, successful people have all experienced going beyond their present knowledge and abilities in order to follow their hunches. Naisbitt and Aburdene, in the quote that begins this chapter, suggest that success lies in looking ahead, and not in the past. This is basically what these people are doing. However, the secret ingredient to their success in doing this is that they've learned to blend the wisdom of the past with the vision of the future.

Let me explain how this is done through our internal marriage. Our feminine embraces the future, while our masculine often tries to stay in the past. When you get a hunch or gut feeling, you are listening to your inner guidance (your feminine), but it is the masculine who actually allows you to follow that guidance. His function is critical in business because although we must follow our feminine's vision, we must never disregard the important lessons learned from the past. Knowing when to take a calculated risk and when not to is critical. Most people are not skillful or adventurous enough to perform in this way. They are either too visionary and get themselves in trouble or too staid—unable or unwilling to try something new. For some of you the task will be to learn to follow your intuition in business, which means trying new things. For others of you, it means building your masculine in business so you learn how to be practical when, based on your skills and abilities, your vision is too far-reaching.

A good example of trying something new is simple "brainstorming," which is very intuitive in nature. Rowan, in his book, *The Intuitive Manager,* talks about the importance of brainstorming your way to business success. He tells the story of how this term was originally created by the head of a New York ad agency to describe the creative process he used in meetings. He would present a problem to everyone present. Then he would ask them to just say whatever popped into their minds, without any fear of criticism. A lot of what was said had no meaning, but because the employees were given permission to free-associate without criticism, unique and innovative solutions would always appear.

When everyone on your team knows how to read their intuitive, meetings can be very creative and accomplish more than you dream. For instance, when I am in a meeting with my staff, all of whom are highly intuitive, we all get into a state of relaxation. Then we open up our intuition by holding our right nostril and breathing through our left. We always begin with a list of the things we need to consider. We go over the items on the list, one by one, and each person tells me what he or she intuitively feels about that item. Then we hold our left nostril and breathe through our right, looking at the projects from a practical, down-to-earth viewpoint. In this way, the intuitive runs my business and the masculine backs it up.

I honor my staff's intuitions during the day. If I tell someone to do something and they come back to me a short time later to say something is wrong with part of the project, I will say, "Tell me what you are sensing." Then I sense and we act.

"Doing Business Intuitively" should be taught in all business schools. When I called Harvard Business College to see if they had courses on intuition in business, they seemed incredulous at the question and assured me that they did not. Of course, until recently, intuition was not something that successful people were even willing to admit they use. So how can we expect prestigious business schools like Harvard to offer this course in their curriculum?

This is unfortunate because they don't teach the very thing that leads to true success. This is easily proven. The majority of our multimillionaires don't have a college education. They were fortunate enough to have avoided training in traditional methods. They didn't know their limitations and they hadn't learned what "couldn't" be done in the business world, so they just forged ahead and did the things that seemed right to them.

My friend Mark is extremely brilliant and highly unconventional. He is the type of person who could be deposited in the center of a strange city with no money and only the clothes on his back and he would be wealthy inside of six months. His ability to create wealth in unusual ways is uncanny. When I asked Mark for the secret of this ability, he told me that it was due totally to his complete lack of formal education. "I never knew until afterward that what I was doing was impossible," he told me.

I mentioned earlier that Abraham Maslow noted that one of the key traits found in successful people was creativity. Maslow found that self-sufficiency was the other key trait demonstrated by successful people. He stated that self-sufficiency is the result of "courage, will, choice and strength in the individual." Self-sufficiency comes from a strongly developed inner masculine. It is the masculine who has the drive to solve the problems that arise, and deal effectively with difficulties that might otherwise crush the vision. When successful business people decide to do something, they do it. I don't mean in the old stereotypical way of pushing through relentlessly, or climbing over everyone else in the well-known P. T. Barnum style. Their perseverance is in staying with something, of never giving up until the dream is fulfilled. If a seemingly insurmountable problem occurs, these people are not willing to compromise their integrity. They find another way to accomplish their goal. A successful businessman once told me, "I can't imagine allowing something to stop me. There is no question that I will go on. Oh, I have certain limits; I won't lie, cheat, or steal to get what I want. I don't have to do that. I always know that there is a more creative solution. When all of those aggravating little details conspire to keep me from following through or people let me down, I just refuse to stop, unless my intuition says to let it go."

The key to this gentleman's statement is, "unless my intuition says to let it go." If your masculine isn't working with your feminine, He can easily become overly focused on building monuments, making a name for Himself, and being important in the eyes of the world. The masculine can become so relentless in His quest for achievement, money, and power that He causes much devastation and suffering.

The ability to combine both creativity and self-sufficiency was the secret to Maslow's successful people. Most of us have the ability to display one or the other traits but not both simultaneously. The creativity that Maslow saw in his successful people came from their feminine; the self-sufficiency came from their masculine. Your internal feminine can uncover opportunities that would not normally be available to you. Your internal masculine can then close the deal. She can find creative solutions to the knottiest business problem and He can bring them to fruition.

In their book, *Personality and Growth,* Frager and Fadiman mention that Maslow noticed that the combination of both these traits led to their being "self-actualized." He stated:

All of my subjects were relatively more spontaneous and expressive than average people. They were more "natural" and less controlled and inhibited in their behavior, which seemed to flow out more easily and freely and with less blocking and self-criticism. This ability to express ideas and impulses without strangulation and without fear of ridicule turned out to be an essential aspect of self-actualizing creativeness.

Catherine illustrates both self-sufficiency and creativity. She was about to retire as an administrative secretary after thirty-five years. Her pension was not going to be enough to retire on, and she was also too energetic to let go of her active life-style. When she came to me, she didn't have the vaguest notion of what to do.

As she opened up to her intuition, she had the inspiration to join the local chamber of commerce. She enjoyed the new people she met there. One of the people who befriended her was a retired schoolteacher. He had never thought about going into business but he had some extra money and when he suggested they do something together, she answered, "Why not?"

Catherine and her friend decided to open up a mediation agency. They had both used mediation skills in their careers but were insecure about their basic business knowledge. It turned out that their lack of knowledge also served them, as they were able to develop totally innovative techniques for mediation. Two years later, after their mediation company had become well known for its unusual but successful problem-solving techniques, Catherine remarked to me, "I never knew what you were supposed to do and what was traditional in this field. I didn't know the prescribed ways of doing things, so I approached them in a completely new way. As a result I can look back now and see that some of the steps I took, although unorthodox, were actually very sound practical business decisions." She further stated, "Now accomplishing new things is the love of my life. I like creating, doing, sharing; and I know that I can handle not only my successes but my failures as well."

As successful people learn to follow their hunches and to use good old-fashioned common sense and intelligence, they gain confidence. The more confidence they gain, the more they are willing to risk and the more determined they are to avoid undue risk. Catherine found that the development of her internal masculine really built her confidence. She says: "Now that I feel confident about my abilities, it's interesting to look back over the years and realize that I did most things well. Yet I have spent most of my adult life having the nagging feeling that I had gotten away with something—that it wasn't really me who did it. Once my visions were strong enough and He developed the ability to back Her up, my views changed dramatically. I now know that I am successful because of my own efforts."

Guidance without Manifestation

You can run into enormous problems if you swing too far into the feminine/intuitive world. If you operate mostly from your intuitive side, you will always have good ideas for business schemes but those schemes will never come to fruition. You may also take too many chances. Remember that the intuitive likes change, expansion and pioneering. She is always ready to leap; but without consulting the masculine, She can easily venture into unsafe situations.

I've had several clients who repeatedly came very close to bankruptcy. It was only when they almost lost everything that they would take corrective action. Four of them learned to pick up the early signals that they were going offtrack by developing sensitivity to their visceral signals, and were then able to avert trouble immediately. This required strengthening their inner marriage relationship. It was a matter of getting these clients to listen more carefully to their feminine, while building their masculine into a fearless partner. I gave them the same exercises to build Her and Him that you find in this book.

I have worked with many companies that are run by creative geniuses who are not very practical about business matters. One such company kept doing big, splashy media affairs when they weren't needed, taking badly needed funds from other areas. The first thing we did was to organize meetings between the top executives and the division managers. In these meetings the executives found out for the first time how frustrated their people were at not having the equipment they needed, while seeing money spent on hype. The boss had to look at the fact that his feminine was running wild and would soon bankrupt him. Based on what they found out, it was possible to work out compromises, and allocate more money to needed equipment and facilities.

Manifestation without Guidance

Todd is an example of someone who was driven by his masculine instead of being lead by his feminine. He is charismatic and handsome as well as very bright and resourceful. As interested as he was in his self-growth, Todd always seemed to get involved in questionable transactions. When he first came to me, Todd sensed that he was in some form of trouble with a large, three-state real estate deal he had been working on for the past two years. It was coming close to completion. Nothing was wrong as far as he could tell, but Todd was suddenly having a lot of anxiety, and he couldn't figure out why.

Todd's feminine, The Crone, wanted him to get out of this real estate deal. To his masculine She said, "I've been telling you that trouble is coming for over a year. Now it is just around the corner." But the masculine was headstrong, and wanted to continue with the deal since Todd had worked so hard on it. Soon even Todd's masculine could smell trouble brewing. We worked together to get Him to the place where He would be fearless enough to walk off the project, if need be.

One day, the sense of danger was extreme. After much thought, Todd met with his partners and said, "I quit." They were visibly more upset than he had figured they would be. Todd was tempted to change his mind, because they truly appeared to need him. Yet somehow he found the courage not to give in to their pressure. It was about ten months later that he read of the arrest of his former partners for a bogus land deal. After that, Todd's masculine began to really listen to the feminine's warnings, as it was clear that the other partners had acted illegally. Fortunately Todd was free and clear, but he was called to testify.

The pretrial period was a long and arduous ordeal that stretched over sixteen months. During this time, Todd's inner marriage became more fully integrated, which created more tranquility in his life. By the time the trial started, Todd was a different man. It turns out that he had had a very narrow escape. There was a strong possibility that the other people involved had tried to set Todd up to take the rap for them. He is now a very conservative businessman but still follows the hunches of his feminine.

This is not an unusual scenario in business when someone has a strong masculine who doesn't listen to the feminine. Out of touch with their intuition, these people have a masculine who may be able to create financial success but the rest of their life is likely to be in trouble. Even on a less dramatic level, many people lose touch with their feminine and live very unsatisfying lives. Have you no-

ticed how many financially successful people in this world don't
have a satisfying family life, or wish they were doing something
else? If you aren't happy with what you're doing for a living, ask
yourself why you have stayed with your job for so long. I'll give
you some probable responses:

"Because I have a family to feed."

"Because I'd have to take a drop in pay to do what I want to
do."

"There's no way I can do what I want to do."

"I (or my parents) spent a lot of time and money for my training;
I can't change now."

"I wouldn't know what else to do."

What part of you do you think is saying these things? Your
masculine or your feminine? If you answered that it was your masculine, you're right. You need to learn to listen more to the voice
of the feminine.

If you are doing well in the business world but are dissatisfied
with what you do or want more from some other area of your life,
I suggest that you open yourself to the possibility that you only
possess half of the equation to business success. Acknowledge the
concept that your masculine isn't working in conjunction with your
feminine. If your masculine were working well with your feminine,
then you would have a balanced personal and professional life, with
each one complementing the other.

Your feminine aspect is expansive enough to allow satisfaction
in your personal life. There is a fine balance needed between your
inner masculine and feminine in order to achieve both business
success and a satisfying personal life.

John is an example of someone who followed his intuition in
creating the life he wanted. He went straight from college to a
small, local company. In his twenties, working for this company
and staying in his hometown was just what he wanted. However,
John soon found out that there was a particular code of operations
and expectations in this company. He was expected to adhere to
these or lose any possibility of upward mobility. He was constantly
being told not to "rock the boat" whenever he questioned company
policy.

John stayed with that company until he was in his late thirties.
He would have left sooner except he had a wife and children and

felt he needed the security that his job provided. However, as he neared the end of his thirty-eighth year, he felt too constricted to continue on in this same way. John quit his job and struck out on his own to follow his heart's desire and become an art dealer. You can imagine the absolute horror his wife felt when he told her his decision. For the family, it meant giving up a rather comfortable life-style. She knew, however, how unhappy John was and decided to support him in achieving his dream. His company associates thought he was crazy. "You'll be back," they said.

John went through many struggles, but he told me that it had been well worth it. He worked hard and he had to keep on his toes, but his love for his new work gave him the zeal and excitement to do that. He could not ask his parents or relatives for financial help and all the banks he approached for loans turned him down. His venture was considered high risk. John became very creative and self-sufficient in order to carry out his vision. His wife became an able partner in dealing with the financial end of the business. She was happy doing this, happier than she had ever been. Neither of them regretted the risky move. John never did return to his old way of life. He went on to become a very successful and highly respected art dealer, appraiser, and writer.

Interestingly enough, John had always talked a lot about listening to his inner voice, but until his career change, he had always been more comfortable with accomplishing his goals through tenacity rather than by his intuition. John told me that he had proved that he was a good manifester in the business world, but that he really honed his intuitive skills only after going off on his own venture. As an entrepreneur, his experiences proved to him that if his gut was telling him something, he'd better listen to it.

To this day, John says things like, "My gut is telling me to call So-and-So; I think he made a mistake with my order." John will follow up on his gut reaction, and invariably he's right. John succeeded through a lot of hard work and by paying attention to the messages from his intuition. He is a perfect example of the kind of success you can have in your life when you operate from the marriage between intuition and ability.

Developing Your Intuitive Guidance

You already know that many people in the Fortune 500 companies put a lot of stock in their hunches. Their ability to use their intuition has set them apart from the average business person. One example is my friend David. Although David has always been highly successful, he is viewed by most people as a renegade. He simply marches to a different drummer than other people. He is a salesman who has an uncanny ability to make highly successful cold calls. He tells me that in order to be successful, he has to really trust his intuition and not let his ego become involved when he gets a negative response. He may make dozens of calls and then call someone who says no, but with whom he feels an opening. Then his logical mind will begin to ask questions about what problems the customer faces and he will explore ways he might serve them. The result is success that is far above average. There are many things that you can do to bring out your intuitive ability. At the end of this chapter you will find a number of very effective exercises.

When working with business people, I attempt to develop individual flexibility and then cultivate an open, inquiring mind. I work on the issues of underlying hostilities found in the internal masculine and feminine. These hostilities can be healed in order for the masculine and feminine to come into Their true power. It is not overworking and rushing around that causes Type A personalities to suffer serious illness. It is their overt or covert inner hostility that is the source of the problem. After dealing with these hostilities, by following the practices in this book you can create an environment that allows for vision as well as the already highly developed, logical way of doing things. It takes integrity and courage to do business this way.

I did a great deal of work with a business owner who felt that there was very little enthusiasm in his company. When I arrived, the first thing I did was just wander around. I quietly observed how people were working and what the emotional atmosphere was. My client was a "systems" man and everyone complained about too much paperwork. As the company grew, so did the complexity of the paperwork. Rowan, in his book, *The Intuitive Manager*, states that "paperwork kills creativity" just like rigid organizations do. I helped my client to see that if he could become less rigid, his employees could become more creative.

One of the things he decided was that the building was too sterile-looking inside. He wanted a different look for the plant, so the walls were painted in soft colors. He had skylights put in, and rearranged the furniture so that work areas were more open. This, coupled with room for people to be more creative, changed things dramatically. The owner said that it was just like it was in the old days, with energy and enthusiasm and new, creative ideas.

It can be risky for a company to encourage creativity and individuality, and it must be done with great care. If you implement changes slowly and with caution then problems will not appear. If businesses are going to support intuition in their people, they will have to create an environment that nurtures its blossoming and still keeps things on a very practical, down-to-earth level. This often means changes in the corporate plan, but it is always worthwhile.

Learn to be creative, regardless of your job. For instance, if you are a supervisor and all the people under you are under high pressure and constant deadlines, you might try giving your employees massage or stretch breaks instead of coffee breaks. A fifteen-minute massage that covers the neck, shoulders, and spine can work wonders. Some companies even hire full-time massage therapists who work throughout the day to give employees a real rest. You will be surprised what a difference this can make in creativity and output.

Over the years I have found that one of the biggest inhibitors of intuition is criticism. I mentioned earlier that judgment comes from the masculine, and creates a block to the feminine's vision. Criticism is a result of judgment. It stifles flexibility and makes one afraid to be open to change. When I think of all the people I know who are highly creative in business, I realize that they tend to surround themselves with people who are positive and open to change, people who encourage free thinking. Of course they also have a few analytical people around, so that they are balanced by someone who will look at the downside risks. These analytical people keep companies from making major mistakes. Your best course of action is to develop your own internal duo, so that you can keep your hand on everything that is occurring in your company rather than having to rely on others.

Guidelines for Building Your Feminine in Business

1. Keep a close eye on the energy in your chest, heart, and solar plexus. Pay attention to the open or pinched feelings you get. When you get a pinched feeling, that is a warning from Her. When you get an open feeling or an uplifting charge that is Her telling you everything is okay.

2. Listen to that little voice in your head and begin to let Her lead you through your day. Act on a few of your hunches and see what happens. Remember to back up your hunches by having your masculine check them out.

3. Try not to ignore Her messages any more than you have to. If you are getting a message to do something that seems absolutely ridiculous to you, like not go back to work after lunch, and you know that will cause problems, tell your feminine you heard Her but She'll have to wait. You want to expand your visions, but you don't want to ruin your life.

4. Try to practice listening to your feminine outside of your business environment as much as possible. Then it will be easier for you to "hear" your intuitive guidance in your business life.

5. Try starting each day by asking your feminine what you should do that day. Organize your day around Her suggestions.

6. Check in with your feminine several times a day to see if you are still following Her lead. Remember that your guidance will come one bread crumb at a time.

7. When someone approaches you with a problem at work, immediately focus on your chest and stomach areas. Conjure up an image of your feminine and listen to that problem with Her ears. You will find an immense source of objective wisdom in dealing with that problem if you do this.

Guidelines for Strengthening Your Masculine in Business

Your inner masculine is essential to your business success. While you must follow Her vision to reach the top of any field, you will also need Him to be strong and capable. Once you strengthen His manifesting abilities and He becomes accustomed to following Her, you will find it easier to incorporate Her vision into your daily routine.

There are a number of things that successful business people do, methodical sorts of things that simply make sure that everything that is necessary gets done. If your masculine is not functioning well, then taking care of mundane things will help Him to build. (Be sure to keep checking in with Her.) Here's a short list:

1. Manage your time well. Start each day knowing what you are going to do, roughly how long each task will take, and the relative importance of each item. It's best to make a list, and to then check off each task as you complete it. Then at the end of each day you can see how well you have done. I always check with Her as I go along, to make sure that my masculine isn't in control. What does She want?

2. Organize your files so you can find things easily. If you are not naturally adept at this, get help. At the end of each day make sure everything you have completed is filed in the right place. This will make it easy for you to find things, and will also help keep your work space clear.

3. If you have a number of people to keep in touch with, make a list of all of them including name, address, telephone, fax number, pertinent information, and the last date you contacted them. It's best to use a tickler card file or a computer for this. Print your list at least once a week, and carry a copy with you if you go out of town. This way you can call people whenever you have time that would otherwise be idle, like waiting for a plane at the airport.

4. Start every business day with a particular activity that stays

the same. This could be something as simple as making a phone call to the East Coast. This stirs Him into action. You will find this familiar routine satisfying and something that you will look forward to. He needs something dependable in the midst of all of the change.

5. As you go through your list of things to do each day, you will find that some of them are pleasant. There are others that you would rather put off, like calling people who owe you money. Do these "difficult" tasks first. Procrastination kills the love affair between Him and Her.

6. At least once a month, go through your entire list of people to call. Pay particular attention to the calls that you imagine will be totally worthless. These are the ones that will often pay off unexpectedly.

7. Maintain very close contact with the people you are currently doing business with. When a project is running, you should be in touch with your customer or your project coordinator at least twice a week, and more likely, once a day. This establishes the personal contact that is so essential to good communication, and to getting a job done right. This close communication will keep you informed of what is going on and will keep your people motivated by knowing that you are interested in them and in what they are doing. This close communication will often be the difference between success and failure on a project.

8. Be sensitive to fatigue. Fatigue is an indication that your masculine is overloaded. If you start to make mistakes, take time off and do something else for a while. Work out, take a short nap, meditate, or do something else that will refresh and revive you.

9. Ask customers, associates, and professional consultants for help and advice often. Don't assume that you know what to do. It may be that your assumptions have gotten you into trouble before. Don't ask them to make your decisions for you, but simply to serve as information sources. You must make your own decisions.

STRENGTHENING THE INNER MASCULINE

Make sure you are seated in a comfortable chair. Play soft music if it helps you to get into a meditative mood. Notice your breathing and take a few slow, deep breaths. Now breathe out in a slow, relaxed manner and then return to your normal breathing. Notice your breathing pattern. Now tense all of your muscles. Tense them even tighter. Squeeze all your muscles including your face, hands, and feet. Hold that tightness. Try to go even tighter. Now relax. As you let go, relax more deeply.

Let go of the cares and concerns of the world and allow yourself to feel the deep relaxation that is now flowing through your mind and body. Continue to breathe easily and naturally. Each time you breathe out just say to yourself, "Relax."

See your masculine turn into a great warrior in full regalia. Some people see themselves as a Samurai and others see themselves as a Knight or an Amazon. The figure you imagine should be one that makes you feel mighty and powerful. Notice that you are fully ready to do battle, to take a strong stand in life and do what must be done.

Continue to breathe deeply and relax. Now let the warrior in you grow taller until it is at least twelve feet tall. Feel the power of the warrior within you. Notice how you relish the call to demonstrate your power. Notice how well prepared you are. Feel this new strength pouring into you and notice how this power actually feels relaxing and leaves you more trusting of all the new possibilities that can arise from the situation you now face.

Now keeping the feeling of the warrior, open your eyes and walk around the room as the warrior. Breathe deeply as you do this.

When you are about to go into a critical meeting, you can quickly recall the warrior in you. Have Him grow tall as you did above and enter your meeting with the sense of His power. Look at everyone there at the meeting from the eyes of that warrior and you will come from a position of strength rather than weakness.

Developing Both Hemispheres

Let's go over some quick techniques for activating the right and left hemispheres so we can integrate and stabilize them. Why should you care about balancing your brain hemispheres? Edu–Kinesthetics (Edu–Kinesthetics, Glendale, California) tells us that balance leads to "enhanced self-esteem, improved communication skills and increased comprehension." This organization also advises us that if we are stuck in one hemisphere or the other we will experience "stress, self-doubt, self-criticism, judgment of others, fatigue, miscommunication, lack of joy and laughter, worry, fear, depression and indecisiveness." Meditation is an excellent way to do this, but successful business people rarely have the time needed for meditation. However, there are some simple techniques with similar results that can assist greatly in opening up the creative right brain. These exercises require relatively little time.

INTEGRATION
A research study conducted by the University of San Diego proved that holding the right nostril closed and breathing through the left nostril stimulates the functions of the right brain hemisphere. Here is one very powerful exercise that you can do just before a meeting to balance your brain hemispheres, putting you at your intuitive/logical best. Before I begin important meetings, I activate both sides of my brain with a similar exercise. This is also a dynamite exercise for relieving exhaustion. It brings oxygen to the brain and perks you up.

Sit up very, very straight. Act as if you are going to pinch your nostrils closed with one of your hands. Place the thumb to one side of the nose and the index finger to the other side but do not pinch your nostrils shut. First, pinch the left nostril closed and breathe through the right. Relax. Then press the right nostril until it is closed, and breathe through the left nostril. Repeat this about six times.

The following exercises are invaluable for integrating both brain hemispheres. They can be done almost anywhere, anytime. Just don't try to do them while walking or driving. You will feel your mind and body relaxing as you do these exercises.

EXERCISE 1:
Put your arm straight out in front of you at about chest height. Use your finger to trace a horizontal infinity sign. (Imagine a figure eight lying on its side.) Follow your finger with your eyes. Then reverse the direction of your hand. As your eyes follow the flowing patterns of the double loop, your two brain hemispheres will integrate. If you are in a meeting, you can draw the horizontal eight on your note paper as if you are doodling.

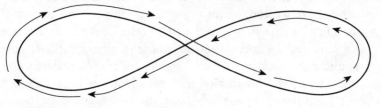

EXERCISE 2:
March in place so that the arm of one side of your body moves up and down with the leg on the opposite side of your body. Start by putting your left arm straight up above your head and at the same time, lift your right knee up. Then switch sides; right arm up at the same time as you lift up your left knee.

EXERCISE 3:
Pat the top of your head with your left hand and use your right hand to rub your tummy in a circle. Reminds you of childhood, doesn't it? It may be harder now for you to do this exercise than it was when you were a child.

EXERCISE 4:
Place your arms out in front of you with your palms facing each other. Now turn the hands in toward center until the backs of the hands are facing each other. Now take your right arm and place it over the top of your left arm. The arms should now be crossed and the palms once again facing each other. Let the fingers grasp each other so that you are holding hands with yourself. Go back to original position and repeat the exercise only this time bring your left arm over your right arm.

     In 1977 I was halfway through my doctoral program and working with Laura Huxley. Through her I was introduced to

Dr. Jean Houston, Margaret Mead's protégé. She made me aware of the concept of developing the full power of the brain through some profoundly simple exercises. One of the exercises that turns on your brain circuits and can be found in her marvelous book, *The Possible Human,* is to keep your eyelids closed and roll your eyeballs down as far as you can. Now move your eyeballs to the right. Now to the left. Keep your eyes closed. Do this several times.

Playing toward Integration

Most of you may have done this exercise as a child. Do you remember how to make a paper airplane? You might recall how exhilarating it was to make those little planes and watch them sail around the room. It seems like child's play because it was so fun to do; but child's play is actually serious business, as any child development expert will attest. The entire process actually strengthens your creative/intuitive abilities and hones your cognitive skills, thus helping to integrate both your feminine and masculine aspects.

The actual steps it takes to make the airplane as well as tracking the movement of the plane when you fly it are the important ingredients of the exercise. When you have reintroduced yourself to these steps, you can then visualize the process whenever you need to.

EXERCISE:
If you have never made a paper airplane here is what you do: Get a sheet of fresh paper in a color that you love and in just the right size for the airplane you desire to make. Make sure the paper is heavy enough to give your airplane body without being too heavy. You can get colored copy paper at any local printing/copy shop or at your stationer.

1. Take your piece of paper and sit at a table or desk with it. Look at the piece of flat paper in front of you. Now hold it and feel its texture. Move it around and notice what happens, how the air moves it, how the paper flutters. Notice everything about that piece of paper.

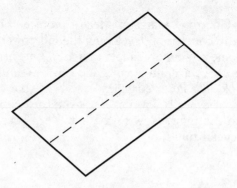

2. Place the paper back down in front of you. Fold it in half lengthwise so that you have a narrow rectangle of paper folded double. Notice how this folded rectangle looks and open the paper on the desk or table in front of you so that the crease is vertical.

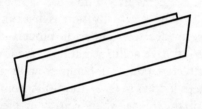

3. Take the right upper corner of the paper and fold it down in a 45 degree angle so that the right, top edge of the paper now rests against the crease. Do the same with the left corner of the paper. Now you have a point at the top of the paper. Feel the sharp point, and notice how the folded paper feels in your hands.

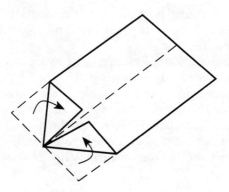

4. Now fold the upper corners into the center once again, making a sharper-angled edge.

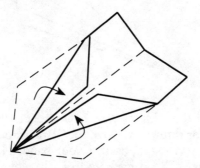

5. Now fold the plane in half at the original fold.

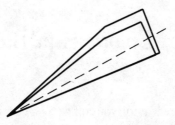

6. Place the paper so that the long, flat edge (the original crease) is at the bottom, nearest you, and the angled edge is at the top as in diagram 5.

7. Starting at the sharp point, fold the angled edge down

to meet the bottom edge (the original crease) of the paper. Turn your paper over and repeat this step with the other side.

8. You have just folded down the two wings for your paper airplane. Fold these wings flat against the body of the airplane and crease the fold well, so it will stay in place.

9. Hold the tightly folded paper in your hands, and notice once again how it feels. Lift the flaps of the two folds you just made, just enough to make the wings of your paper airplane into one flat plane. You now have a paper airplane!

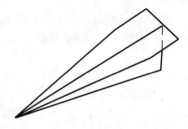

10. Hold the body of your new airplane in the hand you use for throwing. Move the plane through the air, and feel how it lifts against your hand. Now, move your throwing hand back and swiftly move it forward. At the end of your reach, flick the plane forward, releasing your paper airplane at just the right time. Notice how gracefully it glides through the air!

The Role of Emotions in Business Success

Imagine that you are leaving your office for a very important meeting where you will be making a presentation to a prospective client who will be a major account if you can land the deal. You know you must be sharp and on your toes. You are well prepared and have timed your day so that you will arrive with time to spare. Just as you are walking out of the door of your office, your phone rings.

It is an emergency call from one of your largest, long-standing accounts. This important customer tells you that the company is drastically cutting back on expenses and has decided to eliminate the project that involves you.

Crestfallen, frightened, and in shock you have no time to absorb this painful reality as you run for your car. You have a thirty-minute drive to get to your meeting and you can either fret and stew during the drive, or you can use that time to ease your panic and strengthen yourself.

We all have days filled with pressure, unpleasant surprises, heavy demands, and serious confrontations. Being a victim limits possibilities. You have the choice of either being ruled by your emotional reactions to these circumstances, or taking command of them. People who can keep their emotional reactions in check when they are hit with unexpected trouble will be more successful.

If you know simple techniques for releasing your emotions when trouble hits, you will be able to operate out of newfound insight and creativity. Then instead of succumbing to the situation, you will find a creative way to solve the problem. When you are reacting, you are letting your emotions rule you and you actually lose control of the situation. If you are constantly battling emotional reactions, you are at the mercy of your cellular patterning. Your immediate reaction to any troubling event will be a habitual response.

Patterned emotional responses block your feminine/intuitive from operating at Her full prowess. Also, your masculine is unlikely to hear your feminine's messages when you are dealing with strong emotions. Both Her diffuse awareness, which could see a way through the problem, and His ability to work swiftly to move in a new direction are blocked when you are in a state of emotional upheaval.

Learning to handle crisis situations in a new way, just as in any emergency training, will help you to automatically shift gears when the occasion arises. You will then respond in a healthy and powerful manner. You can train yourself to relax just the way you train yourself with any exercise program. All it takes is a small amount of time each day for these exercises. If you do them with commitment and devotion, you will see amazing results in a very short period of time.

Controlling Emotions through Breathing

When we are under tremendous stress, we tend to hold our breath, which locks us into our negative patterns of thinking and feeling. Concentrating on our breathing when we are in stressful situations begins to relax us immediately. Controlling our breathing is the first step in keeping command of a trying situation.

Here are several exercises that utilize breathing and movement as instant tools for change:

EXERCISE 1:
Inhale deeply, allowing the breath to gently push out your abdomen as you fill the chest slowly. Hold your breath until you can't hold it anymore. Now keep your mouth closed and release the breath through your nose in two short spurts of air, tightening your abdomen as you do this. Your abdomen helps push the air out. Repeat this exercise four or five times. Please do not try this in a car until you have perfected it in a chair. Otherwise, you may be distracted while driving.

EXERCISE 2:
Take a few deep breaths, concentrating on slowly breathing out all of the air. Then breathe in deeply, clench your teeth together, grimace with your whole face: eyes, forehead, mouth, and cheeks. Growl loudly two or three times.

Moving toward Success

If you want to be happier and more fulfilled in your professional career, then I would suggest that you put aside at least one hour, twice a week, just to be with yourself and learn some new patterns of behavior. This time should be spent doing anything that is totally outside your normal professional career, and should be oriented toward learning about your inner masculine/feminine. A quiet walk by yourself, for instance, will give you the opportunity to simply monitor Her messages. Most of you will need to develop your intuition if you want to be happier and more successful.

There are many, many activities you can do to gain inner peace, and at the same time, greater intuitive awareness. I have already covered many of these techniques in this book, and there will be more in the next two chapters. Your main emphasis should be on sharpening your intuition and honing the skills of your internal masculine. You can do this through any of the exercises in this book. Both the internal masculine and feminine must be strong and capable so that you will not fall short of your dreams in your business.

When you are first learning to come from your inner power, don't be too rambunctious. For instance, if you are a secretary, don't rush in and tell your boss that you have a plan for reorganizing the whole company. Focus on your particular job and see what needs to be done creatively to make the work flow easier. See if you can take responsibility for making that happen. Then approach your boss and discuss the matter. Let's say that the boss likes your idea and it turns out to be very, very successful. Over time, as the boss begins to trust your insights, you can make more and more suggestions.

If you have been out of touch with your deeper self for a long time, then you may want to do some therapy or you might also consider joining a group of people devoted to inner exploration. You will also want to really get to know Her and Him and to work closely with Them. You should do almost all of the exercises in this book. You will discover, as you engage in your passionate inner journey with Them, that there is a totally unexpected and unaccountable sharpening of your business acumen and your hunches. As both hemispheres of your brain open up and begin to work together, you will become more flexible in your thoughts and emotions and you will find that you automatically become more creative and adaptable. You will be able to perceive opportunities that you might have previously missed, simply because you will now have greater acuity, and will have freed yourself to be sensitive to subtle cues. Your cognitive skills will also vastly increase, as will your ability to bring projects to completion.

Unfortunately, many people never stop to smell the flowers. They tend to place more and more emphasis on their work, which rewards them with money, and less and less energy on a personal life. They may get to the point where they find close relationships puzzling and frustrating.

When Patty came to me she had just left a middle management position where she had done everything from secretarial duties and bookkeeping to publicity for a small corporation. She had learned that she really had a flair for publicity. As her daughter reached junior high school age, Patty decided that she didn't want her to go to high school in the city.

Patty didn't know exactly what to do to make a living, but she and her daughter moved to a small town they both loved. There was no publicity firm in that town, and after checking around she discovered that there really was a need for one. Patty had done fine in her past jobs. However, she had always worked for other people. Her feminine, Miss Sugar and Spice and her masculine, Methuselah, were a good combination for keeping peace and maintaining the status quo. But now that Patty was going into her own business, her intuitive would have to let go of Her "nice little girl" act and become a more mature feminine. Methuselah needed to become younger and more capable of following the feminine's vision. Patty couldn't afford to get caught up in maintaining peace and always being nice when her business was at stake.

Here is a conversation I had with Patty's feminine:

SHE: We have to do something quickly and I don't know what to do.

  I: What would you like to do?

SHE: I don't know, anything He wants to do; but I want Him to do it now.

  I: Unless you are willing to speak up and tell Him what you want, He will just keep going on as He is and your new business won't be very creative.

SHE: He might get mad at me.

  I: I don't think so. In fact, I think He will only get angry if you don't speak up. You have to be very clear about what new changes you want, and not vacillate back and forth.

SHE: I want to get to know people in town. They will be
Patty's clients.

I: Good idea.

Now that the feminine had made her needs very clear, I turned
to Patty's masculine. Could He support the feminine? This was
something Methuselah could easily do. He readily agreed with the
plan, and the first thing He decided to do was spend a week going
to different businesses to let them know about Patty's background.
This would offer invaluable feedback as to the viability of her
business idea. Then Miss Sugar and Spice, who was now about
twelve years old, told Patty to wait for about ten days. Slowly,
people began approaching Patty for advice on how to promote their
small businesses. After counseling a few people, Patty did a workshop that was highly successful. As a result of this workshop a top
television talk show featured her in one of their episodes. This, of
course, was great for her business. Patty soon became very successful.
You see, it does take courage to follow your vision, and it takes
determination. If you are consistent and willing to live in the
uncertainty of things unfolding, you can fulfill your dreams.

Business in the Nineties

In the nineties, it is the creative business that will do more than
be an anomaly and just survive. Years ago, we were just beginning
to hear rumors that businesses were addressing the creative aspect
of success. Where, heretofore, the image of major companies was
that of a cold, ruthless organism, that thrust is slowly changing.

All over the world we see signs of a growing business ethic that
focuses on the individual as well as the globe. We have seen all
kinds of new businesses become more focused on environmental
and ecological concerns. Manufacturers and distributors of water
purifiers, pollutant-free cleaning aids, and other environmentally
sound products have sprung up. Companies are beginning to address
world problems such as dealing with the homeless, world hunger,
and employment of people with physical or mental handicaps. For
example, the two grocery stores in my town have hired several

developmentally disabled adults to bag groceries and help around the store. There is a not-for-profit, multi-level company whose net proceeds go to feeding starving children in the United States and around the world. Some products on your grocery shelves are manufactured by not-for-profit companies who funnel the proceeds to pet projects. Other products are being packaged with recycled materials.

We are now in the midst of one of the largest changes in our work force that we have ever seen. I just recently read an article reporting that because of the high rate of unemployment, many people are being forced to go into business for themselves. So the word *entrepreneur* is fast becoming a more common title. Today's successful entrepreneurial ventures include doing simple tasks such as house-sitting, dog walking, and catering. Many of these small ventures have become major successes. Mo Siegel, who years ago started a small herbal tea company called Celestial Seasonings, eventually sold his business to a major food corporation for millions of dollars. Two young women started a small deli/catering business in New York several years ago called the Silver Palate, and ended up becoming so popular and successful, they wrote cookbooks based on the recipes they used in their business. These cookbooks became best-sellers.

The old ways of operating in our schools, our governments, and our businesses are beginning to crumble: airlines are going broke, banks are collapsing, businesses go bankrupt every day. Since our old stability is being shattered, we have no choice but to go forward in an inventive, creative way.

Now more than ever it is time to be innovative, highly productive, and enthusiastic. Changes are occurring so rapidly in this technologically based society of ours that any business that is going to succeed must have a highly developed motivator and mover. Otherwise the business will suffer greatly and will not be flexible enough to stay on top. You should be able to do much more than just survive in the next decades!

ELEVEN

Romantic Love and Your Inner Marriage

> . . . If we wish to understand romantic love, we must begin by understanding aloneness, the universal condition of us all.
>
> Innovators and creators are persons who can to a higher degree than average accept the condition of aloneness. They are more willing to follow their own vision, even when it takes them far from the human community.
>
> —Nathaniel Branden, *The Psychology of Romantic Love*

All of your life is about relationships. The relationship of self to self, of self to others, of self to career, and most importantly, the relationship of your inner masculine and feminine. I say most importantly, because your inner relationship is the basis for all your other relationships. Interestingly enough, it is an external romantic relationship that gives you the most immediate and in-depth feedback on the state of your inner marriage. It is this type of relationship that allows you to truly understand your vulnerabilities, fears, and personal pitfalls. A romantic relationship is also very likely to put pressure on you to work out your own internal dynamic.

I have heard many people say that they lose their individuality and inner peace when they are in a romantic relationship. It is much easier to operate from a strong sense of self when you are alone and not dealing with the daily needs of a partner. When you are alone, you end up operating in a vacuum with little intimate feedback which shows you how you are doing. When another person enters your everyday life, with another set of needs and another internal marriage, then you experience how solid your own internal relationship really is or isn't. You get immediate feedback as you experience the daily interactions with your partner.

I like to think of relationships as a personal polishing process, similar to that used with stones and gems. An unpolished stone has sharp edges, mineral deposits, and all sorts of blemishes. If you put that stone in a revolving wire basket and tumble it with other stones, its imperfections smooth out and the stone becomes far more beautiful than its original state. The secret is that a stone cannot become polished unless there is at least one more stone in the basket bumping against it. It is the constant interaction of the stones knocking against each other that causes those sharp edges and blemishes to disappear.

It is the same with us. Unless we are willing to love and work with one another, we will remain in an unpolished state, full of bumps and blemishes. We are quite beautiful as we are right now, but just think how much more exquisite we could be through our willingness to become emotionally intimate with friends and lovers.

We all know that romantic love is complex and often difficult. Our divorce statistics show that. What I am about to tell you may offer you some fresh insight as to how truly complicated your interpersonal interactions really are, knowledge that will give you a new way to overcome even the most difficult problems. Whenever you have an intimate relationship with someone, there are actually six of you interacting instead of just the two of you who are physically present. There is the you that you present to the world, your partner as he presents himself to the world, and both of your internal masculines and feminines.

If your internal relationship isn't aligned, you will inevitably find some kind of misalignment in your romantic relationships. You may have both a mature masculine and feminine while your partner may have one mature archetype and one inner child. Your feminine may be battling your lover's feminine or masculine. Your masculine may be battling your lover's feminine or masculine and vice versa. You might even be having an all-out war with both of Them. One thing is certain; it will never be possible for a romantic relationship to work unless everyone (all six of you) can get along.

I was once in a very short-lived relationship with a man who was a gentleman cowboy from Wyoming. When Ted and I first started seeing each other, on the surface Ted seemed mature and confident, but as our relationship progressed, I saw how little he was able to accomplish his goals or lead a productive life. We also began battling over simple power issues. Ted became more and more childish as time progressed. I decided it was time we sat down and started working with the inner dynamics of our relationship. When we did this, the problem behind our external dynamic came to light. Both Ted and I had Attila the Hun for a masculine. They battled incessantly with each other. Ted had The Brat for a feminine and my powerful Wise Woman feminine kept trying to help Ted's Brat to mature. The Brat wouldn't listen.

One day Ted screamed at me, "My feminine hates your feminine." I told Ted that the feminine doesn't hate. I knew that his childish inner feminine was having tantrums. Ted didn't want to listen any more and there was nothing further I could do except deal with my feminine who had believed in his surface image. She really thought that he was a rugged he-man. At that point I did some reality therapy with myself. This means that I sat myself down and looked at how I really wanted to live my life, and found that there was really no place in it for an out-of-work cowboy. That was about the same time that Ted and I decided it was over. I was greatly relieved when Ted decided soon afterwards to leave town and move to another state.

Here's another example of how troubled inner relationships can reflect into the external relationship. Carol and Andrew were having difficulty with their twenty-year marriage. When they came to see me, Carol said that Andrew had become a workaholic, and that his sexual performance was like that of an old, weary man. Andrew said that Carol was growing increasingly angry, rigid, and more demanding of his attention. When I contacted Carol's feminine, She turned out to be a blithe spirit in flowing gowns. Her masculine was a tall, stone pillar, incapable of moving. Andrew's feminine was much like Carol's. His masculine, however, was a very old, frail man. His masculine could hardly walk. Their two masculines together were impossible; Andrew's masculine was too weak to function in the relationship, and Carol's was too rigid.

When we began working together, the first issues we addressed were Carol's anger and Andrew's withholding. In order to break free from the pattern of anger and withholding we had to do some strong work with both of their masculines. Carol and Andrew's masculines had to learn to back up Their two feminines. Carol and Andrew had to help their masculines develop to the point where the two of Them could say no more often than They were used to, particularly to each other.

I instructed Andrew and Carol to spend more individual time apart, pursuing activities that they liked to do alone, and also to be more intimate with each other when they were together. They really had not been spending any time at all on their own personal needs. We began by having both Carol and Andrew individually make lunch dates with a friend without inviting each other. This was not as simple as it might sound. Andrew and Carol were both codependent and very attached to one another.

Although Andrew and Carol were given this same exercise, the effect on each of their masculines was very different. Andrew's masculine became stronger while Carol's masculine became more flexible and began moving more freely. It was the first time that Andrew had developed any boundaries at all, and the first time that Carol had developed any flexibility in her boundaries. Both Andrew and Carol were now developing new boundaries, which gave them much more personal freedom.

Once the separate lunch dates became comfortable to Carol and Andrew, we included an occasional dinner. Then we started to see real breakthroughs. Andrew started doing things that his feminine really wanted to do, like playing handball and tennis. He soon became much happier, and this opened the way for a healthier dynamic with Carol. At first Carol couldn't think of anything that she wanted to do. Then she remembered that when she was younger, she wanted to learn to weave. She decided to take some weaving classes and soon became quite proficient at it. Carol even began to sell a few of her creations.

As Carol grew more excited about her artistic abilities, her masculine became inceasingly flexible and able to work with the feminine. Carol's masculine, who at first was a stone pillar and could move only by walking very stiffly, now began to walk briskly. Andrew's masculine became younger and wanted to do many things. He could now fulfill his feminine's vision fairly rapidly.

Eventually Carol also began to play tennis. She and Andrew would occasionally play together, using the strenuous activity as a way to work out their aggressions and release their anger. Within six months after starting their work together, Carol and Andrew were once again the excited lovers they had been at the beginning of their relationship.

Tension often arises between couples because they each expect something from their partner that should come from within their own internal relationship. Women often get caught up in casting the functions of their internal masculine onto the men in their external relationships. They expect their partner to manifest their particular dreams, instead of relying on their inner masculine. Men do the same by looking to their external woman to feed their vision, rather than turning to their own internal feminine. Men who don't listen to their internal feminine will try to find women who tell them what to do, and will then resent them for doing so.

We are doomed to heartbreak and unfulfilling love relationships as long as we cast parts of our failing inner marriage onto another person, and we will never be happy as long as we do this. Our partners will tend to mirror the parts of ourselves that we are unwilling to face. People who are very angry and won't acknowledge that anger tend to draw angry partners to them, or else stir up anger around them. They actually get other people to act out their own anger. Rather than owning our inner foibles, we tend to act as if someone outside of us is doing something to us. It is impossible for another person to give us what we lack in ourselves.

Shana and Paul had been married about one year when they came to me for counseling. Shana said that Paul had seemed so kind and loving at first, but now he was a brute and mistreated her emotionally. Paul said that at first Shana had seemed strong and capable, and she occasionally still was. But now Shana was either whiny and very needy most of the time, or else she was enraged at something Paul had done. Paul said, "This drives me crazy. I never know who I am dealing with."

Rather than beginning with their external relationship, we had to first work on Shana's and Paul's internal relationships. This meant doing individual work before we could address the couple's external issues. When we checked their internal duos, we found the source of Shana's and Paul's problems.

Paul's masculine was rigid and controlling. He wanted to take charge all of the time. Since Shana also had a strong masculine, who wouldn't allow Paul to take charge, Paul's masculine was usually quite angry. Shana's feminine initially appeared to be lovely and serene, and was clearly the aspect with whom Paul had originally fallen in love. However, as we further talked with Shana, another feminine appeared—a whining, frightened child. She told me "I've tried so hard to be strong. I don't like Paul's masculine, because He never takes care of me." I asked this inner child how She felt about Her own masculine and She said, "Oooh, He's really scary."

When we talked to Paul's feminine, we found that She was also whiny and needy. Paul's feminine whimpered over the way She was treated by Paul's masculine and feared Shana's masculine. When Paul's masculine first appeared He would hardly reveal Himself to me. Finally, when He did, He was very sarcastic. Shana said, "He reminds me of the way Paul is acting."

That sarcastic, nonrevealing image was just the veneer that hid an angry and controlling masculine, who grew even angrier when Shana's feminine went on a whining binge. At first Paul's masculine had total disdain for his internal feminine and for Shana's as well. He had absolutely no intention of following His own whining internal feminine. Paul's masculine absolutely refused to be cooperative, and the feminine began whining even more. He wanted to be in charge of everything, even though I told Him that vision was the feminine's role. Shana's masculine then went into hiding and began to sabotage the feminine. We tried a number of approaches to change this, but were unsuccessful. Paul's feminine was willing to change, but She couldn't as long as the masculine continued to brutalize Her.

It was very hard for Paul's masculine to accept the fact that He had contributed to the whimpering behavior of both His own and Shana's inner feminines. When I pointed out to Paul's masculine that His feminine counterpart was just like the Shana He didn't care for, He became really angry.

I had heard that the Dalai Lama, one of the political/spiritual heads of Tibet, was going to be in town. I decided to use this opportunity to expose both Shana's and Paul's masculine to the energy of a masculine operating in His perfection. The Dalai Lama is a highly intelligent and extremely compassionate man, loved by people the world over. He is the recipient of the Nobel Peace Prize.

I had come to know the Dalai Lama when I traveled with the sixteenth Gyalwa Karmapa (who is also a spiritual head of Tibet), so the three of us were able to meet with the Dalai Lama in a private audience. I had told Shana and Paul before this meeting that both the masculine and feminine of the Dalai Lama were very wise and fully functioning.

It was no easy feat to get Shana to the private audience. She was frightened, and made every excuse she possibly could find to cancel our date to meet this great man. Shana finally did end up going, and both she and Paul were stunned by the love and the strength pouring from the Dalai Lama.

The next time I worked with Shana, her masculine understood that He had a higher function. He seemed to know that His life would be a great deal better if He would fulfill it. He also knew that He needed to limber up, and soon decided to try to follow the feminine. These attempts were rocky at first. Shana's child feminine would occasionally appear, which caused problems.

At one point Shana's feminine was desperate to visit her brother in Alabama. The masculine took two months to do it, but finally did get Shana there. She and her family had a wonderful visit. Several weeks after her visit, Shana's brother was killed in an automobile accident. Shana was grateful that she had gotten to see her brother before he died. After that dramatic incident, Shana's masculine and feminine became inseparable. They fell deeply in love, and the qualities that Paul had originally loved in Shana began to reemerge.

After the audience with the Dalai Lama, Paul's masculine became much kinder. His masculine finally agreed that He would try to back the feminine up in whatever She wanted and began to help and encourage Her. For about six weeks there was still a battle between Paul's masculine and feminine, because She was still weak and his masculine kept forgetting about His newfound love for Her. The feminine's visions were initially sporadic, but She soon began to get a glimmer of what it was like to fulfill Her function.

One day Paul's feminine wanted to take off for two hours and go downtown to a particular restaurant for lunch. The masculine was annoyed because of project deadlines, but He decided to keep His promise to back Her up. At the restaurant Paul ran into a client whom he had been trying to reach by phone for weeks. The masculine began to see the real possibilties of working with Her, even in business.

I began working with the external issues between Paul and Shana as a couple fairly soon after their internal duos became more integrated. We soon discovered that both sets of masculines and feminines were eager to work toward a happy relationship, but had certain concerns. We addressed those concerns. Paul's feminine had loved Shana's feminine but hated her masculine. Shana's own feminine didn't like her masculine, either. Shana's masculine had hated Paul's feminine and was disgusted with her own internal feminine. We had many, many conversations during the course of our work together. After a while the internal duos began to communicate quite well. Through this process Paul and Shana learned to communicate all of their thoughts and feelings. They learned to make immediate corrections by going inside to their own masculine or feminine. They also developed the ability to successfully interact with their partner's masculine and feminine.

Once in a while one would have to say to the other, "Your masculine is battering me," or "Your feminine is whining again." They all began to feel more open to one another. Soon there was a real love affair among all of them. Paul and Shana did fine after that. Today they continue to have a happy relationship, and have three children. Their masculines and feminines are still very much in love.

If you are in a relationship, you and your partner will each have to individually create your own internal harmony before you can experience harmony and excitement in your external relationship. As you both learn to listen to your own internal feminine without neglecting the masculine, you will become two self-reliant individuals with much to contribute to one another.

The Many Levels of Intimacy

It's now clear that successfully loving and living with another person means that you must realize that you are dealing with more than one aspect of that person. If you are in a relationship, you will want to take into consideration your partner's internal dynamic as well as your own. When two people are having a conversation, there are also two inner conversations going on. From the perspective of the inner marriage, a typical conversation between two people will actually have six participants instead of just two.

Let's take a hypothetical couple who are having a difficult time in their relationship. Below is a typical six-way argument that we all get involved in. It includes the couple's heated words to each other as well as their inner dialogues that simultaneously take place. To make this conversation easier to understand, I have placed the couple's quotes in bold, and the conversations between their inner masculine and feminine in regular type. It might sound something like this:

TOM: **Why don't you ever do anything you promise you will do?**

HIS FEMININE: *(To his masculine)* What a wimp her masculine is!

HIS MASCULINE: *(To his feminine)* He can't hold a candle to me. I would like to destroy Him.

JANE: **Tom, I have a career too, and I can't always do what you ask. I told you I might not be able to do it. You're impossible.**

HER FEMININE: *(To her masculine)* Who does he think he is?

HER MASCULINE: *(To her feminine)* I want to leave now.

HER FEMININE: *(To her masculine)* I'm angry with Tom, but I still have the juice to be with him. Calm down.

HER MASCULINE: Fine, do what you want but I won't help you.

HIS FEMININE: Do something. I don't feel seen or heard.

HIS MASCULINE: Okay! *(Jane leaves the room and slams the bedroom door.)*

As Jane's internal conversation continues so does Tom's:

HIS FEMININE: That does it. We're out of here.

HIS MASCULINE: Absolutely. We aren't putting up with that witch.

TOM: *(Yelling)* **I've had it with you.** *(He slams out of the house.)*

JANE: *(Her masculine explodes and she opens the door and screams)* **Don't bother to come back!**

You can see that the war is actually occurring internally as well as externally. That is why it is difficult to deal with the issues of the external relationship until you have dealt with the internal duo.

Even if two people seem to get along, they might be creating an unhealthy web of interdependence in which they need their partner to make up for the lacks in their dysfunctional inner marriage. Jim and Gail are a good example of this. They came to me saying that they had a good relationship, although they seemed to be a most unlikely couple. Jim was a soft-spoken, highly intelligent man, yet obviously controlling. Gail was very spiritually oriented, talented, and bright, but was never able to realize her visions. Both of them told me that they had individual problems that they were interested in working on. They both felt they were in a rut professionally, and were beginning to experience financial problems. They wanted to address those problems by using my masculine/feminine work, which they had recently read about in a magazine article.

When we first met Jim's and Gail's feminines and masculines, both of their internal marriages turned out to be somewhat dysfunctional. Despite these dysfunctions their external relationship seemed harmonious, because Gail relied upon Jim to provide what she couldn't get from her inner marriage. Jim did the same thing with Gail. I was cautious about doing work with them, because I knew that the apparent harmony in their external relationship would vanish as soon as Jim and Gail started working on their inner relationship. I warned them that things could get very bumpy as we reorganized, but the bumpy trip would be worth the results in the end. They both said that they had enough confidence in their love to go ahead, and I believed them.

Jim's feminine was charming but a little too withdrawn and subservient. She wasn't capable of leading the masculine. She had not yet grown into Her full power, and She was certainly no match for Gail's feminine, who was powerful and certain. Because Gail's feminine was so powerful, Jim's masculine actually acquiesced to Her rather than to His own feminine. This made Jim's feminine absolutely jealous and furious. She would beg Her internal masculine to listen to Her. He always did, and then would once again revert to external control, as She was always too weak to give Him the kind of vision that He could follow.

Jim's masculine was as tough as they came. Gail's masculine was willing but weak. Because Jim's masculine was tough and more powerful than Gail's, Gail and her feminine relied on Jim instead of their own masculine. Gail's masculine was hurt and disappointed by this.

As we began to bring Jim's feminine into Her own clarity, his masculine quit following Gail's feminine and started following His own. Whereas Gail had previously been the one to organize their lives, deciding what she and he would do, Jim began to have ideas as to what he wanted to do. Gail's feminine became grief stricken. She cried and cried. She wanted Jim to follow Her once again. Gail started picking on Jim, tearing apart his ideas. At the same time, she became highly insecure, wanting more of his time and attention.

Another form of trouble began to develop in their relationship as we developed Gail's masculine, at which time Jim's masculine fought for control. Gail had always looked to Jim to watch over family finances. Jim was accustomed to directing the budget and liked having the hold on the family purse strings. When Gail's masculine began to grow, Gail wanted to have more say in the budget priorities. She and Jim began arguing on where their money was going. Their internal duos were doing much, much better but Jim and Gail were having a hard time adjusting to the changes in their partners. For almost four months their once-pleasant relationship became almost unbearable for them.

Jim and Gail threatened to break up a number of times during this process, but I always reminded them of their love for one another. As the weeks went by Jim and Gail could see their partner's individual changes. They began to honor each other's process, and grew more patient with each other's struggles. They always got through their troubles and ended up strengthening their relationship. They really admired the growth that was taking place for both of them.

Jim became much more intuitive and his business skyrocketed. Gail began working in a very chic salon, something she never would have been able to do before. They had survived the tempest. Now, as I write this, Jim and Gail have a good relationship and are also radiant, guided, strong, and capable within themselves.

The Battle of the Sexes in a New Light

I first met Martin Cohen when he came to Arizona from his home in New York. He is a powerful teacher and we had a marvelous connection with each other. Martin teaches a relationship course in which he breaks down the generic "battle between the sexes" into the three things that each sex wants from the other. The battle begins when we don't fulfill those three wishes for each other. I describe these three requirements below.

A woman wants the following three things from a man:
• She wants him to be fun.
• She wants him to be certain.
• She wants him to be her passionate lover.

A man wants the following three things from a woman:
• He wants her to be a safe harbor.
• He wants her to carry his vision.
• He wants her to maintain the dance of the relationship.

When a woman doesn't get what she wants from a man—fun, certainty, and passionate love—she begins criticizing him, stops participating in the dance, and/or gives up on her initial vision of the relationship. When a woman is too critical, won't be the catalyst for the dance, or doesn't care about the relationship, the man quits being fun, certain, and/or her passionate lover. When a man stops being fun, certain, and a passionate lover for his partner, the woman usually responds by criticizing him or losing interest in keeping the relationship going. You know how easy it is to create a cycle of criticism and withholding between two partners. Either one of them can desert his or her role in the relationship and start this circle of unhappy interactions.

The truth is that there isn't a single man or woman who doesn't possess many of the very traits the other wants in him or her. It is a matter of bringing out and strengthening these traits in each other. Both sexes can get these qualities from their partners to some degree, but it has to first occur from within. Still, both sexes tend to look outward rather than inward. We must realize it is our feminine and masculine who want these qualities from each other. When They aren't gratified, They look elsewhere for gratification and support. This causes problems in our relationships. Let's look at Cohen's list in more depth and shift our focus to the internal masculine and feminine.

What Our Internal Feminine Wants from Our Internal Masculine

She wants Him to be fun. She needs Him to be fun. She is so busy being diffuse and holding the whole picture of past, present, and future that She often isn't much fun. His abilities to focus and manifest allow Her to have the fun She needs.

This might sound like a frivolous, petty request but it isn't. While it is important for the masculine to skillfully manifest more serious needs, He must also be able to manifest pleasurable and fulfilling activities that fill the feminine's life with joy and beauty. Joy creates the verve that makes us more powerful in our lives. The old adage, "All work and no play makes Jack a dull boy," is a very wise rule to follow, especially for the success of your internal dynamic.

In this case I use the word *dull* in the sense of losing one's edge. Have you ever noticed that it is hard to make decisions when you are feeling down, or to put any energy into the tasks you perform? On the other hand, have you ever noticed how brilliant, radiant, and powerful you are when something wonderful has just happened to you? You literally scintillate with the joy of life. Others can't help but be positively affected. Happy people are simply more powerful than depressed, unhappy people.

She wants Him to be certain. This means that the feminine wants the masculine to take charge of Her visions and to be absolutely certain that He can manifest them. She wants Him to be assertive and confident in His dealings with Her.

Your feminine needs to know that your masculine is there to back Her up. If She can't trust His ability, She will either want to take over and do everything Herself, or else will give up. His task is to build Her trust in Him so that She knows He means it when He says He will do something. If She stops trusting His certainty, She may stop giving Him the vision. If She stops giving Him the vision, He may lose His certainty, or else revert to his old separatist ways.

She wants Him to be Her passionate lover. She wants to know that She is the most important feminine energy in the world to Him and that He is passionately devoted to Her. She wants a lover in every sense of the word: sexually, spiritually, emotionally, and intellectually. In other words, She wants Him to be Her soul mate and Her perfect lover.

Your feminine must always be the only feminine energy your masculine pursues. She is a jealous lover and greatly resents anything taking priority over Her vision. His task is to be fully devoted to Her. If your masculine follows other visions, like those of your partner's feminine, for instance, He will lose sight of your feminine. He will also be incapable of creating the boundaries that guide Her visionary process. This very dynamic is the foundation for addiction and codependency that I discussed in Chapter 9. If the masculine cannot be Her passionate lover, the feminine will turn against Him. If He denies or abuses Her vision She will stop giving it to Him. If that happens you'll have to gently coach Her back into revealing Her truth.

What Our Internal Masculine Wants from Our Internal Feminine

He wants Her to be a safe harbor, working with Him, not against Him. The masculine longs for a feminine who will be so committed to Their relationship that She will stay connected to Him rather than dismissing His needs. Most importantly, He wants Her not to pick on Him when he doesn't do things exactly the way She would like them done.

The feminine, being the visionary, sees only how to get some-where in a straight line that leads to the vision. This may not necessarily be the most successful path. The masculine, in contrast, may go in a wide and erratic circle to accomplish the feminine's vision. If the internal feminine repeatedly berates the masculine for the way He has done something, He will soon lose confidence and stop manifesting for Her. He will also stop being the source of fun and love that She wants Him to be. The role of the feminine in Their relationship is to trust and honor the methodology of the masculine. The feminine also needs to honor the slower pace of His process, as He operates in the world of form, which emphasizes timing and focus on detail.

He wants Her to be the vision. The masculine needs the feminine to do Her job and provide the vision of where They are to go next. If She encourages Him in fulfilling Her vision, He will eventually believe in His ability to manifest with Her.

Since the internal feminine is the visionary, it is imperative to Their relationship that She keep encouraging the masculine. She must enthusiastically support His decisions as He strives to fulfill Her vision. It is not enough to tell Him what She wants. She must also encourage Him and get out of the way so that He can do His job. Once He believes that He can fulfill His function, the pas-sionate inner marriage will be in full flow.

He wants Her to stay involved in the dance with Him and wants Her to keep spurring Him on. This means that She promises to never give up Their connection and to keep maintaining the juice between Them. This keeps Their relationship evolving and strong.

The unfortunate thing is that the feminine is often too willing to give up on Their relationship. She will quit too soon when the going gets rough. When this happens She no longer honors the masculine, and doesn't act as the safe harbor that He desires Her to be. He responds in the only way He knows, and withdraws. Then He is no longer fun, and stops being Her passionate lover. It is a very sad state for both of Them.

Knowing that manifesting is His duty, the masculine may have a hard time expressing Himself. He may be afraid to speak up when He can't accomplish Her vision. When this happens, the feminine must be willing to slow down for Him. She can learn to support Him by realizing how courageous He must be to acknowledge His limits and say, "No, I can't do that."

When He isn't certain about following Her direction, She must ask Him "What isn't clear? What else do you need to know about this?" If He doesn't want to talk, then She needs to lovingly support Him until He can answer Her. She shouldn't go one step further with the vision until He opens up again. He cannot be ignored or put down, because this will always lead to disaster.

How Do You Know You Are Loved?

In order to function well with the desires of your internal masculine and feminine, you will find it helpful if you determine your own list of criteria for how you "know" you are loved. Consult your masculine and feminine when you do this. They will each give you different responses. Write down Their responses and make a list of two hundred qualities that you want in a partner and in a relationship. The point in working with two hundred qualities is you will really refine your desires to a fine point as to what you want in a relationship. Be sure to list the ways that signal love to you. For instance, I know I'm loved when someone keeps in touch by phone or letter.

We usually don't define our criteria for happiness in a relationship, as powerful as they are, even to ourselves. You must discover "how" you know you are loved. This knowledge takes the guesswork out of it for your partner. Your partner will now know exactly what to do to let you know that she or he loves you. You should also have your partner's criteria list for what they want in a mate.

We have a tendency to take whoever comes along without really discerning whether this person is someone we can be happy with over a lifetime. We are much more careful about buying a car than we are about choosing a partner. We research the best cars on the market for our needs, check out the color, the gas mileage, and the options. Isn't it strange that our relationships don't get the same consideration? Your criteria list can change all that. Your internal criteria list becomes a blueprint for future choices, totally without your conscious awareness. It is essential to bring this list out into the open, so you can make conscious decisions.

I was once sharing a house with Lynn, a good friend. We had our first argument and we were both devastated by the anger that arose. That night Lynn came home with a horror video. The significance of that movie was that I love to watch horror movies and Lynn is absolutely repulsed by them. It was very touching to me to know that this was her way of saying that our friendship mattered and that she was sorry. Doing such a simple thing is so healing to our relationships.

As you make your list, please be very precise. Don't just say, "I want a partner who has a sense of humor." After all, they might tell barroom jokes. That may be all right with you, but if it isn't, then define your idea of perfect humor. I would say I want a mate who has a sense of humor and the ability to laugh at himself and life. This will give you the beginning understanding of what you are really looking for. You will be surprised to discover that many of your criteria will have been established during your childhood. You will also want to rewrite your list periodically because as your feminine and masculine grow, your list will change dramatically.

How Their Inner Relationship Affects Your External Love Affair

Most of us long to see the qualities described above in the partners we choose. We all want to be with someone who isn't overly critical of us, who inspires us, who keeps the game going, and is fun—someone who believes in us and who will stay in the relationship with us. Our mistake is that instead of pressuring our mate to provide these qualities, we need to focus on our inner relationship to provide us with these qualities.

Chances are that if you continue to work on your inner marriage, you will more likely get what you want from your partner. When your internal masculine and feminine stop meeting each other's basic needs, Their conflict will show up in your external relationships.

For instance, if your masculine isn't strong and certain, you may draw someone to you who isn't trustworthy in a relationship. If your feminine doesn't trust the masculine, then you will most likely be distrustful of men and will draw a man who doesn't trust women or isn't trustworthy.

Your external problems are often a reflection of an internal discordance. There are always danger signs that indicate any internal war. When the men in your life are acting up, go inside and see what is wrong with your internal masculine. Check to see what He needs and what He is upset about. When the women in your life are acting up, go inside and check with Her and see if you can determine what is going on. In either case, check with both of Them so that you understand Their perspective.

Peggy was a successful young businesswoman who had a fairly good relationship with her husband Dwayne. They were usually able to work out any differences without trouble. Both were very calm people who were able to articulate their desires and needs. Then Peggy started on an exciting new project that had a very strong chance of pushing her close to the top of her corporation. She was very excited about this project and dove into it. She lived, ate, and breathed this project for several weeks, striving to finish it ahead of schedule.

When Peggy first came to me, she told me she and Dwayne were continually arguing, and that these arguments couldn't seem to come to any conclusion. The two of them usually ended up walking away from each other, hurt and disappointed. She said that their arguments were like nightmares. Dwayne wouldn't let go of an issue and would hound her to the point where she would explode in a tantrum. These tantrums of Peggy's were even more upsetting to her than to Dwayne, because she was normally calm natured. Peggy figured that Dwayne was upset at the changes in their relationship that had occurred when she began working so much, but she was surprised at this development. She had been extremely busy at other times because of work and it had never created such a problem before.

We talked to Peggy's masculine and she was surprised by what she discovered. As I suspected, Peggy's masculine was outraged. He had been trying to tell Peggy and her feminine to slow down with this project. The masculine couldn't back up the desire of Peggy's feminine to rise higher in the corporate structure at such a breakneck speed. Peggy wasn't listening to His messages. Then Peggy remembered that she had been having a stiff neck for the last two weeks. She had also pulled her lower back a few days earlier. These back and neck problems were her masculine's messages to slow down.

Once I explained to Peggy that Dwayne's behavior was a reflection of her inner masculine, she then understood her part in the dynamic. I told Peggy that Dwayne would probably calm down if her feminine started listening to her own masculine. Sure enough, after several inner conversations, Peggy slowed down in her feverish attempts to finish the project early, only to find out that she had overlooked a big problem that would have caused a lot of trouble for the project a year down the line. At that point her inner masculine calmed down and so did Dwayne.

How to Follow Her in Your Relationships

Are you looking for a good relationship with a wonderful, loving and supportive, yet exciting person? Stop looking out there and start looking inside. The qualities you desire in a partner are the qualities your masculine and feminine desire in each other. As you work on Their ability to give these qualities to each other, you will begin to see these same qualities reflected in the people you attract.

Working on your external relationships will give you some of the most challenging exercises that you could possibly face in developing your inner marriage because you will have constant feedback on the accuracy of your choices and the strength of your follow-through. When you follow your feminine you learn to pay attention to the juice. You do the same in any external relationship, whether long term or brief. You will want to continually check with your feminine so She can guide you step-by-step. Let me show you how you do this through the experience of a client.

At one of my workshops a woman named Milly stood up and said, "I have a good friend who keeps wanting to make our relationship more romantic. Should I go further or not?" When I first talked to Milly's feminine She didn't know what She wanted. I broke the decision up into small questions to answer:

"Do you want to continue to be his friend?"

"Yes."

"Do you feel sexually attracted to him?"

"Yes."

"What would be the problem if you became his lover?"

Milly's feminine said, "I don't like the way he treats his women. I would get very angry if he tried to control me like he does them."

I instructed Milly to go inside and concentrate on her solar plexus. I then told her I was going to make two statements and she was to listen to each, paying attention to her body's reactions.

First I said, "You are going to be his lover" and allowed a pause. I then said, "You are not going to be his lover."

After another pause, I asked her, "What did you feel?" Milly said, "I felt a tightness in my solar plexus when you said I was going to be his lover. I felt an enormous release and relief when you said I wasn't going to be his lover." Now Milly knew that she needed to keep this man as a friend and not wander into the danger zone of romantic involvement. I told Milly that she should keep checking with her feminine as time went on, because the message could change along the way.

Milly said that the next time she got involved she was going to go much more slowly than she normally did, so she could keep checking in with the feminine. Good advice for everyone. She and her friend never did become romantically involved, but now Milly knows a lot more about how to choose her mates.

You might think to yourself, "I always follow the juice but I still get into trouble." Why? It is only when your inner relationship is finely honed that you can create the balance needed to be sensitive to the subtle signals from Him and Her. It is only then that you can truly understand why you are experiencing the juice for a person, and if that juice is a good sign or not. Your masculine can monitor the juice. If you follow only Her juice, you are bound to create difficulties and heartbreak for yourself and others. With Her we often choose partners who give us a real charge, but the relationship can be unrealistic or even devastating. This is a typical pattern for those who have trouble with codependency. I discussed this in Chapter 9.

Conversely, it rarely works when we allow our internal masculine to choose our relationships. He will pick partners for business reasons, or to ease his survival issues. He will also choose someone who either reflects His own image, or who is like the feminine He wishes He was partnered with. When you are interested in someone, yet feel a deadness, don't get involved. Your feminine isn't turned on to this person and your masculine is pushing the issue.

Your masculine and feminine can create a balanced decision if you consult Them from the very beginning and also along the way. Pay attention to the juice from the feminine, but also let your masculine check out the reality of being in a relationship with that person. If you were to follow these precautions, you would probably not get into most of the relationships that you do, and certainly wouldn't stay as long in the ones that are not right for you.

Your masculine has the ability to make or break a relationship. His highest function is to go in and out of relationships as She wills it. If She is wild and irresponsible He will want to slow Her down. Without His boundaries She can be flighty or sexually addicted and will pick one partner after another, never really choosing a mate who will make Her happy. When He tempers Her, She becomes wiser about Her choices and moves more slowly in relationships.

Your masculine can also help you resolve problems in a relationship. He can also help you remove blocks that are keeping you from having a good relationship. I told Milly that she might consider talking to her friend about her concerns in the relationship that she was considering. I suggested that she tell him she felt strongly that he would have to make some real changes in the way he treated women before she would even think of getting involved with him. This kind of action is a function of your internal masculine.

Your internal duo will need to support each other in successfully choosing a mate and in maintaining a relationship. Remember to never discount the responses you get from either of Them. Never go past His ability to back up a relationship. When He says He can't do it, believe Him. He might not be able to follow Her wishes, but you can acknowledge Her desires and then tell your feminine that She will have to wait. When your masculine can back up the feminine, but is wavering, have your feminine encourage Him to take a chance. You can act as mediator. As you work with both of Them They will come to have what They both desire.

To Stay or Not To Stay

At times in a relationship you may begin to feel a deadness with your partner. This may mean that your feminine's vision is leading you to no longer be with him or her. Don't live with that deadness, especially if it has been there for a long time. This doesn't mean you should give up the dance with your mate easily. When the deadness comes, you should either heal the emotional blocks that led to the deadness or else separate.

I urge you to really try to keep the relationship going. Your feminine may have turned off to your mate for reasons that can be easily rectified. Before you start pointing a finger at your partner as to why you feel dead, turn within. You may discover that the deadness is coming from your own inner marriage. Inner communication may be a way through this dead feeling, and being sensitive to your inner relationship will greatly help you define the real problems in your external relationship. If your internal relationship is in good working order, then She is really turned off to your partner. If this is the case, get your feminine to be really honest about what it is about your partner that bothers Her.

It may be an accumulation of many small things that is causing the problem, rather than one large thing. Often, resolving all of the small problems leads to a breakthrough. You will also have to determine whether or not the problems bother you so much that you can't stay in the relationship without changing them.

Now it's time for real communication between you and your partner. Tell your partner exactly how you feel and why. See what behaviors your mate is willing to change. If your partner is unwilling to change, then the juice will deaden even more, and you will have to leave the relationship—unless you can get your partner involved in his or her own internal journey. Through the integration of your partner's own internal duo he or she may become much more flexible.

If you and your partner are both willing to work at creating change, then set a time period (like three months) by which you expect to see real change. Keep the commitment to work on the relationship, without reservation, until that time even though the juice may still be dead.

Don't make your commitment for too short a term. Change is usually not going to happen rapidly. You should stay in the relationship long enough to clear away any harmful beliefs that your internal masculine and feminine have established during this time. Even if you do break up after the agreed-upon time, you will have stayed in the relationship until you are clear of some of your debilitating thought patterns. Otherwise you will just carry those patterns into a new relationship. *Never, never leave a relationship until your internal masculine is really ready to take that action, or until your feminine is really willing to go.*

Pay attention to the juice. Never take for granted Her continued interest in a partner. Over time, if you still feel a strong juice to be with a person that you know is not right for you, then She is trying to teach you something. Sometimes She chooses mates for you to learn a particular lesson or to expand your ability to love. You will know when She is willing to let go of the relationship and when it is time to move on. You may only discover in retrospect why She wanted you to continue on for a while with this person.

Rachel's masculine was so strong that He always chased away any man who came into Rachel's life. It was simply easier for Him to do it all Himself, and He didn't want anyone else around. As long as Rachel's internal masculine was so strong this same pattern of short-term relationships continued. While Rachel was working with me she met a man whom her feminine loved but whom her masculine didn't care for. Even though He didn't like the feminine's decision, Rachel's masculine agreed to follow and support Her. The relationship was dramatic and filled with turmoil. Rachel's masculine constantly threatened to walk off and forget the whole thing, but her feminine continued to have the juice to stay. Rachel's masculine kept following the feminine's lead, against His better judgment.

The relationship lasted a year, longer than any of Rachel's previous relationships. During that time Rachel softened. She became much more receptive and open to Her internal guidance, and to having a long-term relationship at all. Her tone of voice and demeanor became warmer and more inviting. She began wearing softer, more flowing clothes rather than extremely tailored suits. She also seemed to be happier.

After Rachel finally broke off this chaotic relationship, there was only a short interval before she met a new man. This new relationship turned out to be wonderful. Despite the strain and turmoil of Rachel's previous relationship, and the terrible year that she had gone through, Rachel could look back and see how much she had changed. It was obvious to her how critical these changes were in order for her to be happy now. She could see that her internal feminine had wanted her to stay in that old relationship so that Her masculine and feminine could transform Their own relationship. This enabled Rachel to go on to have a much more suitable relationship. It's now five years since she met her new mate and they plan to wed this summer.

Using Inner Dialogue to Transform Your External Relationships

I'd like to give you some examples of how you can use your masculine and feminine to enhance your external relationships. These examples will help you develop your ability to tell which internal voices are your masculine and feminine, and which are the voices of old patterns.

Joyce came to me because her marriage appeared to be breaking up. She and her husband loved each other very much but it didn't seem to matter anymore. She was having an extra-marital affair but wasn't happy about that either. Joyce and I had the following conversation with her internal masculine and feminine:

I: (*To the feminine*) How do you feel about the internal masculine right now?

FEM: I love Him but He never pays any attention to me. I'm bored.

I: What would He have to do to make things different?

FEM: Well, He is always paying more attention to Joyce's husband than to me. He would have to love me the most.

I: We'll see what we can do about that. But I want to know how you feel about Joyce's husband.

FEM: He's just like my masculine. My masculine is more interested in the outside world, and Joyce's husband is married to his job. I just can't seem to get what I want.

I: Have you told your internal masculine exactly what you want?

FEM: Sort of.

I: Well there's part of the problem. That also means that you haven't clearly discussed this with your husband. I want you to speak with your masculine and to tell Him clearly what your needs are. Tell Him the problems, and tell Him what you want.

FEM: *(She was quiet for almost ten minutes.)* I want you to passionately pursue me, not anyone else. If you will take time for me and be my lover, I will give you all your heart's desires.

I: That's good. Now let me talk to Him. *(I connected Joyce to her internal masculine and then said to Him)* You've heard what the feminine just said. How do you feel about it?

MASC: First of all She has never been direct about wanting more attention from me. She hints at it. I guess She's really unhappy with me because She picks on me all the time. It makes me kind of angry that She didn't speak up because I would have done something about it before it became such a serious problem.

I: How do you feel about Her right now?

MASC: Well, I'm annoyed and surprised. She goes around pretending that She is communicating. I'm not a mind reader, you know; if She wants something from me, She had better tell me more clearly.

I: Well, She just gave you a clear message. Can you take care of it?

MASC: Certainly I can, although I am not quite sure what to do about the husband.

I: How do you like the husband?

MASC: I like him, but I guess we do act alike. What should I do?

I: Well, first of all there is nothing you can do about the husband. He has to make his own changes. We will get the feminine to give you stronger, clearer messages like we just did. Then I want you to use the husband as a reflection of how you are doing. As you change, the pressure will be on the husband to deal with Joyce more effectively.

MASC: Okay, I can do that.

Joyce and I then mapped out a series of discussions she would have with her husband. She would not blame him, but would simply tell him about her own internal dialogue, and about the realization she had of how her own masculine was ignoring her own feminine. She told her husband that she was working hard to change her internal duo. She also told him that her internal masculine was just like him, and that they needed to talk seriously about some changes that needed to be made.

Three weeks later she gave up her affair and began to work in earnest on her marriage. Once she was free of the affair she became much more loving and understanding. Joyce's husband began to soften and ultimately began working with me. Now they work on themselves regularly and on their fifteen-year marriage. They have fallen in love again and have renewed their sexual passion, which had been dying.

A second example concerns Bob, who came to me because he was involved in three relationships at once and sometimes thought he wanted them all and at other times didn't want any of them. He had a wild, wonderful feminine who wanted every woman She saw. (Whether you are a man or a woman, the feminine is the one who chooses the partners.) Bob's masculine was just a young boy who couldn't really back up any relationship at the time. We had the following conversation:

I: The masculine simply isn't grown up enough to be involved in any relationship now.

SHE: That isn't fair. I just feel like spreading my wings and being with lots of people.

I: Wouldn't you like to have what you want deep down inside? Like less hassle from women?

SHE: Well, that would certainly be a relief. But what do I do about the women who are around right now?

I: I think you need to really narrow down the field. Look at the first woman and see if you are really attached to her.

SHE: Actually I'm not. It was fun for a while, but I don't really need that relationship anymore.

I: Now look at the second woman.

SHE: I'm kind of attached to her but I don't want the relationship to become more serious. I think it's time to let go of this one, too.

The feminine wasn't quite through with the one remaining woman. For two months Bob kept meeting with this woman, noticing that little by little the juice was dying and that his perceptions of the possibilities were changing. He began to see that the two of them weren't well suited. Eventually they broke up and now he is not with anyone. He wants time alone to become better acquainted with his own internal love affair.

Guidelines for a Successful Relationship

In his book, *The Psychology of Romantic Love*, Dr. Nathaniel Branden lists the elements common to long-lasting and loving relationships. Many years ago, when I first read Dr. Branden's criteria for romantic love, they seemed impossibly demanding to me. Over the years I have discovered that achieving this kind of love is quite possible, both internally and externally.

I offer you some of those criteria so you can use it as a guideline for developing Him and Her until They have a wonderful romantic love affair. You may want to adapt these criteria to your external relationships. Dr. Branden says that couples who stay in love do things like talking about their love for each other and verbally expressing it. They want to be together because they respect and appreciate each other. They make sure that they have time to be completely alone together. They share their deepest inner feelings and want to hear about their partner's feelings as well. They genuinely want to care for one another and forgive one another for not being perfect. Their lovemaking is above average.

Are you or have you ever been in a relationship like this? The quality of your external relationships, like your internal relationship, is dependent upon the level of communication you can achieve with the other party. I have an exercise below that can help you begin that process. It incorporates the help of the masculines and feminines of you and your partner.

COMMUNICATING

First just talk together for about fifteen minutes, clearly outlining the issues you face in your relationship. At that time, each of you should share your thoughts about what you want from each other. You are not permitted to answer your partner's requests nor is your partner allowed to answer yours. Please do not defend yourselves or make excuses for the way things are. Simply take in the information from your partner.

Now go inside, and each of you access your feminine. Take turns listening to your feminine as She gives you Her perspective of the issues. You might want take a look at the exercise at the end of Chapter 7 for guidance.

Then have each of you access your masculine, and allow the two masculines to speak to each other. You may have to do mediation work, in which case one of you should be the client and the other the mediator. Finally, talk to each other about any new insights and resolutions that might have occurred while both of you listened to your masculine and feminine, and then finish completing the conversation between your mate and yourself.

At the end of such a session you should be well on your way to understanding what behaviors you need to change and how to do it. Here are some guidelines for being in a relationship and staying true to your masculine and feminine:

1. Never forsake your internal feminine.
2. Pay attention to Her signals.

3. Always check with the internal masculine to see if He can or will back up Her vision.
4. Never ignore His inability to back up your feminine's vision.
5. Be willing to live with the outcomes of your actions even if they don't all turn out exactly as you envisioned.

The only relationship that is yours for a lifetime is the one with your internal masculine and feminine. They will always be there for you, no matter what. Cherish Them and love Them, and you will be filled with a love that you have never known. Your whole presence and body will radiate that love. Then you will attract the external love that you've always desired.

TWELVE

Your Passionate Inner Union: The Foundation for Life Mastery

> [The passionate inner marriage] is an evolutionary, neverending process—always exciting, sometimes fearsome, because the direction is unknown, the future unpredictable. It is, however, satisfying beyond anything else in life.
>
> —Shirley Gehrke Luthman,
> *Intimacy: The Essence of Male and Female*

*Y*ou can live your life as a victim or as a master. You have the power to choose. Most people immediately say, "Of course, I would prefer to have mastery over my experiences." The problem is that it takes time and discipline to develop any kind of mastery, especially when that mastery involves all the diverse skills necessary to live modern-day life successfully. Fortunately, your masculine and feminine possess all the necessary skills between the two of Them.

Your mastery can unfold through the passionate union of your internal feminine and masculine. If you have followed the exercises in this book, you have already begun your evolution. As your feminine grows in giving you your direction She becomes the state of wisdom and direct knowing. As your masculine grows in His power, He will develop mastery in fulfilling Her visions. As you develop your inner marriage, you will discover that you have unlimited power and discernment (Him) and unlimited creativity and wisdom (Her). They will embrace in a passionate dance of life and become an invincible team united in a very important cause, which is you. Your words, your actions, your thoughts and feelings, and even your body will all radiate the energy and excitement of Their union. You will become more in tune with your strengths and abilities. Your intuition and logic will create a double flow of energy, which will allow you to live and move in a condition of love.

As a result of your inner love affair, you will have a new life that is filled with more love than you could ever have imagined. A basic law of physics states that the activity of one atom affects the movement of all atoms around it. Like the ripples in a pond that follow after the splash of a rock, this influence progresses out into the far reaches of the universe. The results of the feelings between our internal masculine and feminine fall under this same law of physics, creating a rolling motion that extends out from us toward others. Our internal nature sends out a particular kind of energy that is then reflected back to us. This draws certain conditions and circumstances to us. The miracle is that we can change the nature of the energy that is rippling out from us, and then being reflected back into our lives.

When I speak of mastery, I am not just referring to samurai warriors or gurus who dedicate every waking moment to training and meditating in order to become masters. I am talking about having the power to remain centered, to utilizing both your intuition and logic as you perform your daily functions. This is the core purpose of working on your inner marriage.

I have seen people from every walk of life who I feel exhibit profound mastery. Once, while traveling in Minnesota, I met a farmer at a country store. There was a storm brewing in the sky. We began to talk about his land and the way he farmed it. He said that he simply knew when it was time to plant, when it was time to bring the crop in, and when disaster was coming. He told me that when he was a youth he had sometimes tarried rather than following through on his gut feeling and how he suffered the consequences. He talked about the reverence he felt as he turned the earth over and as he watched the miracle of growth. He told me that when he was working with the earth, he experienced his divinity.

It has been said that when someone is a master, others are affected by his or her presence and are often profoundly changed. When I left the farmer, I could feel myself expand with love and

wisdom. I felt inspired and more whole. He is an example of a true
master living in ordinary circumstances.

Masters have had many labels. In native cultures they are sha-
mans; in medieval cultures they were sorcerers. In business, I call
someone who has this level of mastery a "Corporate Magician."
They seem to pull miracles out of the air, to take risks that seem
crazy to others, and then turn those risks into success. Few people
think of business people as masters, yet some of the most well
balanced and visionary people in the world are found within the
business community. To be a master is to be able to fully use one's
intuitive and logical abilities in a way that not only enhances one's
own life, but the lives of others as well.

Mastery is not necessarily deliberate control and manipulation
of external circumstances. You can't always control what happens
in your life, but you can master your responses to what life brings
you. You can also develop more control over the way your life
progresses simply by realizing that much of life is a mirror of your
internal state. You can't be victimized by life when you know how
to make the internal adjustments that will lead you to success in
every area of your life.

The Patience to Move toward Perfection

Even though you may have now experienced your passionate inner
marriage, you are not automatically at the end of your journey, nor
are you fully integrated. Integration is a process that occurs over
time. There are many pitfalls and stumbling blocks to maintaining
your inner marriage. This is where time and discipline come in.
You can easily become distracted and overconfident as you progress
on the path of mastery. The only way to succeed in the long run
is through patience. Mastery is not an end result. Once you feel
that you are a master, you are really only at the bottom rung of
living your life.

Don't get discouraged when, after a period of falling in love
and experiencing a graceful state, you suddenly find that the grace
is gone and that you once again feel cut off and separated inside.

Your feminine and masculine will, for some time, have to learn to work with one another as new situations emerge. She has to learn to give clear, manageable visions and to adjust the speed of Her vision to His ability to manifest. He has to learn to let go of forms and build new ones as She leaps in a new direction.

For a long time your masculine and feminine will periodically separate, become one, then separate, again and again. At these times you may become concerned that you are dealing with dichotomy and separation rather than the wholeness you really desire. If you can accept these dichotomies, rather than pretending they don't exist, you have a wonderful opportunity to really heal. Your job is to keep focusing on Their passionate union. When you are having problems getting your world of form to match your vision, try these activating phrases, "I want a body that matches spirit" or "I want a masculine who matches my feminine."

As you build toward Their union, your masculine and feminine might waver in the forms in which They appear. You may find yourself falling back on the same old patterns that once plagued you before you started working with your internal duo. For some people this may show up as a feeling of deadness, for others confusion or anger. You may feel a lot of pressure and stress as you work on yourself. This is particularly true if you have more than one feminine or more than one masculine. One day the strong one may be present, whereas the next day the child may appear. When this happens, your task is to keep on with your internal process. You will find that your process of change continues just as long as you don't give up. As Shirley Luthman states at the beginning of this chapter, our inner marriage is an ever-continuing process.

A stumbling block to maintaining your inner marriage is an inability to remain in the present. This simple concept is extremely important. Some people live in the past and are always making comparisons between then and now. Others live in the future, fearing possible outcomes and waiting until "things are different." If you devote your thoughts and emotions to planning for the future or wishing for the past, you will create an internal dialogue so loud you will be incapable of receiving your feminine's messages and acting upon them. When you lose touch with Her vision, you stand the risk of your masculine taking over, or your feminine running off without Him. You will be once again living in the shadow of

Their distorted relationship, the harmony and flow gone again.

Continue to trust in your process. Do not judge your thoughts and actions—merely observe. Self-judgment is one of the biggest stumbling blocks to receiving Her messages. It is a very difficult task for most of us to accept our physical, mental, and emotional limitations. We often deny our weaknesses and vulnerabilities, even to ourselves, and become upset or enraged when someone tries to point out those weaknesses to us. We also become exasperated and unforgiving of ourselves, which devastates the ability of our feminine and masculine to function together. An unforgiving attitude involves placing blame either on oneself or somewhere else. No one can thrive under the shadow of blame. This is true even for our internal masculine and feminine. If your feminine and masculine are blaming each other, then Their dance stops and your growth ceases.

Another major obstacle to the passionate union of your feminine and masculine is the attempt to elevate yourself above the human condition. Mind you, we all do this in one form or another. But, there are many people who thoroughly reject human emotions, desires, and the problems they confront as human beings. These people focus on "higher" pursuits and are somehow above being human. This is an undeniably severe block to personal growth.

I find that individuals who are deeply absorbed in self-growth are the most likely to reject their humanity. While they might be willing to heal and teach the masses, they basically find the human experience discordant with the way they perceive a higher spiritual state. Nothing could be further from the truth. The more enlightened one is, the more human one becomes. Ram Das talks about how much he used to "know" before he was enlightened. The further he went along his spiritual path the more human he became.

The journey toward perfection is actually the opposite of eliminating human foibles. Our challenge is to live in the world as it is, doing what we are doing while we attempt to better ourselves. Those who seek to live only in the "higher realms" of existence, keeping themselves separate from all that they are meant to embrace, are living in a fool's paradise. We must fully own the normal human experience and be willing to jump right into the middle of the fray, to *move through* life's pain and inconsistency rather than trying to deny or avoid our experience. We must develop compassion for our human frailties.

I have a marvelous male friend who just went through this very lesson. He has a profound gift for teaching. While he is warm and people oriented, there was something about him that made people feel uncomfortable. His communications are loving, but there was once something in his demeanor that people subconsciously picked up, which created a lack of trust when they were near him. My friend came to discuss this with me after he had received the same feedback from several people. He was surprised that people perceived him as untrustworthy because he knew that he was honest and loving.

As we explored what there was about him that could be giving this message, I suddenly intuited that, in spite of his wonderful ability to teach and share, my friend's heart was very closed to the human experience. I told this to him. In a moment of surprised revelation, he told me that at an early age he had decided that it was beneath him to be human. His life, he said, was to be a journey of holy communion only with God. This meant he had spent his whole life staying away from the pitfalls of being human. He was afraid that if he became part of life he would be sucked into human depravity. As a result, when this man interacted with others, they felt unseen or a little dismissed by him. How could they not? He was rejecting his own human essence and therefore everyone else's. The more he refused to accept himself as human the more his life fell apart, and the more he embodied the very things he fought against.

Rejection of your own humanity blocks all intimacy, including the intimacy between your feminine and masculine. Your ability to receive the abundance that is rightfully yours begins with the openness and love between these two. All else follows. Your love for others is merely a mirror of the love that He and She hold for one another. Conversely, the degree of love you feel from others is a mirror of your own internal union.

Another stumbling block to maintaining your inner marriage is arrogance. It is deceptively easy to manifest subtle arrogance as one becomes more adept and powerful. Our egos like to hold on to our accomplishments and to exaggerate them. If you are consumed by arrogance, prepare yourself for your hardest lessons as you work with your masculine and feminine. You will be knocked off your feet.

If you keep control of your attachment to end results, you will receive many pleasant surprises. You never know exactly how things will turn out when He backs up Her vision. I call this "living life free fall." Successful business people do this all the time. There have been many examples where people completely changed their business focus only to become a greater success. They were able to deal with what could have been a disastrous twist of circumstances and to flexibly adapt so that things worked in their favor. The famous Post-it Notes™ by 3M manufacturing were the result of a mistake. Instead of throwing the mistake away, the people at 3M started using the glue that "didn't work" to post memos to each other. Because of this, we are now able to use this mistake for our benefit.

You will continually work on the stumbling blocks in your inner marriage just as you do in external relationships. It is this process that likens us to stones tumbling against each other to reveal the gems inside. For this reason we must be willing to continually come in contact with others, as they are our polishing stones. This process can be an adventure filled with joy and new beginnings. The more you do this work the more you establish the foundation of inner love that will radiate out into the world, bringing you all that you have dreamed of.

As a gift to you I have a special wedding invitation. It is to your own inner marriage. When your masculine and feminine are working together and have discovered the harmony of Their love, you can plan Their wedding ceremony. DO NOT DO THIS CEREMONY UNTIL HE AND SHE ARE REALLY IN LOVE AND YOU HAVE CHECKED IN WITH THEM TO SEE IF THIS IS A GOOD IDEA.

You may tape the ceremony you create, so that you can easily experience Their love, or you might want to have one of your friends officiate. Treat this ceremony just as you would if this were a real wedding to a fabulous partner. Set the date and decide where you would really like to be married. Go check this place out and see where everyone will stand. Prepare what you will wear, what kind of flowers you will have, and whether or not you will have candles. Arrange to play special music. You might have more fun at your inner wedding ceremony if you put the following story on tape so that you can play it during the ceremony. Then you can devote your attention to your masculine and feminine completely as They go through the wedding to one another.

THE WEDDING CEREMONY

See your inner masculine and feminine begin the wedding procession and stop in front of the person who is officiating. As They stand together, listen to the story of Their love:

This is the day in which we gather together to celebrate the glory of Their love and Their passion. They have come from the beginning of time for this union. They tell this ancient story:

Once the world was only dichotomy, only black and white. He dressed in black and was mired in the mud of the earth. She dressed in white and moved constantly through the heavens, never able to touch the earth.

She often looked down upon the earth to see Him. Her desire for the earth and for Him was great. She had come near Him for centuries, loving Him, wanting to caress Him. Often She said in His ear, "Come away with me and be my love."

Each time She had whispered this, His heart had leapt and He wanted desperately to go. But always the earth held Him fast.

Each time She touched Him and He turned back to the earth, She wanted to stay but She could not. Movement called Her and She turned to leap through the universe.

Their yearnings for one another grew. She began to see that without Him Her world was nebulous and unreal and She wanted His divine manifestation. He looked at His world and saw the deadness there. He wanted Her movement more than the world of form.

One day as She came toward Him, the radiance of Her beauty brought tears to His eyes; and He reached more toward Her.

As She felt the depth of His sweetness, His strength, and His courage, She reached toward Him more strongly than ever. Their fingertips touched but still They could not maintain Their contact because the mud held Him fast and the movement swept Her away.

She continued to visit Him each day. Each time She beckoned and each time He reached for Her, She became more a part of Him and He a part of Her. They continued to reach for one another.

Day after day They sought each other. Finally, in one grand burst of energy, They managed to embrace and Their embrace lifted Him from the mud. Together, They soared up into the sky. In that moment the world of the rainbow and wholeness was born. Heaven came to earth.

On some days They walked upon the earth and had children and built homes. On other days They soared through the sky, touching the stars and dancing with the clouds.

On special days, in our own lifetime, in special moments of sky and light and water and earth, we can see Them dancing across the sky in the form of a rainbow.

If you listen carefully with your heart, you can still hear Her say, "Come, come with me, and I will take you places you have never been before."

And He, with a masterful stroke, will reach out to Her and say, "I am here my love. I will do anything for you."

We have seen His form emerge to match Her vision. We have seen the splendor of Their dance together. This is the passionate union. This is the love affair that we have all sought.

This love affair is to be found only within. Each time you choose to follow Her energy, you build His radiant form. Each time She says, "Come and I will reveal God to you," and He says, "Yes, I am with you always," She grows in strength, He grows in courage. Their compassion begins to fill your life. They are love.

As they join now in you, in perfect union, have your masculine and feminine face one another.

Internal Feminine, out loud repeat after me these vows:

I will always be with you.

I will give you my vision and energy.

You are my beloved.

Internal Masculine, out loud repeat after me:

I will always be with you.

I will give you strength, courage, and will manifest your dreams.

You are my beloved.

I now declare your inner masculine and feminine as a passionate inner marriage. The groom may now kiss the bride.

Pause.

Feel Her shimmering inside of you, moving to life's music.

Feel your body begin to pulse with His power.

Feel Her beginning to move inside of you and Him beginning to follow Her. Feel Them moving in perfect union and harmony.

Feel Them beginning to entwine in one another's arms passionately and sensuously making love to one another.

May your inner marriage last through the end of time and bring you the manifestation of many joys and dreams. May you bask in the glow of Their unfolding experience of love and may They always dance happily together.

Bibliography

BRANDEN, NATHANIEL. *The Disowned Self*. Nash Publishing: Los Angeles, 1971.

BRANDEN, NATHANIEL. *The Psychology of Romantic Love*. Jeremy P. Tarcher, Inc.: Los Angeles, 1980.

BRANDEN, NATHANIEL. *The Romantic Love Question and Answer Book*. Jeremy P. Tarcher, Inc.: Los Angeles, 1982.

BRONOWSKI, J. *The Ascent of Man*. Little, Brown and Company: Boston/Toronto, 1973.

"Cellular 'Reward Seeking' Offers Clues to Addiction," *Brain/Mind Bulletin*. December, 1989, p. 6.

CLAREMONT DE CASTILLO, IRENE. *Knowing Woman: A Feminine Psychology*. Harper Colophon: New York, 1973.

COLEMAN, WIM AND PAT PERRIN. *Marilyn Ferguson's Book of PragMagic*. Pocket Books: New York, 1990.

COLE–WHITTAKER, TERRY. *The Inner Path From Where You Are to Where You Want to Be*. Valentine Books: New York, 1987.

The Encyclopedia of Religion. 'Androgynes' Vol. 1. Macmillan Publishing: New York, 1987, pp. 276–28.

FADIMAN, JAMES AND ROBERT FRAGER. *Personality and Personal Growth*. Harper & Row: New York, 1976.

FARBER, S.M. AND H.L. WILSON. *The Potential of Woman*. McGraw-Hill Publishing: New York, 1963.

FERGUSON, MARILYN. *PragMagic*. Pocket Books: New York, 1990.

FILLMORE, CHARLES. *Keep A True Lent*. Unity School of Christianity: Lee's Summit, Missouri, 1965.

GAWAIN, SHAKTI. *Creative Visualization.* Bantam Books: New York, 1978.

GAWAIN, SHAKTI. *Living in the Light.* Whatever Publishing: San Rafael, California, 1986.

GERBER, RICHARD, M.D. *Vibrational Medicine: New Choices for Healing Ourselves.* Bear and Co.: Santa Fe, New Mexico, 1988.

GRIFFIN, SUSAN. *Woman and Nature: The Roaring Inside Her.* Harper & Row: New York, 1978.

HOUSTON, JEAN. *The Possible Human: A Course in Enhancing Your Physical, Mental, and Creative Abilities.* Jeremy P. Tarcher Press, Inc.: Los Angeles, 1982.

HOUSTON, JEAN. *The Search for the Beloved: Journeys in Sacred Psychology.* Jeremy P. Tarcher, Inc.: Los Angeles, 1987.

JOHNSON, ROBERT A. *He.* Harper & Row: San Francisco, 1989.

JOHNSON, ROBERT A. *SHE!* Religious Publishing Company: King of Prussia, Pennsylvania, 1976.

JOHNSON, ROBERT A. *We: Understanding the Psychology of Romantic Love.* Harper & Row: San Francisco, 1983.

JUNG, CARL G. *Man and His Symbols.* Doubleday: Garden City, New York, 1964.

JUNG, C. G. *On the Nature of the Psyche.* Princeton University Press: Princeton, N.J., 1960.

KAGAN, JEROME. "Check One: Male, Female," *The Female Experience. Psychology Today,* 1973, pp. 50–53.

LEDERER, WOLFGANG, M.D. *The Fear of Women.* Harcourt Brace Jovanovich, Inc.: New York, 1968.

LUTHMAN, SHIRLEY GEHRKE. *Collection: A Continuation of Intimacy.* Mehetabel and Company, San Rafael, California, 1980.

LUTHMAN, SHIRLEY GEHRKE. *Energy and Personal Power.* Mehetabel and Company: San Rafael, California, 1982.

LUTHMAN, SHIRLEY GEHRKE. *Intimacy: The Essence of Male and Female.* Mehetabel and Company: San Rafael, California, 1972.

MANDINO, OG. *The Greatest Salesman in the World.* Bantam Books: New York, 1968.

NAISBITT, JOHN AND PATRICIA ABURDENE. *Megatrends 2000.* William Morrow & Co, Inc.: New York, 1990.

ROSZAK, BETTY AND THEODORE ROSZAK. *Masculine/Feminine: Readings in Sexual Mythology and the Liberation of Women.* Harper Colophon: New York, 1969.

ROWAN, ROY. *The Intuitive Manager,* Berkley Books: New York, 1986.

RUDHYAR, DANE. *We Can Begin Again Together.* Omen Communications, Inc.: Tucson, Arizona, 1974.

SANFORD, JOHN A. *The Invisible Partners: How the Male and Female in Each* of Us Affects Our Relationships. Paulist Press: New York/Ramsey, New Jersey, 1980.

SCHWARZ, JACK. Voluntary Controls. E.P. Dutton: New York, 1978.

SINGER, JUNE. Androgyny: Toward a New Theory of Sexuality. Anchor Press/Doubleday: New York, 1976.

SMALL, JACQUELYN. Transformers: The Therapists of the Future. Devorss & Company: Marina del Rey, California, 1982.

"Sob Story," New Woman, August 1989, pp. 44–46.

SUJATA, A. Beginning To See. Unity Press: Santa Cruz, California, 1975.

TENDZIN, OZEL. Buddha in the Palm of Your Hand. Shambhala Publications, Inc.: Boulder, Colorado, 1982.

TRUNGPA, CHÖGYAM. Cutting Through Spiritual Materialism. Shambhala Publications, Inc.: Berkeley, California, 1973.

TRUNGPA, CHÖGYAM. Maitreya. 5: Relationship. Shambhala Publications: Berkeley, California, 1974.

TRUNGPA, CHÖGYAM. Shambhala: The Sacred Path of the Warrior. Shambhala Publications, Inc.: Boulder, Colorado, 1984.

WHITE, BETTY. Drawing on the Right Side of the Brain. Jeremy P. Tarcher, Inc.: Los Angeles, 1989.

WILE, DANIEL B. After the Honeymoon. John Wiley & Sons, Inc.: New York, 1988.

Additional Resources

Loretta Ferrier Tapes

ALBUMS

Pathways Publishing offers a number of tapes that I have created especially for you to help you passionately pursue your dance of life. Each time you listen to these tapes you will feel more at peace and more certain that you can learn to trust yourself in every way:

Meeting Your Masculine and Feminine
Building the Masculine and Feminine
A Troubled Marriage
Following the Breadcrumbs
The Unfolding Dance of Your Internal Masculine and Feminine
The Wedding Ceremony

Complete sets of these six tapes are available in The Dance of the Self collection for $59.95. Be sure to add postage and tax per order form. Each of the above tapes is also available as singles for $10.95 each, plus postage and appropriate tax.

Also available, a three-tape set on love and relationships:

The Love of Your Life: A New Approach to Finding and Keeping Love.

This collection of tapes is on the nature of true love and guides you in keeping your own inner dance while in a relationship. Available for $19.95.

These tapes are $10.95 per tape, plus postage and appropriate tax.

I have a newsletter if you are interested in the new methods I develop and new insight I have. I will also keep you informed on the difference in the dance of Him and Her in foreign countries. This newsletter will offer some new exercises as well as keep you informed of new arenas in the work that I am doing. There will also be articles by others in my field as well as a complete schedule of where I will be speaking. For $12 you will receive three issues per year. You may begin receiving this newsletter by writing to: 2675 W. Highway 89A, Suite 1030, Sedona, Arizona 86336.

If you want to be on the mailing list only, write to the above address.

SEMINARS

The Dance of Life and The Spiritual Warrior workshops are offered throughout the country and in various parts of the world. The Dance of Life is a two-and-a-half day workshop that allows you to work with me on personal clearing and advanced techniques to further the dance of the inner masculine and inner feminine. The Spiritual Warrior is a four-day workshop. It offers advanced training for living and responding in the moment. You will be taught Eastern techniques that are normally only given to the advanced teachers.

ANNUAL RETREAT

A yearly retreat and playtime will be held once a year for workshop graduates. The place for this retreat will vary year to year.